JOHN DUBOIS:
FOUNDING FATHER

JOHN DUBOIS: FOUNDING FATHER

By

RICHARD SHAW

The Life and Times of the Founder of Mount St. Mary's College, Emmitsburg; Superior of the Sisters of Charity; and Third Bishop of the Diocese of New York

United States Catholic Historical Society
Yonkers, New York

and

Mount Saint Mary's College
Emmitsburg, Maryland

1983

Frontispiece illustration: *John Dubois as Bishop of New York. Oil painting by Mira Vizzala, dated 1830; said to have been painted from life. The painting now hangs in the Founder's Room in Bradley Hall at Mount Saint Mary's, Emmitsburg. (Courtesy Archives, Mount St. Mary's).*

U.S. Catholic Historical Society

Founded 1884

Monograph
Series
Volume 38

Mount Saint Mary's
175th Anniversary
1808 - 1983
a celebration of values

Official
175th Anniversary
Publication

Published by

U.S. Catholic Historical Society
P.O. Box 498
Yonkers, N.Y. 10702

Mount Saint Mary's College
175th Anniversary Office
Emmitsburg, MD 21727

LC Card number: 83–050646
ISBN: 0–930060–18–0
      0–930060–19–9 pbk.
ISSN: 0146–5651

Book Design and Production: Bookmakers, Inc., Washington, D.C.
Cover Illustrations by: John J. Mahoney

To
my spiritual father
Bishop Edward J. Maginn, D.D.
who was John Dubois to my generation,
and to my brother
Father Dominic Ingemie
who is being John Dubois to the generation following ours.

Preface

"He did everything for us. Everything," said old Sister Martha Daddisman when interviewed by younger Sisters of Charity in 1877, "That's why I'm mad with you. You make so much fuss over Bishop Bruté and you never say anything about Father Dubois and he did a great deal more. How I did cry when he went away to be Bishop and Father Hickey told me he wished I'd cry as much for my sins."[1]

The month after John Dubois' death in December 1842, *The Catholic Expositor and Literary Magazine* wrote: "The details of the life of this lamented prelate would fill a volume and no doubt will, in due time, be collected and preserved for posterity."[2]

They never were. Though John Dubois appears in numerous biographies of contemporaries whose lives he affected—Elizabeth Seton, John Hughes, John Nepomucene Neumann, Simon Bruté, John Carroll, and a number of others—no biography was ever written about him. In time even the whereabouts of his grave was lost. Only in the late 1970s were his remains rediscovered—under the pavement in front of old St. Patrick's on Mott Street in New York City.

John Dubois had played a role in the life of Saint Elizabeth Seton which strongly paralleled the role played by Saint Vincent de Paul in the life of Saint Louise de Marillac. Then, at the age of sixty-two he had left Mount

St. Mary's College and Seminary, which he had established, and the motherhouse of Elizabeth Seton's Sisters of Charity of which he was both builder and Superior, to become bishop of a vast territory inhabited by an evergrowing number of Catholic immigrants—the majority of them Irish.

He moved from holding a position in which he had been loved and respected for decades to one in which he remained somewhat lost until the day he died. A gentle Frenchman, he was no match for the rough-and-tumble New York Irish who resented the appointment of a "foreigner" as their bishop. A missionary whose presence had been welcomed by the Catholics of rural Virginia and Maryland since 1791, he could not effectively cope with the wealthy urban Catholic trustees who were determined to rule their churches spiritually as well as temporally.

For sixteen years he was beleaguered, ridiculed, and rendered ineffectual by those of his people who were concerned with gaining and holding power. By contrast, he seems consistently to have been loved by those who might be termed "little people": the meek of the earth. In this respect the nineteenth-century historian John Gilmary Shea wrote of him:

> It is strange that the papers of a man like Bishop Dubois
> have not [been] preserved here [New York] or at Mount
> St. Mary's. We have little of him but platitudes, generalities
> and newspapers, not always, in fact rarely, friendly. My
> boyish recollections of him are vivid and my harsh father's
> opposition to him as trustee of the Cathedral ranged me
> on his side. Children generally have implicit faith in their
> father but in my case we were negative poles and
> almost spontaneously I took the opposite. As I saw those
> who went to their duties cling to the bishop it gave him a halo
> in my boyish fancy and I felt great veneration for him.[3]

It is hoped that this narrative will help to place the accomplishments of John Dubois into a proper perspective in American Church history, and render him some of the veneration which is due to him as a good— in fact in would seem—great and holy man.

Prologue: The Lost Bishop

Bricks shattered the windows, startling into wakefulness the sick old man who was in his seventy-eighth year. Terrified and confused, he lay in bed in his ground floor room while an angry mob bashed in the front door of the house. The orange glow of torches lit the night. Above the tumult individual screams of anger filled the air: "Blood will flow"—"The Pope rules the Republic." Were they coming to get him for not taking the oath? The clatter of hoofbeats pierced the noise in the streets. The riot act was being read. Was it Lafayette again? Was the National Guard saving the priests from death? Where were the cries: "To the lamp post"?

What was it? Was his Mountain school on fire again? Were the students safe? Cries were discernable in the din, cries about infidel Papist schools poisoning children's minds. Which was it? Louis Le Grand, about to be turned into "Equity College" to please the ruling Directory? Mount St. Mary's, folding in debt and about to be sold as a school for cadets? The doomed college at Nyack or the sisters' orphanage, both burned to the ground?

The hollow crash of splintering glass and the frenzied cheers told him that the stained windows in the church across the street were now the object of destruction. Which church? Was it St. Sulpice? Was it St. Mary's on Grand Street again being put to the torch? He was caught up once more in the sounds of revolution. But which revolution? 1789? 1830? A new one?

Gradually the police gained control. The howling mob dispersed. Fully awake, the old man was calmed. It was not St. Sulpice which was threatened. It was St. Patrick's on Mott Street in New York—his cathedral—a small building which might have fit into Our Lady's Chapel in St. Sulpice in Paris. The mob had cried out for the blood of the bishop. He was the bishop. But only in name. The mob did not want him. Their wrath was aimed at his absent auxiliary, a virile young fighter who, in this year of 1842, manipulated the local elections to show the voting clout of the Irish immigrants.

The old man tried to resume his rest. He had escaped from death so many times before. The noise might have frightened him as well as the violence of the mob, for a lifetime of turmoil had not hardened his child-like heart. But death itself did not frighten him. Preparing for it was the only work which was left to him in this life.

Contents

Illustration Credits

See list on pages xv-xviii for reference numbers.

American Catholic Historical Society of Philadelphia: 68, 69; Artaud de Montor, *Lives & Times of Popes, IX*: 64; Barbant, C.H., after F. Lix. Ducoudray, G. *Cent Récits D'Histoire de Frances, 1902*: 7, 65; Bertarelli Collection: 78; Bibliotheque Nationale: 1, 2; Burdet, after Raffet. Thiers, *Histoire de la Revolution Française, II, 1865*: 10, 11; Calyo, N. (aquatint): 79; Carlyle, T., *French Revolution*: 8, 9, 38; *Catholic Church in the U.S.A., III, 1914*: 16; Corrigan Memorial Library, St. Joseph's Seminary, Yonkers, NY.: 70, 75; Daughters of Charity, St. Joseph's Provincial House, Archives, Emmitsburg, Md.: 28, 29, 30, 31, 32, 33, 34, 35, 39, 40, 41, 44, 45, 46, 48, 49, 76, 91; Farley, J., *Life of John Cardinal McCloskey*: 77; Fortier, J.A. (photo). Cheronnet, *L'église Saint Sulpice de Paris, 1971*: 6; Girodet (1812), Musée de Châteauroux: 23, Hamel, C., *Histoire de L'Église Saint-Sulpice, Paris, 1900*: 4, 5; Harper's Weekly, June 22, 1872: 71; Home Insurance Company: 67; *Metropolitan Catholic Calendar & Laity's Directory, Baltimore, 1834*: 53, 80; Mount Saint Mary's College, Emmitsburg, Maryland, Archives: 12, 14, 18, 19, 22, 23, 24, 25, 26, 27, 36, 37, 42, 43, 47, 50, 52, 55, 59, 62, 68, 69, 82, 83, 84, 90, 92, 95, frontispiece; Museum of the city of New York: 54; New York Public Library: 20; —(Schomburg Collection): 21; —(Stokes Collection): 17, 58, 60; Old Print Shop: 60; Pratt Library, Philadelphia: 23; Diocese of Rochester, N.Y., Archives: 72; Seton Hall University (NJ Catholic Historical Records Commission): 73; Shea, J.G., *History of the Catholic Church in the U.S., III*: 86, 87; Sheehan, *Pierre Toussaint*: 63; Sisters of Charity of Mount St. Vincent, N.Y. (oil by G.P.A. Healy): 81; Sully, Thomas. Fiske, *American Revolution I, 1896*: 15; Taylor, Sr. C., *History of Catholicism in the North Country*: 74; Turgot, M.E., in Bretez, L., *Plan de Paris, 1739*: 3; U.S. Catholic Historical Society; 57, 66, 85, 88, 89, 93, 94; *U.S. Catholic Miscellany, June 23, 1824*: 51; *Nov. 9, 1825*:56.

List of Illustrations

CHAPTER 1

The Child of the Ancien Régime

The child, John Dubois, just entering his second decade of life, poked his head out of the seventh-story dormer cut into the roof of the school of Louis Le Grand. Situated almost at the top of a hill on the rue St. Jacques, the height gave him a view of Paris which seemed almost from the clouds. The Seine was only a short distance down the hill, its ancient bridges still crowded with houses. At the river's closest point was the Ile de la Cité where the towers of Notre Dame rose majestically over the city. At the very crest of the hill, directly at the end of the school's property, could be seen the slowly progressing construction of the mammoth romanesque church being built in honor of Saint Genevieve. Construction had begun in 1764, the year of his birth,* the intent being to replace the small Gothic church to the rear of the rising edifice with a shrine worthy of the city's patroness. Yet, even if Paris was considered one of the great cities of the world, the boy could see, from his window, neighboring farmlands. The countryside was so close that the masters of the school had found it necessary to warn the students while on their free time against trampling through vineyards, wheatfields, and chasing after game.

---

*His birthdate was August 24th.

Younger than his classmates by as much as two years, the child John's innocent brown eyes, soft face and small size made him seem younger still. Nonetheless, he had a natural merriment of nature and a precocious intelligence beyond his years. This intelligence had won him a scholarship which only a year earlier would have been denied to him because of his lack of noble birth.

In 1763 the Jesuits had been suppressed in France. King Louis XV, faced with replacing them as instructors in educational institutions throughout the nation, chose Louis Le Grand as a vehicle for training a whole new generation of teachers. According to the King's orders, entry was to be gained by intelligence rather than blood. The ironic effect of this decision by this most absolute of monarchs was the democratization of this school, once run by the Jesuits exclusively for the sons of the nobility. The sons of the lower classes now paced its halls, and their places were won by nomination, strict testing and fairly-won scholarships. So it was that the precocious child John Dubois, the son of a bourgeois widow, was named to the school by some observant and sympathetic curé or civic official. Nonetheless, John—so intellectually advanced for his years—had to prove himself on his own. That he had done so and won his scholarship in so prestigious a school remained a source of quiet pride for him till the end of his life. Other boys of poor backgrounds also gained entry into this great experiment of the king and became John's companions and schoolmates. One of these was Camille Desmoulins. Another, from Arras, was Maximilien Robespierre.

If the latter two in later life were to make their mark in other fields, John Dubois would someday have much to do in the field of education in a new nation yet to be formed. The rules and the spirit of the school in which he lived for the next dozen years of his life would be deeply ingrained in him and would become the tools of discipline with which he would build his own schools.

With his schoolmates, he followed a rigorous schedule. Awakened each morning at 5:30, he was given half an hour to be dressed and in place for prayers and devotional readings. At 6:15 he went to a study hall which included "the learning and recitation of verses from scripture." At 7:45, two hours and fifteen minutes after rising, he went to breakfast. Morning classes were followed by daily attendance at Mass and then by another study hall. An hour and fifteen minutes was allowed for lunch and recreation. At 1:15 the afternoon classes and study halls began, continuing until 4:30 when a half hour of recreation refreshed the boys for another hour and fifteen minutes of supervised study. At 6:15 individual conferences were given for each class. Supper at 7:15 was followed by recreation until 8:45 when night prayers were said, followed by devotional reading. At nine o'clock the students were packed off to their dormitories. Even at this late hour John was permitted few mind wanderings, for, as the boys prepared for bed, they listened to a reading from the life of the saint whose feast day was being celebrated.[1]

Externally it seemed forbidding, yet according to the spirit of the rules personally written by the king, discipline was purposefully moderate. If boys entered Louis Le Grand as young children and remained there the full twelve years until they were in their early twenties, it was only right to hope, as did the king, that they should "consider themselves as brothers and children of one family." Professors were discouraged from using "severe" punishments "unless they have exhausted all other means" and if severe punishments were necessary they were to be administered "in a way that tempers bitterness." The students on their part were taught respect for their home ("It is expressly forbidden to write on the tables or desks . . .") and cleanliness ("They will wash their hands at least once a day and change their linen several times a week.")

In short the king ordered that the young men learn to be gentlemen.

"Students will acquire from an early age the habit of mild and honest intercourse with others," the king directed, "In outward action and speech they will avoid whatever may jar upon well-bred people such as conceited airs, haughtiness, scorn, sarcasm, ridicule, gesticulation, etc."[2]

To help instill these gentlemanly graces, the boys, at mealtimes, were not herded into a hall to eat barrack style. Meals were designed to be a time of gentle conviviality. Tablecloths were used and every boy was given his own silver utensils with which to eat.

Daily Mass and prayers were mandatory and the oldest students (called as a class, Theologians) had to meet regularly for philosophy discussions in which they were "expected to take part in the argument." One of John's professors, the Abbé Proyart, had written a book of meditations based on the life of a student who died shortly before John arrived.

John, small and timid by nature, was thoroughly malleable to all of this. On one occasion his confessor set out to curb in him a habit of exaggerating tales into lies. The priest ordered that he should catch himself as soon as he realized he was committing this fault and retract his false assertions on the spot. John remembered this order halfway through fabricating a tale. He stopped, struggled with his conscience and won the day for virtue's sake by suddenly blurting out the truth of the matter. The triumph of self-humiliation was too much for him. He fainted dead away.

John shared a talent for classical languages with the older Maximilien Robespierre. Maximilien, an aloof loner, withdrawn from the schoolboy pleasantries of his classmates, liked the shy, happy-natured younger boy, a happenstance which would one day become a life-saving factor for the latter. As students, both boys would win their class Latin prize as they graduated.

The school placed a heavy emphasis on the political literature of ancient Rome, and some observers felt that this was an incipient danger in the minds of young men of lower class. Louis Sebastian Mercier warned in his pre-revolutionary work *Tableau de Paris* that "after hearing so much of the Senate, of the liberty and majesty of the Roman people . . . of the justified death of Caesar . . . it is a hard lot to leave Rome and find one's self again a bourgeois in the rue des Noyers."[3] Events were to prove him a prophet. Louis Le Grand would afterward be labelled "the school of the French Revolution."

The atmosphere in which Desmoulins, Robespierre and Dubois grew was a mixture of philosophical extremes. Abbé Proyart would remain strongly conservative throughout and long after the Revolution. By contrast the students were constantly exposed to the thinking of radical professors such as the Abbé Yves-Marie Audrein, the assistant headmaster, Abbé J. B. Dumouchel and Jean François Champagne.

Abbé Audrein, who authored an ultra-liberal book on education before the Revolution, would take the revolutionary oath, marry, and accept a state-issued bishopric in Brittany. He would eventually be assassinated by a rightist group which would stop a public coach in which he was riding, drag him into the road, and shoot him.

Abbé Dumouchel would likewise become a state bishop, but would ride through all the storms and become the head of public instruction under Napoleon.

Jean François Champagne, who had ended his studies for the priesthood while a subdeacon, would take the oath to the state, and then renounce Christianity altogether. Taking over as head of Louis Le Grand, he would change its name to "Equity College" in 1792 and keep it open— the only college in France to be kept open—through every twist and turn of the Revolution.

Some students were ripe for the radical new philosophies; among them the pale, grim-faced adolescent Robespierre whose coldly staring, steel-colored eyes disquieted adults. Another was Camille Desmoulins who, though younger by several years, was a close friend of Maximilien. Desmoulins, closer still in age to John Dubois, was not liked by the student who could faint at the prospect of telling a lie. Dubois would one day recall for his own students that the acid-tongued Camille wore a perpetual scowl and was a bully over smaller boys—smaller boys such as himself.

The timid Dubois was readily drawn under the influence of Proyart's ideas and sought friendships with like-minded students. Among these was John Cheverus, as much his junior as Desmoulins was to Robespierre. Cheverus would follow in Dubois' footsteps through Louis Le Grand, through the seminary, and then to the new United States of America.

In the summer of 1775 a new king, young Louis XVI, returned from his coronation at Rheims and attended a Solemn Mass at Notre Dame. His entourage crossed the Seine to the left bank and made its way up the rue St. Jacques to pay respect to the remains of Saint Genevieve. By arrangement, he stopped at Louis Le Grand to assume the king's role as the school's special benefactor. John crowded into the entranceway with the rest of his schoolmates, for the king did not leave his carriage to enter the courtyard. Robespierre, so gifted in the classics, stepped forward to represent his fellow students. The soft, fat young king and his soft, pale-faced queen, Marie Antoinette, sat impassively while the seventeen-year-old student rendered to his ruler a polite address telling the king only what he was inclined to hear.

Whether or not Louis listened at all to this, one of many speeches of coronation praise, he nonetheless bowed politely to Maximilien before the immense, gilded carriage lumbered away, moving up the hill to the shrine of the city's patron saint.

Paris was a city of churches and John paid great attention to them as his ideas about the priesthood matured into a vocation. As the idea grew within him, so too did the nearby Church of St. Genevieve grow towards completion. Walking a short distance from Louis Le Grand, he could watch construction on the massive Church of St. Sulpice where a second tower, mismatched with the first, was being added. Attached to the church was a seminary of the same name. Watching the seminarians, while wondering about his own vocation, he saw there and later at the Sorbonne across the street from Louis Le Grand one seminarian who dragged his right foot in a constant limp. The seminarian became in time more notable since gossip scored him for being openly careless in his companionship with an actress who lived in the vicinity. Such conduct might have created open scandal in other times and places, but it was only cause for raised eyebrows in these last years of France's ancien régime. Neither the seminary nor the Archbishop of Paris would do anything, for the young man, Charles Maurice de Talleyrand-Périgord, was of the nobility.

France's long-standing class orders divided society into three "estates": clergy, nobility and commoners. In reality, the first category was twofold, for the ranks of the clergy were filled from both of the other estates and the separation caused by their origins remained intact. The caste system within the Church was as notable as that in secular society. The nobility, seeking titles and riches for younger sons had long since preempted the ranks of the hierarchy. Almost without exception the Sees of France, as well as the lofty titles and financial revenues attached to the wealthy religious orders, belonged to the sons of the second estate. It was expected that those of the third estate who felt called to the priesthood would be confined to serve in the lower ranks of the clergy. The abuses of wealth and power in the Church were parallel and often identical with those in the kingdom at large. The need for purgation was realized by many from within the Church, but the hierarchy, in control of the machinery needed to effect reform, remained complacent and comfortable. Purgation would come—as it had before in history—from without.

Talleyrand was but one of a legion of examples. Even before he was ordained for the diocese of his uncle, the Archbishop of Rheims, this doting relative granted him the benefices from the Abbey of St. Remy—a yearly income some one hundred times that received by a curate in an ordinary parish. Ordained in 1779, the limping young man never worked as a priest in his diocese but remained in the salons of Paris, active in the getting of mistresses, an illegitimate child, and, above all, prestige at Versailles.

The priesthood, despite the inequities, still attracted men of good character. Almost all historians of the Revolution would eventually agree in saying that, no matter how indolent the religious orders had become and how corrupt the hierarchy was, parish curés and curates throughout France were generally holy men, living simply (of necessity) and giving goodly service to their people. Ironically, when the Revolution came many of these men, so immediately available, would suffer the brunt of hatreds meant for the noble clergy while many of these latter, having the means to do so, escaped at the first signs that the long-overdue deluge was on the way.

In the early 1780s the academically gifted John Dubois, certainly aware that his origins in the third estate would limit any ambitions he might have with regard to a clerical career, nonetheless decided to give his life to God and join the lower ranks of the first estate. It would have been vain for him to think of the possibility of ever becoming a bishop. He entered the Seminary of Saint Magloire planning to live and die in the ranks of the priesthood in Paris.

College Louis-le-Grand, Paris. Above, *the main courtyard showing boys at recreation, about 1780.* Below, *as it appeared in the 1860s. The College is in the foreground, and the dome of the Pantheon looms at upper right. Note the similarity of the architecture to Dubois' college at Emmitsburg.*

An overview of the neighborhood around College Louis-le-Grand, as seen in the 1730s. It appears left of center as "Col. des Jesuites," as it was known in those days, along the Rue Saint Jacques. The dome of the Sorbonne church faces the college at lower center.

3

CHAPTER 2

The Deluge

In 1787 official France began to yield slowly to the ideas of the Enlightenment. An edict of toleration was passed allowing at least some civil status for the 5% of citizens who were Protestant. The provisions of the edict included such basic rights as legitimizing marriages and births (such records in France had been legally kept by the Catholic parishes). In September of that same year John Dubois was ordained to the priesthood by M. de Juigne, Archbishop of Paris. Dubois, precocious and younger than his classmates as a student, was, at 23, too young for the priesthood according to Canon Law. His appearance could only have added to making him appear too young for ordination. He was small of stature and his features, with his dominant nose and cleft chin, were soft. His dark eyes carried an expression of vulnerability. A dispensation was granted to him because of his age.

He was assigned to the huge parish of St. Sulpice, the towers of which he had watched being constructed while he was at Louis Le Grand. It was a parish of some 90,000 communicants in an area of 120,000 inhabitants. The church itself inspired extremes of opinion from admirers and from detractors. Massive in size, its facade, with high columns and stories of porches, looked like an overly ornate Roman temple. The funds for the

construction of the recently completed, mismatched towers had been raised
by special lotteries—a rage with the French at the time. The seminary attached to the parish was run by the Sulpicians, and this, along with the
great population of the parish, caused some sixty priests to be assigned
there. People who admired pomp and majesty set against marble and stone
could attend religious ceremonies at which some two hundred ecclesiastics
participated.

Others, less impressed with size, found the place aesthetically appalling.
Gouverneur Morris, the United States Minister, accustomed to small
wooden churches, judged the exterior to be "disproportionate and fan-
tastic"; the interior, "immensely heavy."[1] Visitors could view the mammoth, clamshell-shaped holy water fonts and the famous silver statue
dubbed "Our Lady of the second-hand plate"—made from melted-down
dinnerware stolen over the years from weddings and banquets by a former
Curé, M. Languet de Gergy.

Just as the edifice itself inspired wide-ranging reactions, the population
of the parish included a wide range of society. Among the nobility who
were parishioners were members of the Noailles family. The women of
this family were a rarity for that age and class, being at the same time well
educated and deeply religious. One of the Noailles daughters, Adrienne,
had married the Marquis de Lafayette who made his house a center for
the representatives of the new republic he had helped to bring about.
Thomas Jefferson lived in Paris for several years and enrolled his daughters
in a convent school in the vicinity of St. Sulpice. They remained there
until one of them began to express an interest in Romanism, whereupon
Jefferson promptly pulled them out. The Marquis de Lafayette himself,
after a brief period of piety as a young man, adopted an attitude not far
from Jefferson's deism and remained for the rest of his life a Catholic only
in name. Discussing the possibility of a United States' military invasion of
Catholic Canada in a 1785 letter to George Washington, Lafayette offered
himself as a potential commander, the advantages being both his French
nationality and his Catholicism. This latter advantage he qualified in his
awkward English as "my Roman Catholic Creed or supposed to be so at
least if anything."[2] In contrast his wife Adrienne made religion the center
of her life and was an active parishioner at St. Sulpice.

Voltaire had died in the parish in 1778. One of the curates, Abbé
Gauthier, had visited the writer and had brought him to the point of reconciliation with the Church. Unfortunately, this was destroyed by the rigor-
istic behavior of the Curé, Jean-Joseph Tersac, who followed up his assistant's interview with a righteous and demanding one of his own.

The sternly aggressive Tersac was still Curé when John Dubois arrived.
He assigned the newly ordained priest as chaplain at the Petites Maisons
run by the Daughters of Charity on the rue de Sevres. Originally founded
in 1497 for the care of lepers, the hospital had become under the sisters a

home for the elderly and the insane. It was in a neighborhood crowded
with unfortunates and with institutions dedicated to helping them. Near
the Petites Maisons, the Daughters of St. Thomas de Villeneuve lived in a
community dedicated to working with the poor. At the Petites Maisons,
newly enlarged in 1785 to give housing for 400 patients, the twenty-three-
year-old John Dubois practiced a daily routine caring for those who suffered both mentally and physically, which demanded both patience and
gentleness for any kind of effectiveness. The forty sisters with whom he
worked and prayed lived under the rule of St. Vincent de Paul. Dubois
learned the spirit of this rule by living within it himself. It was an assignment of historic significance, for in the coming century, on the other side
of the Atlantic, he would adapt it to suit the needs of a convert to Catholicism whom he would direct in forming America's first native religious
order for women.

Curé Tersac died in the summer of 1788 and was replaced by M. Antoine
Pancemont, Vicar General of the diocese of Autun. A high forehead under
curly white hair and deep-set pensive eyes gave him an air of both dignity
and strength. He would need both qualities to endure the humiliations and
dangers which the last decades of the century were to bring to him. He
became an important influence in Dubois' life, as he was in the lives of the
sixty-some priests under his charge. Historians have noted that in the
larger parishes of Paris during the religious confusion of the Revolution
the clergy tended to act according to parish rather than as individuals. If a
Curé pushed them towards compliance with the revolutionary government,
the curates did so together; if a strong Curé held them to long-standing
hierarchical discipline, they held firm together. In the capital only the
Church of St. Roch on the right bank matched St. Sulpice in size. Thus,
Curé Pancemont as a leader was an important figure in Paris. The community of men at St. Sulpice had the advantage of living under the guidance
of a man not only firm in his ideals as was his predecessor Tersac, but
whose active devotion to the poor in his parish rivaled that of St. Vincent
de Paul who had worked in the same vicinity.

Owing largely to France's involvement in the American Revolution, the
nation was on the verge of bankruptcy. While royalty and nobility continued to live opulently, heedless of the worsening state of the middle class
and the poor, the unusually harsh winter of 1788–1789 pushed matters to
a point where revolution was unavoidable. Paris was the scene of tight
money and bread shortages. Curé Pancemont threw himself wholeheartedly
into the service of the people of his parish, concentrating not only the energies of his priests but also his own family's ample financial resources to
alleviate suffering. Dubois, returning from his work at the Petites Maisons,
could oftentimes encounter his pastor who ran his parish, not from behind
a desk, but by going from door to door helping his people. From the rich
Pancemont personally begged assistance; from the poor he took statistics

of their needs, drawing up a list of some 25,000 names of those to whom charity was to be directed.

The king, in an effort to avert financial disaster, summoned the Estates-General to meet for the first time in a century and a half. In spring the representatives were chosen from the three estates—clergy, nobility and commons. The limping priest Talleyrand, still living in Paris, had been serving as agent general of the clergy. In this public role he had won almost as great a reputation for political ability as his private life had won him for being a voluptuary. Seeing a road to political advancement in the Estates-General he manipulated to obtain a bishopric. John Dubois, living with Curé Pancemont, must certainly have had his attentions drawn to the machinations of this ambitious cleric, for the vacant office he succeeded in grasping was the same Diocese of Autun where Pancemont had been Vicar General until the previous year. Talleyrand obtained the diocese and was duly elected as deputy to the Estates-General. To seasoned men such as Pancemont, and to spiritually-oriented young men under his tutelage such as Dubois, it was galling to watch the progress of this Bishop Talleyrand who, before he left Autun on his first and only visit, agreed to celebrate a Solemn High Mass. The rubrics and his priestly vestments were so unfamiliar to him he stumbled over both and evoked laughter from the congregation.

The Estates-General convened at Versailles, May 5, 1789, inaugurated by a procession to the Church of St. Louis. Thomas Jefferson, no friend to organized religion, watched the proceedings and judged: "This is the first time that churches have been made good use of."[3]

Members of the third estate were resentful from the start at both the seating arrangements and the social distinctions which separated them from the nobility and the clergy. Again, the more observant of them might have noticed that there were four, not three, groupings. Dressed in ermine and purple, the bishops, along with the powerful heads of religious orders, were carefully separated by the ceremony's musicians from the diocesan priests clad in simple black.

In the weeks that ensued, while the nation's economic crisis deepened, the argument as to whether voting would depend on separate ballots in each estate or balloting as a single assembly held all other work at a standstill. On the 28th of May the Archbishop of Aix came into the Commons dramatically carrying a loaf of black bread and exhorted the members to move on to important business for the sake of people in France who were starving. One delegate to the Commons, a young lawyer from Arras, voiced the pent-up feelings of many against the clerical estate and won the approval of the clergy who were commoners like himself. He retorted:

> Go tell your colleagues not to hold up our discussions
> with spurious delays. They are ministers of a sublime religion
> founded on a scorn of wealth. Let them copy their Divine

> Master and give up their displays of luxury which offend
> the people in their dire need. The ancient Canon Law
> states that one may sell sacred vessels to relieve the poor, but
> there is no need for such a desperate remedy. Dismiss
> your proud servants, sell your coaches, your sumptuous
> furniture and the luxuries which are an offense to Christian
> humility. Give the unfortunate the immense fortune you
> hold in the name of charity.[4]

This young lawyer's fame was growing fast owing to his gift for words and the courage to express them. He especially won the interest of John Dubois. It was his schoolmate from Louis Le Grand, Maximilien Robespierre.

The impoverished curates of France agreed with Robespierre's sentiments. On June 13, a handful of them deserted their estate to sit with the Commons. Others followed, and by June 17, the third estate could declare itself with this crucial support of the clergy, a new entity—the National Assembly. The Revolution had begun.

In Paris, eleven miles from Versailles, violent demonstrations had been breaking out sporadically throughout the spring. Mercenary troops were stationed to keep order. On July 12, when the king reacted against the National Assembly by choosing a reactionary Ministry, he tipped over a national powder keg. At a café in the Palais Royal Garden, a meeting place for political extremists, another schoolmate of John Dubois, Camille Desmoulins, now a sometimes employed barrister and fledgling pamphleteer, touched the spark to the powder. Leaping to a table and crying "to arms" he rallied a crowd, which became a mob, which then became an undisciplined army. For two days rioting filled the city, and on July 14th, the prison of the Bastille was attacked and taken by the populace.

This seemed, at first, to be unalloyed good. It gave a sense of emergency to the voice of commoners as expressed in the National Assembly. The king advisedly came to Paris and half-heartedly sanctioned what had occurred by donning the tricolor cockade which had become a symbol of the Revolution.

The priests who were serving the common people in the churches of Paris saw reason to rejoice in the changing order of things and John Dubois eagerly joined those who rejoiced. At St. Sulpice, a *Te Deum* was sung immediately after the Bastille's fall, and later a Mass was said for those who had died storming the prison. In August, Curé Pancemont celebrated a Solemn High Mass at which batallion flags of the newly formed National Guard were blessed. Lafayette, the commander of the Guard, was present accompanied by his wife. At the same time, however, there were ominous outbursts of zeal which went beyond reason. One cleric preaching at St. Sulpice earned a rebuke from the pastor for praising the memory of the anticlerical Voltaire who had been denied burial at the same church only a dozen years earlier. On another occasion the ever-stronger sentiments of anticlericalism were felt when members of the National Guard spoke out publicly against the clergy. Curé Pancemont angrily went to Lafayette's home and demanded a retraction. The Marquis was a weak man who wanted to be smiled upon by the established order and by the revolutionaries. Hampered by what Jefferson labelled as his "canine appetite for popularity and fame"[5] Lafayette always sought to please whomever was in front of him, and to Pancemont he offered the sought apology.

Nonetheless, others saw clearly that the Church would become the scapegoat of the new order. One who recognized this was the Bishop of Autun, Talleyrand, who, on October 10, suggested the Church as "a source of revenue as immense as it is yet untapped."[6] He proposed a nationalization of Church property. In early November it was approved by the National Assembly. In the months that followed, as the trappings of the nobility were destroyed, so too were the lordly trappings of the Church. Along with the trappings, however, the fabric of religion began to be torn away. In early 1790 religious vows were declared to be without official recognition; contemplative houses were to be suppressed. Only orders engaged in educational and charitable works could remain in existence. The statistical result was that men's religious orders generally opted to abandon their vows; women's orders, more actively involved in social work, remained at their tasks. Dubois' work with the Daughters of Charity among the elderly and the insane remained for the moment untouched.

The winter of 1789–1790 was again unusually cold and again there were shortages of necessities. The work of distributing food to the poor, so well organized by Pancemont, was hindered since the growing numbers of nobility fleeing the country left him with fewer sources for funds. Only a sizeable gift from the Prince de Condé allowed the parish to continue its charities with any success that winter.

Camille Desmoulins, like Maximilien Robespierre, had become one of the voices of the Revolution. Famous because of his table-top harangue at the Palais-Royal, he had gone on to become an inflammatory journalist. With the same bullying thrust for the jugular he had employed as a boy, he went after the Revolution's targets, in particular the Church. Camille went beyond attacking clericalism. He belittled Christianity itself. In the midst of these attacks, he came to St. Sulpice with his fiancée Lucille Duplessis and demanded that the Curé marry them. Pancemont refused, saying that Desmoulins was no longer a Catholic. In proof of this he quoted Camille's newspaper wherein Desmoulins had stated that the religion of Mohammed was as good for him as that of Jesus Christ.

Desmoulins appealed the matter in the National Assembly. Honoré Mirabeau sent word to St. Sulpice that Camille and Lucille were to be married. Pancemont still refused. Finally, Desmoulins circumvented the Curé's authority by recourse to one of the professors from Louis Le

Grand, L'Abbé Berardier. Pancemont allowed the priest to perform the ceremony in St. Sulpice. Robespierre stood up for his boyhood friend as witness. If it had ever occurred to Camille to ask the curate Dubois to perform the ceremony, he left no record of his consideration. The curate Dubois, working with nuns, spending his days with the elderly and insane, could not have grown any in Camille's estimation since the days when Dubois had been bullied by him in school. Camille Desmoulins concerned himself with men who were prominent in the Revolutionary arena and not with chaplains to lunatics.

In the beginning of 1791 the Revolution took a direction which forced the involvement of even those priests who would have preferred a quiet, nonpolitical life of Christian service.

In the summer of 1790 the government had voted into law the Civil Constitution of the Clergy. This nationalized religion in discipline as well as in property and remodelled the Gallican Church along lines of the Anglican Church. The government instead of Rome was to be the final authority. Dioceses were reduced in number to parallel civil departments, curés and bishops were to be elected democratically, those outside the Church being able to vote as well as Catholics. Priests were to become paid functionaries of the State. In January of 1791 all priests were to be required to take publicly an oath to this new order of affairs.

The decision to take or refuse this oath was not a clear or easy one for priests living through the confusion of the Revolution. Good men came down on both sides. Rome had for too long remained silent about internal corruption in religious orders, about absentee abbots and multiple benefices, about nonbelievers in the nobility taking positions in the hierarchy. Moreover, the Papacy had allowed interference on the part of kings in the Church's affairs for centuries. Should there not be interference by a government which reflected the will of the people? Thus, the interference by the government in purely spiritual matters had increased since the days of May, 1789. By 1791 voices of authority among those steering the Revolution seemed more antireligious than merely anticlerical. Thus, Desmoulins spoke of his preference for Mohammed while being married in the Church and Robespierre hinted that those who performed priestly functions should be chosen at random from among the people at large.

One strong argument against a priest submitting to the new decree was that priests were being forced to take a special oath of loyalty not demanded of any other citizens. In confusion, the priests of Paris divided into two almost equal stances, tending to group by parish communities. The civil authorities looked especially to St. Sulpice for leadership, not only because of the size of the parish but because of its location at the very center of Paris.

On January 9, the deadline for taking the oath, St. Sulpice was packed for Mass with groups of parishioners including Madame Lafayette, sym-

pathetic to the priests. Other, actively hostile groups had also gathered as
if to pass immediate judgment on the priests if they refused the oath.
Because of this volatile atmosphere, the National Guard was called to the
scene. Curé Pancemont entered the sanctuary surrounded, as if for protec-
tion, by all of his curates. The sermon which he began to give was about
the needs of the poor in his parish. It quickly became evident that he would
not address himself to the political situation, and sections of the crowd
began to yell, "The oath . . . the oath."

At length he stopped and declared simply:

"I cannot take the oath, my conscience will not allow me."

Spontaneously, all the priests around him, including the young Dubois,
repeated in unison:

"I cannot take the oath, my conscience will not allow me."

An uproar began over which could be heard the cry:

"The oath or the lamp post."

These last words were understood only too well. They threatened immediate lynching. Paris had been filled with enough mob violence in the
previous two years for the threat to be taken as real. Many heads had
already been borne through the streets on top of pikes.

The uproar made continuation of the Mass impossible. Forming a
phalanx around the curé, the priests moved him toward the sacristy. The
angry crowd surged around them and the National Guard moved in to clear
a path. A man brandished a pistol which someone quickly wrested from
him. Another reached Pancemont, seized him by the hair and struck him
across his head. He remained silent, the priests pressing as best they could
toward the sacristy. Inside, safe for a moment from the crowd, Pancemont succumbed to the emotional pressure and fell, unconscious.[7] Dubois, who would
ever deplore confrontations, could not have been far from following suit.

Almost immediately afterward the Mayor of Paris, M. Bailly, arrived at
the parish house and harangued Pancemont to lead the priests into
obedience.

"When the law speaks," he told the curé, "the conscience must be silenced."

When Pancemont refused to yield, Bailly told him he had made a "fatal
decision."[8]

In the next months the Civil Constitution badly divided an already confused people. Talleyrand resigned his bishopric, not to protest the new order
but to become more fully part of it. Before setting aside his priesthood,
however, he consecrated two bishops to represent the new Constitutional
Church. It was his last ecclesiastical act. In Paris, Bishop Gobel, the auxiliary of Bâle, took over as Constitutional Bishop of Paris.* The govern-

---

*Before the revolutionary storm would be over he too would renounce his Church after
having, while still archbishop, taken a wife. He eventually lost his head under the guillotine
during the Terror.

ment's replacement for Pancemont, Jean Poirée, had been an order priest
in charge of the Oratory where Talleyrand consecrated the constitutional
bishops. As if in payment, he was awarded the job as Curé of St. Sulpice.
Accepting his office in a sermon at Notre Dame he told the congregation
that the voice of heaven had told him to fight against the "rage of super-
stition" represented by the nonjuring priests by zealously accepting this
"immense parish without a pastor in the eyes of the law."[9]

In April, the so-called "nonjuring clergy" were forced out of their parishes. The law, however, only forbade nonjurors to serve the public and to
receive pay from the State. For a brief interim they were allowed to serve
private residences and religious houses. Dubois still maintained his position
with the sisters at the Petites Maisons. The community of nonjuring priests
of St. Sulpice were, nonetheless, without a home. Pancemont hoped to use
a loophole by which the law allowed priests to serve as did Dubois. He
rented an abandoned chapel near the Seine which had belonged to the religious order of the Theatins. At Eastertime he opened this chapel for those
of St. Sulpice who wished to remain with the nonjuring priests. To the
evident embarrassment of the nonbeliever Lafayette, his devout wife
Adrienne was among these people. So, too, was the wife of Mayor Bailly.

To be safe within the law, the nonjuring, former priests of St. Sulpice
placed a carefully phrased placard over the entranceway:

"Building consecrated for religious worship by a particular society.
Peace and Liberty."

The sign was torn down by a crowd and replaced by another:

"Notice for Pious aristocrats; Purgative medicine distributed free."

When Bailly ordered local police to replace the original placard, the
second was again put up over it by revolutionaries along with an added
statement:

"Removed by order of M. Bailly; replaced by that of citizens."[10]

On June 2, the feast of the Ascension, Mass there was interrupted by an
angry mob. Lafayette, frightened for the safety of his wife, arrived on the
scene with a battalion of the National Guard and quelled the disturbance
without making any arrests.

This marked the end of the nonjurors' attempt to serve the parishioners
of St. Sulpice. The hostile atmosphere made it increasingly dangerous for
any Catholics to remain loyal to this group of priests. Pancemont left
Paris for Brussels; others of the parish priests went to Switzerland or
Rome. John Dubois had grown up in a sheltered, well-ordered world that
was dying. The magnificent Church of St. Genevieve, the construction of
which he had watched as a student, had been de-christened. It was no longer
to honor something so foolish as a patron saint of Paris. It was to be the
Pantheon of France's heroes, and the government had just ordered that
Voltaire's body be triumphantly reinterred within its walls. The Pope,
almost a year too late, came out with a condemnation of the Civil Consti-

tution of the Clergy. Such condemnation meant little to France now. There
was a new state church. Dubois did not belong to this church and, despite
the published *Rights of Man* which aped the United States' Bill of Rights
in assuring freedom of religion, Dubois was marked for persecution because
of his beliefs.

He approached the Lafayettes. The Marquis had, at the beginning of
June, written to George Washington that the nonjuring priests were "playing the devil."[11] But as always he was gracious. He was continually un-
faithful to his wife; but he loved her dearly. She would appreciate a kindness to the Roman priesthood which had just been destroyed in France
and which had meant so much to her. He complied and wrote a letter of
introduction for Dubois to use should he succeed in reaching the United
States.

In June the royal family attempted to escape. Foolishly they set out from
Paris in an oversized, elaborate coach. The king was recognized near the
border at Varennes. They were brought back as prisoners, and Louis heard
his death called for by the onetime schoolboy who had praised him at the
front gate of Louis Le Grand. Robespierre was a self-tortured man whose
actions were often contradictory. In this same month he and John Dubois
chanced to bump into each other on the street. Robespierre invited his
former schoolmate home to share breakfast with him. Though he had done
so much to create the extreme dangers in which the nonjuring priests were
placed, he could not particularize these upon the gentle, fellow Latin scholar
who visited with him now. Against all that he stood for in theory, he wrote
papers—falsified papers—which would get the outlawed priest safely out
of the country.[12]

That same month John Dubois said goodbye to his mother, never to see
her again. He turned his back on the beautiful city which had reduced itself
to a communal madness worse than any madness he had known within the
walls of the Petites Maisons. The perimeters of Paris had been the totality
of his world. The city had filled him with its culture, with what had once
been its Faith, and now with its pervading threat of violent death. Wiser
than the king in regard to his safety, he removed whatever might identify
him as a cleric. The only priest leaving the country at this time would be a
nonjuring priest and recognition would place him in jeopardy of his life. At
Le Havre he booked passage for America.

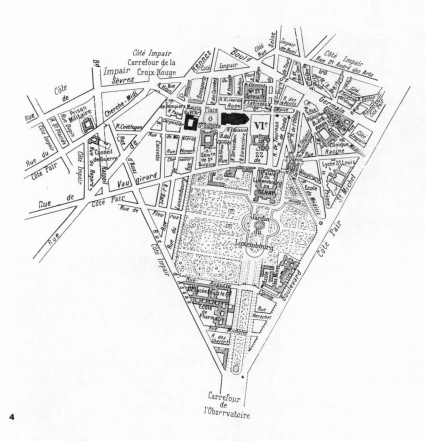

4

Above, *map of the parish of Saint Sulpice, Paris where John Dubois served for four years. The large church is the dark outline in* upper center, *and to its left is the Seminary of Saint Sulpice. The lower portion includes the famous Gardens of Luxembourg.*
Following page: above, *the exterior of the Church of Saint Sulpice with its mismatched towers;* below, *the vast interior of the church.*

5

6

Camille Desmoulins (1760–1794) delivering his famous tabletop speech: A Call to Arms! July 12, 1789. Two days later the Bastille fell to the revolutionists. Dubois remembered him as a bully over smaller boys. Desmoulins, like Robespierre, ended his career at the guillotine.

8

Above, *Charles Maurice de Talleyrand-Périgord (1754–1838) the "chameleon-like" ex-bishop who was a Parisian scandal when Dubois was a schoolboy.* Right, *Maximilien Robespierre (1758–1794)—Dubois' slightly older friend at school. Robespierre forged papers to enable the young priest to escape France in 1791.*

9

10

Above, *while John Dubois was a parish priest in Paris, the desperate Louis XVI donned the "tri-color cockade" on a hat to show he had sanctioned the demands of the mob.* Below, *public riots were common in Paris, but by the time Robespierre led this insurrection on August 10, 1792, John Dubois was safe in exile in Virginia.*

11

12

Marie Joseph Motier, marquis de Lafayette (1757–1834). Although himself a nominal Catholic, Lafayette's wife was a devout member of Dubois' parish. It was probably through Madame Adrienne Lafayette's influence that the Marquis wrote Dubois a letter of introduction to his friend in America, James Monroe.

At left, *Napoleon I (Napoleon Bonaparte)*, to whom John Dubois was likened by his students at Emmitsburg, and dubbed the "Little Napoleon."

13

CHAPTER 3

Politics and Politicians of This World

No great numbers of French emigrés came to America. Other European countries, and even hostile England, seemed more attractive to the wellborn and to the great majority of escaping priests than did a voyage across the vast Atlantic. Only some two dozen clerics made their way to the United States—not counting the ex-Bishop Talleyrand whose politics rather than his faith turned out to be his downfall.

Madame La Tour du Pin was a lady-in-waiting to Marie Antoinette. Protecting her ailing husband and two infant children, she engineered a harrowing escape from under the very shadow of the guillotine. In the United States she quickly saw that those French who had remained after fighting in the American Revolution judged the newcomers as "aristocrats fortunate enough to have escaped from death, which according to them, we fully merited for our past tyranny."[1]

John Dubois, at twenty-seven, with four years of the priesthood behind him, was of this oppressor class according to the Revolutionary rhetoric. Disembarking at the seaport of Norfolk, Virginia, where the sharp smell of raw tobacco exports filled the air, he could only stand in confusion. He could not speak a word of English, and the sparsely populated continent before him was a wilderness. Talleyrand, Dubois' fellow Parisian, one-time

17

fellow clergyman, and fellow exile in the United States recorded that an
urban Frenchman might as well have migrated to another planet:

"I found myself in that vast country where whatever I saw reminded me
of nothing I had ever seen before," he wrote, ". . . At less than one hundred
and fifty miles distance from the Capital all traces of men's presence dis-
appeared."[2]

The one valuable property Dubois had in hand was the letter of introduction from the Marquis de Lafayette. Yet, for all he knew, even this was
fast diminishing in value. Lafayette (whom Madame La Tour du Pin remembered from Paris as "that simpleton")[3] could never make up his mind
as to which side to take in the revolution. In the summer of 1791 the Virginia newspapers reported Lafayette's resignation, then his rejoining of the
National Guard, and finally his fainting spell when attempting publicly to
explain his position.

After the royal family's attempted escape while Lafayette was in charge
of them, he had been called by some Frenchmen "a vile tool of con-
spiracy"[4] and demands were made that he be called to an account. Rumors
were printed that he planned to flee to America with his wife and children.

James Monroe had fought as an officer in the Continental Army alongside Lafayette in the Revolutionary War and had nursed him when he had
been wounded at the battle of Brandywine. The two young soldiers had
become fast friends. It was most natural that Lafayette would have told
Dubois that this was the man he should seek out. And yet, Monroe was at
that moment passionately declaring in Freneau's *National Gazette:*

"I rejoice in the French Revolution."

By way of explanation, he married his past to the present events in
France.

"Whoever owns the principles of one Revolution," he wrote, "must
cherish those of the other."[5]

In the summer of 1791, freed from his winter duties as a United States
Senator, Monroe announced to the public that he would be practicing law
in the superior courts at Richmond. It was only a short distance from Norfolk. Dubois travelled to the state capital—barely a village compared to
his own native city—and there called upon Monroe.

A tall, well-built man of thirty-three, Senator Monroe had, at this time,
just written to Jefferson and had reached deeply into his own American-
formed bias to describe a battle he was having with what he labelled as the
"Monarchist party." Though he had been made to endure precious few
Catholics in his lifetime other than the Frenchmen who had helped him
fight for independence, he told Jefferson that it was impossible for any
well-thinking person to be passive in such a controversy "unless the person
had been bred a priest in the principles of the Romish Church."[6]

Shortly thereafter a priest of the Romish Church called on him. Dubois'
letter from Lafayette gained him hospitality, for Monroe was, like the

Marquis, a gentleman. Beyond that, the success of Dubois' visit depended upon his own personality. Some seventy years later a man who had been a boy at the time remembered that Dubois had impressed Richmond as being "learned, accomplished and amiable."[7] Though Monroe and Dubois were at opposite poles in politics and belief, amiability became a bridge for acceptance. The two young men developed an enduring friendship. Dubois had a way with children and Monroe's little daughter Eliza immediately responded to his happy personality. Later, as an adult schooled in Paris, she would maintain a friendship in correspondence with him.

The American fascination with anything or anybody from France—regardless of political standing—helped to make Dubois attractive to Monroe. Had Richmond been flooded with exiles, the learned priest, amiable or not, would have drawn no special attention. There were but few, and Dubois was a sophisticated social find. Moreover, Americans have always shown an immediate compassion for manageable numbers of those who are suffering persecution, regardless of politics. One French exile declared that his new countrymen had "treated us like brothers," and thus had "rendered America a native home."[8]

The city fathers could not do enough in offering hospitality to the guest Lafayette had sent to Monroe. Richmond, the state capital, was still raw enough as a new town to lack adequate church facilities. At the invitation of the General Assembly, two Protestant ministers regularly alternated religious services on Sunday mornings in the new state capital building—a Roman temple design which imitated at Thomas Jefferson's suggestion the "Maison Carrée" at Nimes, France. The General Assembly broadened its invitation to include John Dubois. He accepted and celebrated Mass in the courtroom of the capital.

In learning English, Dubois could only have been confused by the inconsistencies shown by his hosts. Monroe was thoroughly gracious to him, yet continued to speak demogogically against the Roman Catholic priesthood. The Virginia newspapers expressed shock that "to the great scandal of Frenchmen and the law" some nonjuring priests were still functioning in France.[9] This while he was invited to celebrate Mass in the courtroom of the State Capital building. American legislators decried the marriage of Church and State in European nations, yet at the same time began to slide into sticky official liaisons with organized religions.

In the Virginia State legislature that year a "committee of religions" was appointed "to take under their consideration all matters and things relating to religion and morality." A chaplain was appointed to read daily prayers to the legislators. No one went on record as objecting except for "the people called Quakers," who spoke up against any public support of a "hireling ministry."[10]

Dubois wisely kept a low profile. After accepting the initial invitation of the General Assembly, he took to celebrating Mass in rented rooms and in the homes of Catholics. There was, however, one long-lasting effect of his experience with the legislature. In the thoroughly Roman Catholic world in which he had been born and raised, Dubois had never known any Protestant laity let alone clergymen. The Reverends John Buchanan and John Blair were merry social lions sometimes criticized by local bluenoses for their bon vivant approach to life. John Dubois was, if anything, a merry man whose childlike outlook on life had been undimmed by insane asylums or by religious persecution, and whose childlike merriment would remain undimmed through many more sufferings until the day of his death. The three Johns struck an immediate liking for one another, and maintained a happy friendship for as long as they served together in Richmond.

The local paper, *The Virginia Gazette,* was a means by which Dubois could hear of events in France, study English and learn about his new countrymen. The French colonies were in turmoil. In San Domingo the black slaves had risen against their masters massacring them and pushing them into the sea.

"They are destroying everything they come across," the paper reported in September, "There is now in sight of the harbour eleven plantations all in flames."[11]

Scores of French colonists began to arrive in the United States and state legislatures, including that sitting in Richmond, passed bills allotting money for their relief.

At the same time, Americans were perpetrating their own racial wars. The United States was doing its best to exterminate the Indians who stood in the path of westward expansions. General Charles Scott fought them along the Wabash River and at Fort Jefferson with the Kentucky militia. General St. Clair was defeated by a force of some three thousand Indians.

Flaming revolutionary rhetoric colored any news from France. The French, noted the *Gazette* early in the fall, were "bursting their chains and throwing off, almost in an instant, the degrading yoke of slavery."[12]

In the same paper a confused Dubois could learn that Americans made quite a profit of their own from the "degrading yoke of slavery."

"For sale," called out a typical ad, "One hundred likely slaves consisting of men, women and children."

Wanted notices called for the return of those who dared to throw off in an instant this degrading yoke in America:

"Buck, about 4 feet 10 inches high . . . branded on the near buttock with a long 8."

"Jesse . . . one of his wrists when young got cut with an axe. The scar still remains and can be seen by pulling up his shirt sleeve."

"A mulatto woman went off with the above. As she can write she probably has furnished the others with passes."[13]

Dubois learned of other American financial practices. Lotteries to pay for public finances were as popular as they had been in France. Americans did not blush at publishing personal matters when it came to money. One man disavowed any debts made by his wife, she having "betaken herself to drink."[14] In what must have been a shocking revelation to a man raised in the well-ordered, if corrupt, Church in France, advertisements by Protestant trustees showed that laymen took care of hiring and firing their clergymen.

"The vestry are desirous of treating with a gentleman of the Protestant Episcopal Church to fill that office," began one such notice offering a salary of 100 pounds per annum.[15] In somewhat the same manner, Roman Catholics began to seek out Dubois. While he was staying at a Captain Coleman's in Richmond,* a William Hunter, in October, informed him that "several respectable Catholics" living in Alexandria were "continually deprived of the consolations of their religion."[16]

Writing to a Colonel Fitzgerald there, Dubois told him that it would eventually be a matter "subject to the Bishop of Baltimore whether I settle for a while at Richmond." If he did remain, he said, he would be glad to serve them "from time to time."

Then, reflecting an attitude toward personal wealth about which he would remain consistent for the rest of his life he offered:

"I do not ask any contribution for this; I wish but the consolation of being of use. Only if it will be necessary for me to go there frequently I will ask that a horse be furnished me upon which I may make the trip."

"Although a Frenchman," he concluded, "I begin to speak several words of your English and I hope to speak it perfectly in time."

He signed the letter simply with his last name—"Dubois."[17]

In November 1791 Patrick Henry retired from public office and re-entered his law practice in order to get himself out of debt. Coming in to Richmond from his estate, some forty miles away, he packed a courtroom to the rafters for several days while he argued forcefully against the pre-revolutionary debt claims of British merchants. Dubois was an eager student amidst all of this. Someone introduced him to Henry—probably, once again, on the strength of his relationship with Lafayette. The two men shared enough time together that Dubois would later tell students that he was indebted to the great patriot for "many friendly lessons in our language."[18]

He began to ride a circuit to the Catholics in Norfolk, Alexandria, and Harpers Ferry, and learned that he was in traditionally unfriendly territory despite the cordial reception he had received. Catholicism had long been proscribed in the colony of Virginia. The few Catholics who lived there, post-revolution, were either widely settled stragglers or recent French arrivals such as himself. The only priest the older settlers had occasionally seen was the German, Jacob Frambach, and he had been shot at several

---

*James Monroe left Richmond for the national capital, Philadelphia, in October 1791.

times by the local citizenry—perhaps owing as much to the role of the
German Hessians in the Revolution as to his being a papist.

The papist Dubois with his amiability and intelligence easily won
respect wherever he travelled. By reputation he won the respect of Bishop
John Carroll whose diocese was, quite simply, the entire United States.
Carroll thought that the arriving French immigrants might form a settlement in Virginia such as the Gallipolis community begun the year before
on the banks of the Ohio River. He measured the priest who served the
community at Gallipolis against what he heard of the newcomer Dubois
and compared the former to the latter as "a vigorous and active man but
not quite so fervent I fear as the one just arrived."[19]

Bishop Carroll was wrong in his anticipation of French enclaves. In contrast to the multitude of soft, royalist emigrés who lived a passive existence
in European countries, the French who crossed the Atlantic were an energetic lot. Rather than being closed into the settlements such as Carroll
imagined, they were assimilated into an American society fascinated by
anything Gallic. Madame La Tour du Pin and her husband learned to milk
cows and operated a successful dairy farm outside of Troy, N.Y. There,
ex-Bishop Talleyrand visited her and did his best to charm her as if they
were still at Versailles.

"One might in one's mind," she wrote, less than fully charmed, "regret
having so many reasons for not holding him in respect."

She decided the turncoat bishop was "worthless." With what she described as "diabolical shrewdness,"[20] he was pursuing a lust for wealth. In
this newly born country he sought opportunities for land speculation,
building in his imagination, so he wrote, "cities, villages and hamlets."[21]

Many of the emigrés turned their nationality into a living. In Richmond
Louis Russell opened a dancing school, John Bourchette advertised himself as a staymaker from Paris (". . . To give and preserve a shape truly
perfect; not drooping or falling in before"),[22] and John Dubois, as he con-
quered English, took a job teaching French in a school run by a Mr. Harris.
He rented lodgings in a small wooden house next to the James River and
by Christmas, 1791, he felt confident enough in his abilities to place an ad
in the *Virginia Gazette:*

> The Public are herebye informed that the
> Rev. Mr. Du BOIS
> from Paris
> will in January next open school for the French language.
> He will also teach in private families and will receive a small
> number of boarders who will be instructed in the English,
> French, Latin and Greek languages, writing, arithmetic
> and bookkeeping. Such as desire to employ him are requested
> to leave a line for him at his house next the bridge on the
> right hand from the capital.[23]

Dubois' school was a success; so much so that within the year he broadened the invitation in his ad. He added a second set of classes on three days a week for "such gentlemen who cannot with convenience attend in the forenoon," and began tutoring families in their homes.[24]

The routine of school, circuit travelling to Catholics, and the rustic enjoyments of American society could not obscure for Dubois what was happening in France. In the summer of 1792 the Revolutionary government rounded up all the remaining nonjuring priests. Hundreds of them in Paris were crowded into jails and makeshift prisons such as the converted Carmelite monastery several blocks from Saint Sulpice. At the beginning of September, with the city in panic because of news of an Austrian invasion, the priests were given a last chance to take the oath. When they refused, one hundred and ninety-one priests were massacred, ninety-five of them in the Carmelite monastery. Sixteen of these men had lived with Dubois. Had he remained in Paris he would have been counted among them.

Death stalked the revolutionary city. The king and queen were beheaded and, after them, thousands of victims in an ongoing terror.

"Blood flowed everywhere in Paris," wrote Madame La Tour du Pin who like all the emigrés could only look back helplessly, "Each of us had relatives and friends among the victims of the terror, nor could we see an end to it."[25]

Lafayette was in prison. A law was passed forbidding emigrés to return under pain of death. Revenge was being laid upon the relatives of emigrés. Dubois could only pray that his mother would escape a death for which he would be the cause. Christianity was obliterated by law. At Saint Sulpice as at Notre Dame, young women were enthroned upon the altars to personify Reason.

Robespierre, standing for the moment atop the wheel of power, changed the dedication of Saint Sulpice so that a new inscription was placed over the door, "To the Goddess of Reason." Then the wheel of power turned and Robespierre the persecutor became himself victim of the guillotine. All philosophies forgotten, the government used the empty, cavernous Saint Sulpice Church as a warehouse.

In 1793 when Citizen Genêt arrived in the United States representing the revolutionary government, he stirred up angry factions. Federalists under President Washington's lead drew back from the bloody excess of the terror. Reacting to the law punishing emigrés, one citizen wondered publicly:

"Is not such a decree contrary to the spirit of the treaties subsisting between the United States and France?"[26]

Admirers of the Revolution, led by James Monroe and James Madison, continued to applaud any revolutionary extreme as long as the word "Liberty" was used by the extremists.

In Richmond John Marshall organized a public meeting to support President Washington's rebuke to Genêt. As an antidote to this, Monroe and Madison proclaimed that the people of France were but defending their liberties against the onslaughts of "priests and nobles."

Closing his eyes to what was going on during the Terror, Monroe wrote Jefferson in May of 1793:

"In my route I scarcely find a man unfriendly to the French Revolution as now modified. Many regret the unhappy fate of the Marquis of Lafayette. But they seem to consider these events as incidents to a much greater one and which they wish to see accomplished."[27]

Sent shortly thereafter to France as an acceptable minister to the government in power, Monroe prudently took with him white, paid servants, lest the presence of his slaves ruin his reputation as a lover of the "rights of man."

Dubois had received a painful education from the double-faced revolutionaries of the old world and the new. He began to pull back from all involvement with politics and politicians. Whereas others of the clergy, both then and thereafter, would consider themselves successful when they could bask in the favor of government leaders, Dubois, for the rest of his life, shunned it. In the half century left to him, his accomplishments would brush him against the great and near great of the young and then not-so-young Republic. But he always would keep aloof. Many years later, in the midst of a sermon, he revealed how deeply it all had affected him:

> God forbid I should sully this holy place with the scandalous
> recital of all the sacrileges, murders, and impieties which
> disgraced those stormy times. Minister of the God of Peace
> I have nothing to do with wars which revolt humanity.
> Much less have I to do with politics and politicians of this
> world. Let it suffice for me to observe that licentiousness
> under the name of liberty; impiety under that of philosophy;
> barbarism under the cloak of humanity; persecution under
> that of tolerance had involved under the same ruins;
> thrones, altars, rich and poor, peaceable citizens and
> ambitious revolutionists, and had disappointed the warmest
> but honest friends of humanity who, by deceitful promises
> were made to believe that man was to become at last
> the friend of man.[28]

Memory of the victims of the September massacres might have shamed Dubois. They had remained in Paris to serve as priests regardless of the consequences. In time the names of those martyred men with whom he had lived would be carved into the wall of the chapel of St. Denis in the Church of Saint Sulpice. Yet, if Dubois had denied himself a crown of martyrdom, he had set out upon a mission of heroic proportions. There were hordes of emigré priests who in the seventeen nineties, lived out a safe existence in European friaries. A report from Italy, published in the *Virginia Gazette* in 1793, noted that "the compassion which at first induced the inhabitants of this capital to receive in an hospitable manner the French priests and clergy has been suddenly changed into hatred and contempt."[29] Viewing these clerics as the cause of revolution and war the animosity of the people made it necessary to move them into two convents outside Rome, protected by guards.

If any substantial number of these unemployed priests had come to the United States, the immigrant church would have been greatly strengthened. As it was, there was too much work for the few who were present.

Catholics were often left without priests for great stretches of time. Some easily lost their faith. The abortive Gallipolis community of French refugees on the Ohio River were Parisians who, according to the prejudice of Bishop Carroll, "brought with them the vices of the large cities and a hatred for religion."[30] In the mid-1790s Father Stephen Badin reported to the Bishop that he had visited and found them to be a community without religion or morals. Others, left on their own, found God in the adversities of pioneer life. The nobly born Madame La Tour du Pin, by her own confession irreligious, awakened in soul when her infant daughter died. Without the presence of a priest (perhaps the reason why she would so disdain the memory of Talleyrand who had abandoned the priesthood), her husband performed the last rites as best he could and buried the child on their farm. With touching simplicity Madame La Tour du Pin recorded her spiritual awakening:

> . . . It was there . . . that God bided his time to work a
> change of heart in me . . . I could not describe exactly the
> change which took place in me. It was as if a voice cried out
> to me to change my whole nature. Kneeling on my child's
> grave I implored her to obtain for me from God, who
> had taken her back to be with Him, and to give me a little
> comfort in my distress. My prayer was heard. God granted
> me the grace of knowing him and serving him . . .[31]

French refugees from the slave uprising in San Domingo continued to pour in. In August of 1793 the *Virginia Gazette* numbered four hundred of these in Norfolk. While this would form a sizeable parish for the work of a priest, it was to the more Catholic Maryland that the great majority of the refugees fled. Over fifty ships that summer deposited some fifteen-hundred escapees in Baltimore. While the state took up charity collections to care for the newcomers, Bishop John Carroll had to stretch further his priestly personnel.

Dubois was doing good work in Virginia. But there was more that he could do northward where there were more Catholics and almost no priests.

In early 1794 Bishop Carroll asked him to move to Frederick, Maryland. Dubois did so immediately, ending his career in Virginia. Before he left Richmond, however, a banquet was organized for him by his fellow teachers. Present at this farewell were his two good friends of the Protestant clergy, the Reverends John Buchanan and John Blair.

It was a touching tribute to Dubois as a person. It was, as well, an indication as to what direction nascent Nativism might have taken had it been met with amiability.

14

Above, *James Monroe (1758–1831) sheltered John Dubois at his home
in Richmond when the French priest arrived with an introduction
from Lafayette.* Below, *although Dubois never lost his heavy French
accent, he understood English quite well. When first learning the language,
he spent considerable time with the patriot, Patrick Henry (1736–1799).*

15

16

Above, *while residing in Richmond, Dubois was hospitably received by its citizens. The state legislature allowed him to offer Mass in the courtroom at the new capital building. It is said to have been the first public Catholic mass offered in that city.*

17

Above, *View of Richmond, Virginia in the early nineteenth century, by the artist St. Mémin.*

CHAPTER 4

We Poor Backwoods Clowns

Bishop John Carroll, born and bred in upper-class gentility, could not be classed with the early American bishops who were missionaries on horseback. He spent each summer, the time best suited for diocesan visitations, visiting his mother at the family estate in Maryland. If sedentary, he was however a good man and a careful desk administrator. He had an awesome diocese to administrate. The Church in the United States was huge in size, had no real ecclesiastical structure, was manned by a handful of priests, and was sparsely yet widely populated by Irish, German, and French Catholics who clashed with one another and with the few native Catholics. Unlike Protestant denominations which claimed no overall unity, Catholics were bound to one another whether they liked it or not, and very often they did not.

Priests acted individually and often in opposition to Church authority. A weakened papacy had bowed to political pressure and suppressed the Jesuits. For decades thereafter the former members of that society clung tenaciously, almost inordinately, to their property. Before he was a bishop, John Carroll had angrily written to a fellow ex-Jesuit that should the Congregation of Propaganda Fide in Rome ever gain title to Jesuit real estate in the United States "our civil government would be called upon to wrest it again out of their dominion."[1]

After he became bishop, the tables were turned with regard to the exercise of authority. In this capacity he was made to endure a plague of priests he labelled "rambling friars,"[2] unhappy in Europe and seeking fortunes in the New World.

In New York, two Irish Franciscans divided their small congregation in a small civil war as to who should be pastor. In Philadelphia, German priests took their parish into schism and Carroll into court disputing his authority over them. An Irish priest, Patrick Smyth, who preceded John Dubois at Frederick, Maryland, found the work of this widespread mission too burdensome.

"The load is become so heavy that I cannot possibly bear it," he groaned, ". . . I must go back to Ireland."[3]

When he got there he published a scathing attack on the mismanagement of the United States missions by ex-Jesuits.

In 1793 another Franciscan, Francis Fromm, left his assigned parish to move into a comfortable estate bequeathed by a late priest to whatever "priest shall succeed him." When Carroll attempted to remove him, the friar took the Bishop to court. Defeated by a civil judgment Fromm continued to carry his case to higher courts until 1798 when a bout with yellow fever carried him off to the highest court of all.[4]

Wishing to ward off clerics who set sail for America with great expectations of fortunes to be made, John Carroll warned prospective missionaries of "labour, hardships of every kind, coarse living," and then added, as only a gentleman could, "great scarcity of wine (especially out of the towns) must be borne with."[5]

It was refreshing to Carroll to gain the two dozen refugee priests from the French Revolution. To a man, having chosen "la mission d'Amerique" over the safe European havens chosen by thousands of their fellow exiled clergymen, they were selflessly dedicated to the work of Christ. Sulpicians, exiled from Paris, began for him a seminary in Baltimore. John Dubois, who had asked of the Catholics of Alexandria only a horse for transportation was well suited to the burdens in rural ministry which Patrick Smyth had declared unbearable.

The town of Frederick, a bustling Maryland crossroads of some seven hundred houses was a center of iron ore, slate limestone, copper and glass industries. Nevertheless, it was as primitive as any frontier settlement. The streets were ill-graded and ill-drained, and there was little attempt at pavement. In dry weather the dust blinded citizens and in rain the town became a Venice of mud. "To cross a street on a wet night," wrote one native historian, "was a bold undertaking."[6]

Frederick became the hub from which John Dubois served vast areas of Maryland and Virginia for the next decade and a half. Living on horseback amidst rolling hills and heavy woods, the energetic thirty-year-old Dubois bought two horses, afraid that he would wear one out. His lonely mission was to travel about seeking out and serving Catholics wherever they might be. He centered himself at various "stations" throughout Montgomery, Frederick and Washington counties. Over the Potomac River, he served Virginians at Harpers Ferry, Martinsburg and Winchester. At the northern border of the state he visited Hagerstown and Emmitsburg—at this last town drawing Catholics from Gettysburg, Pennsylvania, ten miles northward. Wherever he travelled, he could see evidence of the old anti-Catholic laws which had been swept away with the Revolution. Typical was the "Mass house" at "Elder's Station" outside of Emmitsburg. There, where colonial law had forbidden any public entranceway to a Catholic Church, a fake chimney to an ordinary looking house opened up to make a doorway into a good-sized chapel.

The social range of his ministry was total. He became friends over the years with the signer of the Declaration of Independence, Charles Carroll. At Petersville, in western Maryland, he served the Catholic family of Governor Thomas Sim Lee who left office the year Dubois arrived. Grateful that his wife had recovered from a serious illness Governor Lee helped construct Petersville's first Catholic church. Many of Dubois' widespread flock were, like the Elders, old stock descendants of the Catholics who had founded the colony of Maryland. Others were immigrants, arriving in ever-increasing numbers. In Frederick's newspaper, notices in German began to intermingle with those in English. Emmitsburg, established in 1788 when James and Joseph Hughes settled in the area with their families, quickly grew as an immigrant center. These immigrants were soon at odds with the native Catholics who gathered for Mass at Elder's station two miles away.

"It was newcomers, Irish, who raised the town church and separated,"[7] remembered an elderly woman in 1853. For a brief while they attached to themselves a priest, Matthew Ryan, who created wounds which John Dubois had to heal.

"When I used to live in Frederick Town," he later wrote, "a scandalous priest was in charge of Emmitsburg; a character queer, violent, in fact insisting on money even to the extent of creating scenes at the Altar against those who contradicted him. He was ridiculed, accused of drunkenness. The event had created a schism."[8]

With this situation he encountered a problem which would plague him for the remainder of his life. Whereas the French immigrants worked to sell their culture to Americans, and the Germans tended to form ghettos, the Irish, speaking the same language as Americans, demanded immediate acceptance. Embittered by England's penal laws at home and their own abortive revolutionary attempts—one in 1798 instigated by the French— they arrived in the new Republic determined to have a full share in citizenship. Meeting prejudice and opposition they returned fire. During Dubois' pastorate the *Frederick Town Herald* printed the resentful political protest of one such immigrant, angry because the New York Irish were "excluded from all the ward and nomination committees."

"Tell us no more of the yearning in your heart toward the friends of freedom," he spat, "In your mouths it is all a lying vanity; a miserable farce."[9]

It was a type of anger which could only breed greater anger to come.

The lowest of those on the social scale whom Dubois had to serve were Catholic slaves. One must look at a map to realize that Maryland, in some places more than a hundred miles south of the northern tip of Virginia, was very much a southern state with southern manners and laws. One plantation near Frederick boasted some two hundred slaves. Liberal young men of intelligence, such as the fellow students of law—Roger Brooke Taney and Francis Scott Key, were raised with the conviction that slaves were undistinguished from anything else that was owned. A typical notice announced the auction of a dead man's personal property consisting of "fourteen or fifteen negroes, twelve horses, twenty horned cattle, thirty head of hogs, hammer, anvil and all kinds of farming equipment."

"Wanted" notices for runaway slaves in Maryland included those posted by the most prominant Catholic in the country:

"Fifty dollars reward. Ran away from the manor of C. Carroll, esq. of Carrollton distant fifteen miles from Baltimore on the Frederick Town Road, on the twelfth dist, a negro man named Moses . . ."[10]

Patrick Smyth, the bitter Irish priest who published his intended exposé of ex-Jesuit control of the American missions, included in his attack charges that they owned and beat slaves.

Defensively, Bishop John Carroll sought to justify slave ownership by churchmen. The slaves owned by Jesuits, he claimed, were "much better fed, lodged and clothed than laboring men in almost any part of Europe . . . the instances are rare indeed and almost unknown of corporal punishment being inflicted on any of them who are come to the age of manhood . . ."[11] To Carroll, it was the manner of treatment and not the ownership of slaves which was a moral issue.

In this milieu, Dubois became acculturated not only as an American but as a Southern American. He would eventually own slaves. Nevertheless, he saw the slaves as part of his missionary responsibility. Visiting plantations and farms, he carefully instructed them and listened to their catechism lessons. Concentrating on persons rather than systems, Dubois saw slaves as individuals with rights. The only time in his life that he used his political connections for any personal advantage was on the behalf of a slave awaiting execution in Virginia for having killed his master.

In 1802 Dubois wrote James Monroe, then Governor of the state, appealing to the same sense of kindness which had prompted him to take in a refugee priest:

"I know too well of your benevolent disposition," he entreated, "to hesitate a moment to solicit your executive interference in a case where both justice and humanity claim it."

A slave blacksmith, Jack Neale, had been sold from one master to another, separating him from his wife and children. Industriously he had set out to buy his own freedom. Wrote Dubois:

"It was generally reported that the fellow had already paid two hundred dollars towards his freedom to his master and would have paid the whole had not people abused his being a black man to keep him out of his money."

Betraying a trust, his owner suddenly sold him to a man heading for Spanish territory. "The idea of being torn thus from his wife and children and from his native country drove the poor fellow to despair," judged Dubois. A powerful man, Neale broke the chains which held his wrists while he was being transported. A stronger chain replaced it, with an iron hook placed around his body.

"Thus he was dragged as far as the Ohio," Dubois continued, "An opportunity having offered in the boat, Jack, in defense of his natural rights executed his threats and killed his tyrant . . . When he and his fellow slaves were taken up he cleared the others immediately and declared that he was the guilty man."

Couching his plea in the language of revolution which Monroe claimed as his own philosophy, Dubois asked "whether the law has a right to punish a murder committed in defense of a right which no one could lawfully rob him of."

After signing, with "great respect and affection," Dubois personalized the letter in a postscript:

"Please do present my respects to Mrs. Monroe and Miss Eliza to whom I will write in a few days. I would have written this time if I had not feared that the least delay in this business might be fatal to that poor black man."[12]

No records in the Virginia State Archives indicate whether Dubois was successful with his plea. The attitude of the times, however, calls for a pessimistic supposition. Shortly before this, Virginia had moved to quell a rumored slave uprising. Monroe, the lover of civil liberties, executed thirty-five slaves as an example to others who might want to start their own revolution.

Not long after Dubois moved to Frederick, the Whiskey Rebellion broke out. Belittled in history because of its name, it was nonetheless a serious challenge aimed at the Federal government's right to tax and govern. It was not unlike the mob revolutions which had overthrown the first moderate revolutionaries of France. Under President Washington's leadership it took fifteen thousand men and the militias of four states, including Maryland, to put it down. Frederick already had a standing militia for campaigns against the western Indians, and it was augmented during this

rebellion. It was not disbanded afterwards. Frenchmen had become suspect
when the arrival of San Domingo refugees coincided with a scourge of
Yellow Fever. Francophobia continued to grow in the latter part of the
1790s when the United States and France found themselves to be less-
than-loving sister republics. Talleyrand, sensing a shift of political winds,
had returned home to gain power as Foreign Minister. In that capacity he
now baited the land of his exile with the insults of the XYZ affair. American public opinion exploded into anger against France. In that country a
new and rising star dominated affairs. Dubois' Saint Sulpice, having served
as a warehouse, its chapel of communion destroyed by the fires of an incendiary, was cleaned up in 1799. Redecorated with tapestries and a grand
statue dedicated to victory, it was made to serve as a mammoth banquet
hall to honor Napoleon Bonaparte.

An undeclared naval war developed between the United States and the
ever more powerful France. In 1801, Dubois' flock in Frederick was increased by the crew of the French frigate, *L'Insurgente,* captured by the
U.S.S. *Constellation.* These men were imprisoned in barracks which
twenty-five years before had been used to incarcerate Hessian troops captured by French and American soldiers fighting as allies. It was a time for
a naturalized French American to lay low. Dubois had already learned
through long, drawn-out periods of danger to do so successfully. He quietly
kept on his rounds, avoiding involvement with politics. In a few years' time
he would be teaching his charges that in his native land "constitutions
sprang up like mushrooms and perished as quickly."

The United States' constitution, modeled on that of England, seemed to
him more stable. Nevertheless he had seen changes made in it since his
arrival. With what seemed almost a stoic shrug he concluded:

"If these changes are adapted to the genius of the people and to circumstances of the time it will stand; if they have been forced upon the nation
by factions it will fall to pieces in a few years."[13]

Living on horseback he waved off political considerations and worked
with the individual souls who lived throughout the hills of Maryland and
Virginia. The immigrant Catholics he found had often been untended by
priests for many years and their religion was at best a distant memory.
Many had intermarried with Protestants while still clinging to their remembered Church. With no clergy of their own, they had married civilly or
before Protestant ministers.

In the early 1790s Bishop Carroll dictated regulations which seemed
too harsh for the existing conditions. He ordered his priests to make known
that those guilty of marrying outside the Church were to be barred from
the sacraments "till they shall agree to make public acknowledgment of
their disobedience before the assembled congregation and beg pardon for
the scandal they have given."[14]

The pastoral man in the field, John Dubois, found these regulations hard to live with and sought to soften them because of mitigating circumstances. He wrote to Carroll of one widower whose sister-in-law had come to settle matters after his wife's death. Young people, they fell in love and remained together. They encountered a priest, but his treatment of them was curt and hurtful. Turned away by him, they married before a minister and had children. Dubois entered their lives.

"She threw herself at my feet the other day all in tears," he wrote, "begging me to save her from despair. Her husband is not so pressing but anxious to repair his fault." Dubois just could not bring himself to make the couple shame themselves publicly. Pleading, "I feel for that unhappy woman," he argued that the crime "has been willful but some allowance must be made for the youth and ignorance of the girl, and her repentance is sincere."[15]

A Parisian, thus raised within what Carroll saw as the vices of that large city, Dubois turned to the manor-bred Carroll for expertise in bucolic American marriage problems. One man, Peter, was a heavy drinker and because his breath made his spouse sick she had an "invincible aversion to lie in bed with him," though "she is willing to grant the marriage debt." Peter was adamant. He wanted her in bed for warmth. Dubois claimed to be at a loss.

"Which of the two ought to be compelled to give up," he asked Carroll innocently, "Must not the sacraments be refused to the one who refuses and to which of the two?"[16]

Eventually, churches had to be built. In Frederick, Dubois began the new century by planning an edifice far beyond the needs or means of the community at hand. A budding politician, Roger Brooke Taney, joined forces with him in the venture, though afterwards he admitted that he had held doubts about his pastor's foresight:

"We all thought that the means could never be raised to pay for such a building," he remembered, "that the church would never be completed, and if it were completed it would never be filled with Catholics."[17]

A twenty-two-year-old immigrant, John McElroy, was an up-and-coming merchant who responded generously to the appeal for funds. In time he decided to give more than money. He abandoned his career and entered the seminary. Later, in between teaching at Georgetown, travelling with Zachary Taylor's army as chaplain during the Mexican War, and founding Boston College he would serve as this church's pastor for twenty-three years.

Dubois and Taney won authorization from the state in 1804 to raise funds with a lottery. It was, at best, a thorny success. A confusing newspaper ad caused many people to return tickets before the fall harvest which Dubois had counted upon for loose, flowing cash. "I am at a loss what to do,"[18] he bemoaned. Taney lost out as well for his political opponents made hay out of his involvement in money-making schemes to build a Catholic Church. If money and prestige were lost, however, friendship was not. For decades thereafter Taney was Dubois' advisor on legal and financial matters. In turn Dubois—whether because of friendship or because of his previously demonstrated ecumenical attitude—did not insist upon a prenuptial agreement when he officiated at Taney's wedding to Anne Key, the sister of his friend Francis Scott Key. The Keys were Episcopalian. Many years later, family descendants would argue about what kind of an arrangement had been agreed upon, but it would seem that it was understood that the boys were to follow the religion of the father and the girls that of the mother. The one boy, who died in infancy, was baptized Roman Catholic. The girls were all raised as Episcopalians. Taney, who refused thereafter to discuss the point with others, remained correctly Catholic all of his life.

In Emmitsburg, the Irish town dwellers had quickly put up a church in the 1790s. The native Catholics who gathered at Elder's farm only two miles away, still determined to build a church there. The house-chapel, near the base of a low picturesque mountain, had served the community during the days of anti-Catholic legislation. Having worshipped there as outlaws, they felt that the site deserved a church. Tradition was on their side. So was Dubois. He agreed to take land for such purpose from the Elder family. Only after accepting this did he happen, "while rambling over the mountains with a couple of gentlemen," to come upon a level space well up on a hillside which commanded an awesome view of the entire valley. It struck him as being perfect to consecrate for prayer.

He also saw practical advantages: "An ever flowing spring which at the base of the hill adds to the convenience of the place . . . the firewood which is abundant there and which in a country Church is very necessary, rendered it much more suitable than the barren piece of ground which was intended formerly for the Church."[19]

Given Dubois' stubbornness, the area might have seen three Catholic churches dotting the landscape when one would have been a rarity. Finding that several people laid claim to the land, he had it resurveyed. To his surprise, "it fell into the hands of the very person whom I had requested to buy it for me." Arnold Elder, at length dragged there by Dubois, was stunned to see that it was a site which claimed as much tradition for the community's purpose as did Elder's station. As Dubois recorded: ". . . it was the very place which more than thirty years ago his father had pointed out to him as a desirable spot to build a church upon."[20]

The matter was settled and the deed transferred, whereupon one more coincidence was unearthed:

"What was my astonishment," exclaimed Dubois, "when I got the title, to see that the valley round that place where I intended to build St. Mary's

Church had been called by the Protestant who took it up, St. Mary's Valley."[21]

The whole procedure seemed almost providential. If the shifting and reshifting of deeds seemed less than such to Bishop Carroll, Dubois simply and cheerfully told him to consult with lawyers about any formalities "which we poor backwoods clowns are not acquainted with."[22]

In November 1805, united, if by nothing else than the decade-long service of their mutual priest, the two communities gathered on the mountainside. Local Protestants joined them, including a long-bearded Mennonite preacher.

"Mr. Dubois . . . ," remembered an old woman present as a young girl, "with his usual energy, walked about the lines of the spot he then selected."[23]

He picked up an axe, chopped into a tree trunk and the communal project was launched. One tree fell and killed a dog. His owner stopped, commented laconically: "I didn't ask him to come," and continued his work. Slaves and freemen, Catholics and Protestants, immigrants and natives—labored throughout the day, and then finished the event with an ox roast.[24]

Dubois had found an idyllic situation both with people and with the physical beauty of the land itself. He continued his circuitous pastorate, but this, now, was his home, the center of his activities. In 1807, as he approached the age of forty-three, he made the first—in fact the only— move in his life to provide anything for himself. Purchasing, on his own, land around St. Mary's Church, he kept the deed in his own name. His apology to Carroll showed clearly that, having experienced one holocaust in France, he felt little security about the Church's ability to take care of him in the New World. Of these twenty-six acres he wrote to his bishop:

> I give you my word that I will give them for the use of
> the Church there although I wish to keep them in my
> hands as a refuge in my old age. Could I be sure to quit this
> world before you I would not hesitate a moment to put it
> and my whole self at your commands. But as I know
> not what may happen I think the best is to keep it in my hands
> until my decease.[25]

When Carroll showed disapproval, Dubois pointedly reminded him that he had withheld Jesuit land from the control of the hierarchy. "Surely when so many Churches were built on the Jesuits' property," he wrote, "both before and after it was invested a corporation, it was not intended to encroach upon the Episcopal authority."[26]

In the light of the next thirty-five years of his life this momentary self-consideration seems almost comic. To the end of his days Dubois would burn himself out working for other people and for the physical development of the church. Even this property was signed over to the church in one year's time.

Prophetically, the paragraph which followed his apology about land ownership concerned a James Moynihan, an Irish immigrant the same age as Dubois. He had decided that he wanted to be a priest, and had written to Bishop Carroll but had gotten no response. In late 1805 he had introduced himself to Dubois who was impressed with him.

"His modest and pious deportment induced me to invite him to stay with me," he wrote Carroll, "until he should get a recommendation from you, which I insisted upon as a first necessary step."[27]

Dubois had already accepted the task of educating a handful of area boys, and several of these boarded with him at his log house on the side of the mountain. The middle-aged immigrant Moynihan joined them, and Dubois tutored him in "languages, philosophy and divinity."

In 1808, Moynihan was accepted by Carroll and sent to the preparatory seminary just begun by the Sulpicians at a private estate in Pennsylvania, some twenty-five miles north of Emmitsburg. He later returned for further studies at Emmitsburg and finished his seminary training in Baltimore. There, in 1813, at the age of forty-seven, James Moynihan was ordained a priest and was stationed to a successful ministry in St. Mary's County.

He was the first man instructed for the priesthood at the Mountain. He was the first of many.

18

As the Bishop of Baltimore, John Carroll (1735–1815) brought Father
Dubois from Virginia to the mission in Maryland in 1794. Although
the bishop respected Dubois, he was often troubled by the zeal with which
the priest made demands and exercised his authority.

At left, *Roger Brooke Taney
(1777–1864) was married to the
sister of Francis Scott Key by
Father Dubois. Taney remained
his advisor on legal and financial
matters, and was to become
Chief Justice of the Supreme
Court in 1836.*

19

20

Above, *an 1817 anti-slavery tract depicting the kidnapping of slaves;* at left, *a typical poster advertising the sale of slaves.*

21

St. John's Church at Frederick,
Maryland, begun by Dubois with the
aid of the young politician Roger
Taney.

22

23

The famous painting "Scene on the National Pike from Baltimore
to Fredericktown" from about 1817. It shows the amount of travel in
Dubois' vicinity during the early expansion to the West.

24

When Father Dubois wanted a church built at Emmitsburg he organized the community. "He picked up an axe, chopped into a tree trunk" and the project was launched. St. Mary's, later known as the "old Church on the Hill," was situated just above the grounds of the college, and served as a parish church until 1897. It burned in 1913.

CHAPTER 5

On Condition That I Would Not Have to Conduct It

In France John Dubois had lived almost all of his life in praying communities; at Louis Le Grand, at St. Magliore, with the sixty priests of St. Sulpice, and with the forty Daughters of Charity at the Petites Maisons. In America he lived starkly alone. He led communities of lay people in prayer and preached to them, but no longer experienced the luxury of listening to others preach or of letting others lead prayers for him to follow. He prayed the Divine Office, meant to be sung in common, by firelight in the empty quiet of his cabin or while sharing the company of his horse as he trekked over dusty country roads.

For the first generation of his missionary life, Dubois periodically left his hills to visit the French Sulpicians in Baltimore. In Paris they had run the seminary attached to the parish of St. Sulpice where Dubois had been stationed. Exiled to the United States, they purchased a tavern in Baltimore and converted it into a seminary which at first showed little promise of success. In the decade after Dubois had arrived at Frederick they often had only one student and never more than five. Nonetheless, hoping for eventual success they built an exquisite chapel—as beautiful as any church in the country. There Dubois could pray in community with brother priests in an atmosphere that brought back warm memories of earlier days. There, each year he took time for an extended retreat.

He longed for this on a permanent basis so deeply that he applied several times for admission into the Society of St. Sulpice. Each time he was refused. It was not mere callousness on the Sulpicians' part. In their present circumstances they were overstaffed to the point of embarrassment in their nearly empty seminary. This overabundance of priests in one place in a priest-starved nation led to a reassignment of several of the Baltimore Sulpicians. The roundabout adventures of several of these men—most notably Fathers Louis William Valentine DuBourg and Pierre Babade would affect the entire course of John Dubois' life.

In the late nineties, Bishop Carroll asked the Sulpicians of St. Mary's Seminary to provide help for the ex-Jesuits who ran a small college at Georgetown. The bishop felt that under the "torpid" leadership of the professors at hand the school had "sunk lamentably in character."[1] Perhaps new blood might help. All concerned, however, got more than they bargained for when the Sulpicians sent Father DuBourg to take over as the college's president.

DuBourg, whose placid, princely face hid a mind overly active with chimerical schemes, had a lifelong habit of starting grand projects, then walking away and letting others take over the responsibility involved.

Two months before leaving Baltimore for Georgetown, he had started and left to others a religious education program for the slaves of San Domingan refugees. In Georgetown he rattled the conservative professors with so many changes that they cried out to Bishop Carroll against his "scheme" to make the place over into a French school under Sulpician direction.[2]

DuBourg quit after one year of battling with the faculty and went to Cuba, where with two companion Sulpicians—Benedict Flaget and Pierre Babade—he attempted to start a seminary. Running afoul of Havana's authorities both civil and religious, the trio made a second attempt in another Cuban diocese. From Paris where the Church was newly resurgent under the Emperor Napoleon, the Sulpician Father James Emery sought to moderate DuBourg, warning him against his habit of "presuming success too easily and of not seeing the difficulties when they are stretched out before you."

"Mistrust the ardor of your zeal," he pleaded, "which you have communicated to poor Flaget. (Babade had no need of any communication on this point.)"

He further scored Babade in a criticism, significant because he would soon be measured against Dubois as a spiritual director. The Sulpician superior thought Babade was tactless.

"He says all that he thinks and says it crudely," wrote Emery, adding that Babade lacked "enough discretion to deal with a situation which requires more than zeal and spirit."[3]

DuBourg returned to Baltimore with several Cuban boys in tow and, principally to care for them, started a new college alongside the Sulpician seminary. The fathers of Georgetown were immediately in arms. No one could foresee that the United States would ever be able to support more than one Catholic college. Emery wrote to DuBourg that Georgetown had every right to think that he had started a second college out of revenge "to ruin their establishment."[4]

A year after DuBourg's college was opened, Georgetown found a way to return fire. Seven young graduates were preparing to leave there for the seminary at Baltimore. Suddenly their departure was cancelled and the announcement was made that they could study philosophy where they were. In direct competition with the Sulpicians, the faculty at Georgetown had opened a seminary. DuBourg then expanded the enrollment of his college beyond that agreed upon between himself and Bishop Carroll. The reverberations of all of this, reaching Paris, roused Emery to anger. Sternly he admonished DuBourg:

"Get rid of grand ideas and act like a man of the Gospel."[5]

The Sulpicians were embarrassed. The purpose of their society was to conduct seminaries, not colleges. Emery had continually advised them to develop preparatory seminaries in various localities in order to foster vocations. DuBourg's secular college was a galling reminder to them that this remained undone. Then in 1806 Joseph Harent, a pious emigré who had settled in Pennsylvania, offered the use of his farm to the Society while he visited France. The septuagenarian superior in Baltimore, Father Charles Nagot, travelled to Harent's farm in August of that year to begin a school for ten students in the first steps of training for the priesthood.

The limitation of this undertaking was, of course, the intended return of Harent. The Sulpicians who travelled to and from Pennsylvania could ponder this when they stopped to enjoy hospitality at John Dubois' delightful mountain. Dubois, starved for companionship, was the happiest of hosts. He had never stopped visiting the seminary in Baltimore, never stopped his yearly retreats under the guidance of the Sulpicians, and had never stopped petitioning to join the Society. DuBourg at one point had taken Dubois under wing and had written a hearty recommendation for him and sent it to Emery in Paris. This, of course, was like a kiss of death. Emery informed his man of grand enterprises:

"You tell me, my dear DuBourg, à propos of Father Dubois' vocation to St. Sulpice, that he is more fit than you for it. I do not know him, but this is the fact; that the life of a Sulpician in his strict and ordinary milieu is certainly not for you."[6]

Then, during 1806–1807 as the Sulpicians made their frequent stops at this scenic mountain they began to take a closer look at the man who came to retreat. Standing on this well-situated land which he owned outright, Dubois seemed ever more likely a community candidate. He showed DuBourg over the acreage "to which I intended to retire after eighteen years of fatigue and hardships in missionary journeys."[7] The man of great enterprises began to think. Turning on the "affable and eloquent" charm by which, as Emery noted, "he takes ascendancy of those around him,"[8] DuBourg made a proposal. Dubois later recorded:

". . . he conceived the idea of building a preparatory seminary on this land. I consented to this on the condition that I would not have to conduct it and promised to give the land to St. Sulpice of which I hoped then to become a member."[9]

The Sulpicians had previously told Dubois that his acceptance would depend upon a trial period wherein he lived with and was judged by the community. At the end of 1807 Dubois arrived in Baltimore to find that this had been waived and that he had been voted into the Society. In lieu of a novitiate, he was told by DuBourg to return "immediately to the mountain to clear the land and prepare the material for the projected building." As Dubois understood the situation he was not in charge but was to act as "the agent of Father DuBourg who was to furnish the funds and give the orders."[10]

Returning to Emmitsburg, Dubois cut a terrace into the mountain for the site of the seminary building. Workmen were paid only sporadically when DuBourg chose to visit the scene or send money.

At Sunday Mass, Dubois appealed for volunteers to hew additional logs and on the appointed day he took his crew up into the hills, accompanied by an unexpected cloudburst. The aristocratic DuBourg, masterminding this great enterprise from Baltimore might have laid claim to being the founder of the new school at Emmitsburg, but it was Dubois, acting as his "agent" whose sweat and muscle brought it into being. A young Protestant, volunteering his help, recorded a remembrance of Dubois.

"The Reverend himself," he wrote, set to work, "with his coat off, doing his share and all of us wet through with the rain so that it was quite a cheerless task. We succeeded in loading the first log and were on the point of starting with it when the holdings gave way and it rolled down the hillside for a considerable distance, we having barely escaped being crushed."[11]

Having escaped this, Dubois then was crushed financially, both at the time and for years afterward, beneath debts contracted by DuBourg.

"It was also at this time," Dubois wrote, "That Father DuBourg had the idea of arranging for the plantation of Arnold Elder . . . "[12]

Elder had decided to leave this adjoining farm to the seminary "after his own and his wife's death." But she was, as Dubois observed, "surrounded by her relatives who wanted the property for themselves despite Mr. Elder's will." DuBourg judged the plantation to be "essential to the seminary" and moved to ensure the school's ownership. He offered that the Sulpicians would pay the Elders six hundred dollars annually if the property could be signed over while they lived. Dubois accepted this, but when the final dickering was done, DuBourg returned with a contract which Dubois felt was impossible to live with. The annual payment was to be eight hundred dollars, with another two hundred added to the initial payment to pay some of Elder's debts. The Elders were to keep their house; were to retain pasturage for their animals; and the seminary was to be obliged to cut and deliver winter firewood to their door. In return the seminary was to be given the farm's moveable property and slaves.[13]

Dubois sputtered an incredulous refusal to the terms but DuBourg waved him off, calling him a "man for objections."[14]

To Dubois' horror the Sulpicians, whom he presumed would reject this contract, voted their approval of it. Suddenly, Dubois was the master of several slaves and of a large farm, further indebted "to buy provisions and clothing for the negroes and harness for the horses for a year since the plantation had been given over to us entirely stripped."

With funds slipping away, DuBourg told Dubois to forget the large building which was planned and to content himself with a second log building. After accomplishing this with logs "which I made myself," a self-satisfied Dubois stood back and observed:

"I made such a good job of this second building that when it was up, the first building, composed of uneven and queer logs [gotten from an abandoned distillery] appeared to fit with it badly. What was there to do?"

Ever practical as well as a perfectionist, Dubois decided not to demolish the building as DuBourg suggested. Instead, he detached it from its chimneys and rolled it over ("not done without trouble," he noted) to a background where it served the school as a kitchen and servants' quarters. He replaced this with a third building to match the second.[15]

Quite apart from all this, DuBourg meanwhile had latched onto another great enterprise—a newly formed women's religious community with a convert from Protestantism as its foundress. Proportionately, as DuBourg interested himself in this new venture, funds for the seminary began to dry up. Construction bogged down. Mr. Harent returned to his farm and an accident crippled Father Nagot, the rector, with a broken leg. Thus, in the spring of 1809 eighteen students were dumped on Dubois while he was still busy hewing and hauling logs. The Elders, now secure with an old age pension provided by the school, cheerfully agreed to house the students— for a fee of eighty dollars plus five dollars for washing.*

In November 1809, DuBourg wrote Dubois telling him, quite simply, that he had no more money. Dubois panicked. He had hired carpenters and masons on DuBourg's orders. They were working without receiving their pay and the buildings for the seminary were nowhere near finished.

---

*Statistics recorded by the U.S. Department of Commerce help to place money amounts in context. In 1810 room and board cost an average of $120 per year. In 1814 a farm laborer earned, on the average, $1.25 a day.[17]

DuBourg was no longer interested. He was involved in his new project with the convert Mrs. Seton. Shrugging off his undertaking in Emmitsburg, he airily wrote back to Dubois in classic terms, telling him:

"Nemo dat quod non habet."[16]

As had happened so often in the past, DuBourg dropped the responsibility for what he had started squarely on the shoulders of someone else.

Mount St. Mary's began its existence under an unbearable financial burden. The new seminary could claim only one asset—the indomitable will of John Dubois.

William Louis Valentine DuBourg, S.S. (1766–1833) priest, educator, and later Bishop of New Orleans. Called by another author a "dreamer of dreams and impresario of the grandiose," he urged Dubois to start a seminary at Emmitsburg. He left Dubois to cope with a large debt and a huge construction project.

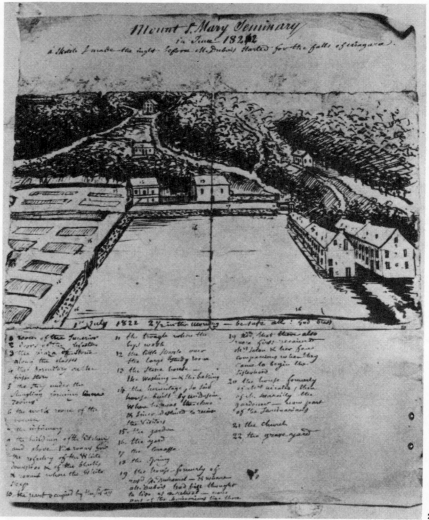

The night before Father Dubois went away for a trip to Niagara Falls with some students, Father Bruté drew this sketch of Mount St. Mary's at Emmitsburg. It is the earliest surviving view of "the Mountain." Shown at top center *is the old Church (1806);* below *that, Dubois' original cabin, where Mother Seton first stayed in 1809; on the same line at far right is the gardener's house. Lower center, at left "the hermitage" or guest house; and on its right a stone house for the laundry and baking; at far right, the residence for students and faculty, known as the "White House"; and next to that a house for the kitchen and staff. On the* extreme left, *along the side, are the gardens.*

CHAPTER 6

Mother is a Saint

Times were bad. Thomas Jefferson, now a strongly authoritarian President, instead of a liberal revolutionist, declared an embargo to combat Napoleon's continental system and blockade against England. The results were disastrous to the economy.

"Ruin encompasses us on every side," bitterly complained the *Frederick Herald*, "The farmer, the mechanic and every other class of people feel most heavily the consequences of the embargo. But they are not at all felt by our beloved president, and to the distresses of his people he is too much of a philosopher to attend."[1]

John Carroll, by necessity more a pragmatist than philosopher, worried whether the Sulpicians would be able to send more priests from bellicose France to staff their schools in Baltimore and in Emmitsburg at "the settlement of the Elders called by Mr. Dubois, the Mountain."[2]

Indeed Dubois felt so burdened while fighting this encompassing ruin that he asked his bishop if he might be relieved of his missions to Frederick and Governor Lee's—"my health declining and inadequate to the hardships which I had to undergo for fifteen years."[3]

Then a turn of events occurred which would place John Dubois in history books. It was a turn of events created by a thirty-nine-year-old, redheaded, toothless seminarian, Samuel Cooper.

Cooper was a mentally tortured man all of his life. Physically ugly, erratic in nature but wildly romantic, he was incapable of remaining in one place for any great length of time. Born in Norfolk, Virginia, a sense of wanderlust would keep him roaming the continents of the earth until the day of his death. As a sea captain he amassed a fortune from his travels, and in 1807 he converted to Roman Catholicism. The next year he was accepted into the Sulpician seminary as a candidate for priesthood under the wary eye of Bishop Carroll, who saw in him "many symptoms of a disordered imagination."[4]

In June of 1808 Cooper happened to share a stagecoach to Washington with Mrs. Elizabeth Seton, a widow, and like himself a recent convert to Catholicism. She had just moved to Baltimore at the urging of DuBourg who had met her in New York and became her mentor. Barely settled with her three young daughters, she was en route to pick up her two sons who had been placed in Georgetown College.

It was a singular encounter. Both had decided to enter a life of celibacy. Cooper, always described as rough and ugly, was a stark contrast to the delicate husband Elizabeth had buried. Yet Elizabeth, whose dark eyes and fair face still made her a handsome woman at thirty-four, felt herself drawn by an "involuntary attraction" to Cooper.

"If we had not devoted ourselves to the heavenly spouse before we met," she later reflected, "I do not know how the attraction would have terminated."[5]

Cooper began to watch her and to study her relationship with the Church which they had both so recently joined.

When her financially ruined and chronically ill husband had died in Italy five years earlier, Elizabeth Seton had been comforted and cared for by the Filicchis, a family of wealthy merchants with business in the Old World and the New. Returning to her Episcopalian family in New York, she converted to Catholicism in March 1805. Her action brought a wave of negative reactions from her aristocratic family, for she had abandoned not only the church of her birth but her social caste as well.

"... Anything in the world but a Roman Catholic.—A Methodist, Quaker, anything," protested her sister, Mary, "... but a Catholic ...! Dirty, filthy, red-faced—the Church a horrid place of spits and pushing, ragged ..."

Elizabeth, moving uncomfortably into the society of immigrant Irish, could only agree:

"Alas, I found it all that indeed."[6]

It wasn't just the congregation; it was the priests. At the time of her profession of faith, Fathers Matthew and William O'Brien had reached a divisive point where they refused to live or speak with each other. Matthew, who had received Elizabeth into the Church, had taken to drink and was a scandal to New York. John Carroll when he recommended candidates for the new Sees of Bardstown, Philadelphia, Boston and New York refused to name a man for the last.

"Amongst the clergy resident in New York when my letters went to Rome," he explained, "there was no one there whom I ventured to recommend for the episcopacy."[7]

The worst of them all, preaching in St. Peter's the last year of Elizabeth's stay in New York, was the hot-headed Patrick Kelly who had taken to lambasting his personal foes from the pulpit.

Throwing the young cleric's own defense of this back in his face, Carroll scolded:

"It is a wretched excuse for a priest to allege that he is an Irishman and subject to his national impetuosity." Suspending both Matthew O'Brien and Kelly, Carroll told the latter:

"The sooner you quit New York the better for you, the other clergymen, and generally for the welfare of the Church."[8]

From this discouraging scene Elizabeth Seton moved—at DuBourg's insistence—to what her brother-in-law described as "The Frenchified State of Maryland."[9] Though she had five young children, she sought to live a vowed, religious life. She might have gone to Georgetown where her two boys were in school and joined the several pious and patient ladies who were waiting for the torpid ex-Jesuit Father Leonard Neale to get around to organizing them into a formal religious order. They had been waiting since 1799 and would have laid claim to being the first native order for women in the United States, but that he made them wait until 1814 when he managed to put them under the rule of the Visitation order. As it was Elizabeth had come into the realm of the "affable and eloquent" William DuBourg. The ever cautious John Carroll was angry when she pulled her sons from Georgetown to place them in DuBourg's St. Mary's College in Baltimore. Yet, he exonerated her and, while doing so, anticipated Rome's official canonization by a century and a half:

"Their mother is a saint," he decided, ". . . she is not in fault." Rather, he feared that "Mr. DuBourg may have induced her to form some plan of which I shall fear bad consequences if carried into execution."[10]

After several years on her own meager resources, the once-wealthy Elizabeth became the guest of Catholics who were the social equal of Episcopalian high society in New York. Not only old families such as the Carrolls and Harpers, but wealthy exiles from France and San Domingo showered attention on her. DuBourg's sister, Madame Victoire Fournier, helped establish her in a house which was also to be a school. She had servants to care for her and she had her choice of intelligent pious priests to whom she could turn for spiritual direction.

For a year's time, from June 1808 to June 1809, she enjoyed the rich

Roman liturgy celebrated by the Sulpicians in Baltimore. The situation fed not only her religious needs but her strongly romantic nature as well.

"Imagine," she enthused, "twenty priests all with the devotion of saints, clothed in white, accompanied by the whole troop of the young seminarians in surplices also, all in order surrounding the Blessed Sacrament . . ."[11]

It was thus natural to her personality that she was drawn immediately to the poetic but erratic Pierre Babade, the partner of DuBourg's Cuban misadventures. She labelled the forty-eight-year-old man her "venerable patriarch"[12] and was enchanted by his proclivity for slipping into unconsciousness.

"He faints almost entirely three or four times a day,"[13] she exulted.

She prepared a first Communion class of girls for him and described the occasion in terms as emotional as they were religious. When Father Babade "dispensed the Sacred Passover," she wrote, "his tears fell fast over his precious hands while he gave it and we had the liberty to sob aloud . . ."[14]

In the shadow of Saint Mary's college she seemed completely happy. However, once again DuBourg showed that his grand plans extended far beyond his ability to produce results. The embargo had dried up the economy and a great deal of money was needed if Mrs. Seton was going to run a school. Unsuccessfully she sought funds from her wealthy friends in New York and from the Filicchis in Italy. Then Samuel Cooper stepped in.

Perhaps he had watched Dubois during the three years in the 1790s when the newly arrived Frenchman had visited Norfolk to serve Catholics there. In any event he knew him well from visits to the Mountain at Emmitsburg when Sulpicians stopped on the way to their Pennsylvania seminary. Cooper cared greatly for Elizabeth Seton. At the moment her future was in the hands of a man who made a career of flitting disastrously from one great enterprise to another. For a generation now, another man near at hand, Dubois, had shown himself to be as solid as a rock. He was beloved by Catholics and Protestants alike all throughout rural Maryland, Virginia and southern Pennsylvania. The comparison, in Cooper's mind, between the two priests led to an obvious conclusion. He called upon DuBourg who was his spritual director in the seminary and offered ten thousand dollars of his wealth to back Mrs. Seton's proposed religious community. He then added a stipulation which left DuBourg dumbfounded.

"Sir," he announced, "this establishment will be made at Emmitsburg."[15]

DuBourg objected strenuously. Mrs. Seton's school for girls was meant to be a sister school to Saint Mary's college for boys. She was to be directed in her new religious life by the Sulpician fathers. Cooper remained adamant. As DuBourg recorded:

". . . Mr. Cooper, while asserting that he would exert no influence in regard to locality, nor in the direction of the work, repeated in a confident tone that it would be at Emmitsburg."[16]

DuBourg was unhappy with the idea. John Carroll expressed the strongest opposition to the plan." Most significantly, the proposal was "contrary
to all the former convictions"[17] of Elizabeth Seton. Cooper as a lowly
seminarian was at the bottom of this pile of ecclesial superiors; but he was
at the bottom of the pile holding ten thousand dollars, and he stubbornly
insisted on Dubois' settlement at Emmitsburg.

In late February 1809, a resigned William DuBourg, a project-laden
Dubois, and a contented Samuel Cooper fought the winter winds and
tramped about inspecting the abandoned Fleming farm two miles from the
Mountain and one-half mile from the center of Emmitsburg. The deed was
signed in the name of all three men. Dubois was ordered by the man of
great enterprises to clear out the underbrush and to ready the house for
occupation by however many ladies might join Mrs. Seton.

All of this coincided with Father Nagot's broken leg and the arrival of
eighteen young seminarians at the Mountain. Until that year Dubois had
been pastor of a vast rural area. Now along with that, on land he had purchased for his own retirement, he was physically to build and then maintain a seminary for young men as well as a separate religious establishment for women. Any sort of retirement would be a long way off.

John Dubois needed more help, or more time, or better still, both. He
was taking care of pastoral duties, teaching school, building his seminary,
and laying foundations for a handsome colonial house large enough to serve
as a home for as many as thirty sisters. Under the best of circumstances it
would be months before he would be ready to take care of the physical
needs of a group of women. But in Baltimore DuBourg, unhampered by
anyone with common sense, continued to hurl thunderbolts of decisions in
Dubois' direction. For no better reason than that the lease had run out on
her house in Baltimore, Elizabeth Seton was encouraged to start out for
Emmitsburg where no one was ready to receive her. She precipitously arrived in Dubois' front yard on a hot June afternoon of 1809, accompanied
by her eldest daughter, two sickly sisters-in-law and one candidate for her
order.

Dubois, set aback by this untimely arrival, saw in Elizabeth Seton a
begrimed and exhausted woman dressed in a makeshift religious habit she
had designed of a black dress and a white bonnet. She was in something of
a culture shock. Thanks to the ten thousand dollar insistence of Samuel
Cooper, she, bred in an upper class urban world, accustomed even in genteel poverty to the finer things in life, was thrust into a pioneer setting.
The dusty roads, the four-day trek walking behind a canvas-covered wagon,
the primitive frontier countryside; all of this was a rough experience for
which she had been little prepared.

In John Dubois she saw a short, beefy workman with stubby hands
roughened by farm and building tools. Burdened by the demands of his
two huge construction projects, he wore the dirt of a man who cut terraces

and spread manure. He seemed worlds apart from the other aesthetical Sulpicians: Nagot whom she saw as "graced with all the venerable qualities of seventy-five" and who was to have been her Superior at Emmitsburg until his accident; Babade, her "dear, dear dear, cherished beloved father"; and DuBourg, who, she confessed "awes me extremely."[18] With a conservation of adjectives that was unusual to her, she wrote only that Dubois was "a venerable fine looking man."[19]

If he was chagrined by the untimely arrival of the women, Dubois kept it to himself. Still, there was no place to put them. The old stone house at the Fleming farm was in no fit condition for habitation. It would take a month of work before it could be cleaned and repaired even half properly. Still, he was never a man to quibble or waste time. He did the most practical immediate thing. He had the seminarians unpack the covered wagon and move the women into his own cabin just below the church up on the Mountain. He then moved his belongings into the long, log cabin which was to serve as Mount St. Mary's dormitory.

Throughout the next several weeks of summer while the stone house— even that a makeshift temporary residence—was readied, Dubois fed the sisters and cared for their physical needs while he worked at constructing his seminary. According to his own notes this work included: uprooting the stumps of over fifty trees, levelling a terrain, building a brick house near a spring for a bakery and laundry, converting a cellar into a refectory and paving it with flagstones, making tables and benches, and plastering the inside walls of his school.

As best as he could under the circumstances, he tried to fulfill the spiritual needs of the community of women. They were disappointed. They had left a jewel of a chapel filled with the sounds of Gregorian chant and priests who had time to construct perfect liturgies. At Emmitsburg they attended a silent Mass in a chapel which John Dubois had hewn out of hillside logs with his parishioners' help. Often he said Mass having to clean from himself the dirt of the earth to do so. Six weeks after her arrival the highest accolade Elizabeth Seton could lay upon him was:

"Mr. Dubois, who in all kindness and charity to us, we begin to get accustomed to . . ."[20]

To one friend she wrote of her temporary home in Dubois' mountainside cabin: "We are half in the sky. The height of our situation is almost incredible."[21] It was unfortunate that she could not see that the careful choice of this startling, romantic spot might have said something about the nature of the man who chose it.

By the end of summer Dubois had the women into their temporary home on the Fleming Farm. The sisters, joined by several more candidates, were all set to make their contribution in return; weaving cloth and making socks for the boys in what Elizabeth Seton still insisted upon referring to as the seminary "of Mr. DuBourg."[22]

The Sulpicians had initially transferred their minor seminarians to Harent's farm to separate them from the collegians at DuBourg's secular Baltimore school. Dubois' pastoral commitment to educate Emmitsburg area children preceded, in time, his commitment to run a seminary for the Sulpicians. As the school year began he continued teaching these boys, as well as Mrs. Seton's sons, William and Richard, aged thirteen and eleven. The two boys were not only not seminarians, they were at best scrcely comfortable in the Catholic religion into which they had been brought with their mother.

The Sulpicians might well raise their hands in questioning consternation. Was Dubois going to run a seminary or an open college boarding school? The answer, given in practice, became a bone of contention, and then a raging argument between Emmitsburg and Baltimore over the next decade of time. Mount St. Mary's, from its first days, was a jumble of both. Dubois just did not have the heart to turn the children away.

Orphaned by the loss of their father, socially ostracized because of the conversion of their mother, the confused Seton boys had been shuffled to three Catholic schools in as many years. The arrival of these two boys was followed by that of the son of Sister Rose White, the widow of a captain lost at sea. Dubois as always was the pastoral, practical man, never the abstract theoretician. So his seminary would be a college as well. He opened his arms to embrace the children. For each of them he would become the father that was lost.

Despite this the women failed to see that this practical laborer might ever be any kind of a spiritual father. Harriet Seton, one of Elizabeth's frail sisters-in-law, had known Pierre Babade for the space of only one week in Baltimore. Throughout the summer in Emmitsburg she wrestled with the decision to follow her sister Cecilia and Elizabeth into Catholicism. Dubois said Mass for them daily. His liturgy was simple and quiet, the very opposite of the glorious pageantry of chant, twenty priests and a whole troop of seminarians which had been so pleasing at the Sulpician seminary. When Harriet finally decided to enter the Church, the sisters ignored Dubois and waited two months until Babade could find time to come to Emmitsburg to receive her. Babade wrote a special poem for the occasion. Dubois, who had good reason to be hurt by this slight, busied himself with writing the rules for his new school. He was to be aided by older seminarians sent from Baltimore to be prefects and teachers. For them, for himself, and for the students, he constructed a discipline of work and prayer which echoed the life he had lived as a child in Louis Le Grand. The entire spirit, however, was tempered and made different from the Paris school by the pioneer setting and by Dubois' good-humored personality.

There was plenty of time slotted for outdoor recreation. During chapel anyone who felt ill could always leave, but, Dubois stipulated, unless the illness was evident, an equal amount of time was to be subtracted from the

ill person's next recreation period. As at Louis Le Grand, unkindness was
forbidden. So, too, were outbursts of laughter, especially in chapel. However, Dubois the amiable realist made exception for such times as when
laughter would be "rendered unavoidable by some accident." During meals
all members of the community including himself were to take a turn waiting on tables. In listing times for religious instruction Dubois carefully assigned equal classes for the youngsters of slaves.[23]

It was, overall, a rule which showed itself to be written by a man who
loved and understood children. He seemed less successful in dealing with
their elders, especially those in religious orders.

Archbishop Carroll had discouraged the aged Father Nagot from going
to Emmitsburg as the sisters' director. Because of missionary duties, he
told him, "Mr. Dubois must often be obligated to be absent."[24] The out-
come was that the sisters were assigned a director who would always be
absent, living in Baltimore. It was to be DuBourg, which must at first have
pleased Elizabeth. Almost immediately, however, the two of them clashed
headlong about the sisters' relationship with Babade. Whether jealous of
Babade's popularity, or angry that Babade allowed them to receive communion daily when twice a week was the norm, DuBourg stirred up a
hornets' nest by forbidding the sisters to use Babade as a confessor.

Elizabeth Seton often expressed herself in a manner that was flowery in
the extreme. Friends who had experienced her iron will and sometimes
headstrong temper accepted with good grace her constant references to
"poor little self" and the quickly adopted, religious self-appelation "little
mother." When her anger stirred, however, she quickly enough let the object of her temper know where mother stood.

Still new in all that was Catholic, she learned readily how to play a
hierarchical game. She went over DuBourg's head to a man superior to
them both: Archbishop Carroll.

Beginning with an attempt at her "poor little self" style, and avowing
"the adored will be ever done," she soon dropped the moonlight and
magnolias and came bluntly to the point.

"There have been some very busy persons making exaggerations to our
Superior about my writing large packages to Father Babade," she complained. The result was that DuBourg had started to act "like a tyrant."
Moreover, DuBourg's decision, she claimed, could only add to "the reserve
we all felt to the excellent Mr. Dubois knowing that he and the superior
had but one soul."

"Well," she concluded, attempting to raise the argument from an emotional to a spiritual plane, "my own troubles teach me I hope how to comfort others."[25]

Her fury shocked the chimerical DuBourg. His feelings wounded, he
quit his job as superior. Until this point, Mrs. Seton had been thoroughly

catered to by the Catholic clergy. Stricken by this, the first negative reaction she had gotten from any one of them, she returned to her "little self" demeanor, taking her community perhaps too far into penitence when she wrote the Bishop:

"All the girls would beg to be laid at your feet if they knew of this hasty scrawl."

Admitting that she had been "made a superior before being initiated," Elizabeth still wanted Babade back as the sisters' confessor. She began to realize however that DuBourg and Dubois were not quite one soul. DuBourg, hurt, had walked away from the sisterhood regardless of the consequences. Dubois, caught in the middle, had been continually frozen out by the sisters. He remained steadfast, supplying the community's temporal and spiritual needs. While she still overlooked him as a possible director she at least began to be aware that he was capable of being offended. She asked Carroll to keep the sisters' preference for Babade from him.

"If Mr. Dubois should know this request was made," she admitted, "his feelings would be hurt and it would answer no purpose."[26]

Dubois, however, was fully perceptive of what was going on and sought to soothe the hurts of the others. Ignoring the insensitivity of the women who accepted his ministry as merely functionary, he asked the more pleasing Babade if he would want to stay at the Mountain and serve the community as a resident priest. At this point none of the major buildings were completed. The newly recruited sisters and Elizabeth's relatives, altogether numbering sixteen, were crowded into the old four-room stone house on the Fleming farm. The Mountain school was a collection of primitive log buildings; its scholars a group of young children. Babade thanked Dubois but chose to write his poetry to the sisters from Baltimore.

Mrs. Seton wrote emotional apologies to DuBourg, and an argumentative plea for his reinstatement to the Sulpician Superior Nagot. Having previously misread the temperament of the priests, she sought out John Dubois; this time for advice on how to deal with them. He generously took her side and suggested that she wait for the Bishop's impending visit, or for some positive response from DuBourg. At the same time, he rebuked her for her display of temperament in addressing Nagot.

"I send your letter back to you," Dubois advised, "after having underlined what I consider rather too harsh coming from you."[27]

Archbishop Carroll arrived, and regardless of whether or not the girls did lay themselves at his feet they still did not get their way. Though Elizabeth promised that he would see "how good a child I am going to be,"[28] the bishop saw "formidable objections"[29] to the reappointment of DuBourg who was beginning to melt after months of a glacial mood. Father Nagot, as well, refused to appoint him or Babade as Superior. He chose instead, Father John Baptiste David, a man whose labors in the United States paralleled, in many respects, those of John Dubois. There is no indication that Dubois, already on the scene in Emmitsburg, was ever considered for the post.

Elizabeth Seton, as a religious had been a protégée of DuBourg. Rose White, another of the first sisters, had been the protégée of David. During this squabble Dubois, when not building or teaching, tried to convince a protégée of his own to enter the sisterhood. Had he succeeded in drawing into the community Charlotte Melmouth, it would have made news all along the Atlantic coast. During the previous two decades she had been one of the nation's leading tragic actresses.

An Irish Protestant, she had run from school as a girl, married and gone into the theater. Her star had risen, and she played a successful year at Covent Garden (1785) and then another at Drury Lane. On tour in Dublin, she made a public pronouncement. As recorded in the prejudicial 18th century account of the *Annals of the English Stage:*

"To fill the house the actress gave out that she was being converted to the Roman Catholic religion, and she went daily and ostentatiously to Mass. The house, however, was a poor one and Mrs. Melmouth became thereby convinced that the Romish Church had not that efficacy she hoped to find in it and she remained in her original belief."[30]

Only the first part of the report was true, for Mrs. Melmouth remained steadfastly Catholic. In 1791, the same year as Dubois' escape from Paris, she came to conquer the New World. "She towers above all competition,"[31] praised the *New York Diary*. She was controversial. Loyal to her adopted faith she refused, in 1794, to voice a violently proterrorist French Revolution speech in a play called *Tammany*. Reacting to this, the *New York Journal* declared the next day: "She ought not be suffered to go on the New York stage again."[32]

But she was, and enjoyed continual accolades as the "grand dame of tragedy."[33]

Unfortunately she also enjoyed the pleasures of the table and her beauty became lost in fat. Reviews would invariably begin with polite qualifications such as: "Not withstanding the disadvantages of figure . . ."[34] In one play, *The Grecian Daughter,* her healthy queen-size caused an audience to burst into laughter at a critically tragic moment as she cried: "Strike here, there's blood enough."[35]

In the major cities up and down the Atlantic seaboard, Mrs. Melmouth performed to audiences who liked to inject their immediate reactions into the script. In 1804 she played Lady Macbeth to a Macbeth so bad that when she finally reached the line—'the king grows worse and worse,'—"a killing shout was the response of the audience and little more of the play was heard."[36]

She was at an age where she was tiring of all this glamour. John Dubois was the connection which almost drew her into Elizabeth Seton's sisterhood. She visited Emmitsburg and stayed with the sisters, unfortunately in the midst of their unhappy squabbles about a spiritual director. She did not remain, but then having left, decided to ask Dubois to obtain lodging for her in town where she might live and make up her mind. His advice, unsought by Mrs. Seton and her sisters, he happily gave to Mrs. Melmouth. To her he wrote:

> I was afraid you would yield to the invitation of your friends
> to remain either at New York or Philadelphia. Believe
> me it is not in these busy and noisy cities that your heart
> can rest. Pleasing as might be the society of the numerous
> friends you have at either place it would take up too
> much of your time. The world has had its full share of it.
> Give the rest to Him for whom the whole of your life
> would not have been too much and who mercifully accepts
> the last hours labour when it is the heart that leads the hand.[37]

If he never wrote poems, there was nonetheless poetry in Dubois' soul.

Mrs. Melmouth lived in Emmitsburg for two years, but never joined the sisters. One cool reference is made to her by Elizabeth Seton who referred to her in a letter only as "an old lady in the village near us."[38]

Discouraged, she returned to New York and en route was in a carriage accident. Though at first she was reported killed, she escaped with a fractured arm. Three months after this she went onstage for the last time. A New York reviewer hoped that this farewell benefit would "be attended with a liberality worthy of the sympathy of a generous public for an old, respectable and faithful servant."[39]

She bought a farm in Brooklyn, kept cows and tutored the children of neighboring farmers. One boy, John McCloskey, who later said she taught him all that he knew about diction, she sent on to her friend John Dubois. He eventually followed John Dubois into the priesthood, followed him in assuming the episcopal See of New York, and became the first cardinal named from the United States.

The winter of 1809 hit unexpectedly early and hard. Dubois made light of the cold to Mrs. Melmouth, writing her:

"As for my little gang at Mount St. Mary's they are as hardy as the Mountaineers in Scotland. We have been like to be caught by the weather which for a few days was very severe, having no stores put up yet, but they bore their trial like men, and like true tars, laughed at the storm when it was over.[40]

In the Valley of St. Joseph's the women were not so hardy. The Setons were a frail lot, and Harriet too sick at the time of the storm. She lingered for a month and died 3 days before Christmas. Bypassed as a director when she was received into the Church, Dubois annointed her into eternity. Several of the sisters took seriously ill, and before the warmth of spring could renew energies, Harriet's sister Cecilia succumbed to the family enemy, tuberculosis.

Dubois cared for them throughout. Sister Rose White remembered:

"Our good Father Dubois would come to say Mass for us on mornings when the cold was so intense and his hands so stiff that he could scarcely hold the reins of his horse."[41]

He kept his sights on practical necessities. Arriving, he would generally stop to pull such items as legs of mutton or loaves of bread from his saddlebags before entering the convent.

In the midst of her personal tragedies, Elizabeth Seton sought solace in communicating with the highly cultured priests who had been her correspondents from the days of her conversion. One of these, the newly appointed Bishop of Boston, John Cheverus, gently tried to push her back toward strength that was nearer at hand:

"Your present worthy pastor is," he wrote, "like myself an élève of Louis Le Grand and St. Magloire. I recollect perfectly that he was then, as he is now, amiable and pious. Have the goodness to give him my respectful and affectionate compliments."[42]

The sisters had moved into the still unfinished, large white house in the depths of winter, unable to endure their temporary, cramped quarters. The builders had to work with them underfoot, and the nuns in turn caught fleas from the hair used in mixing plaster. Mrs. Seton wrote to John Carroll, and still carefully referring to Dubois as the "representative of Mr. DuBourg," allowed that he was "making some exertions for the settlement of the establishment which gives a better appearance to things in general." In the wake of her two sisters-in-law's deaths, she referred almost bitterly to the effects of his work and his steadfast attitude:

"The masons have nearly finished the lower part of the house but the work falls so heavy on our good sisters who have stood it out the longest that every one of them is now almost bent double . . . Fortunately for us Mr. Dubois never thinks any sickness worth minding till the doctor gives over and therefore everyone keeps up with courage."[43]

In her grief Elizabeth forgot that the religious community of women had been foisted upon Dubois before he could finish the enormous construction tasks assigned to him. It was not his fault that he ended up building over their heads in the dead of winter. It had been lack of foresight which allowed the sisters to be sent into the country with their sickly guests. The blame for this must be laid upon DuBourg, Cooper, and even Elizabeth herself. Dubois, suddenly made responsible for the total welfare of some fifty people was performing a herculean task. It is rather to his credit that he tried to maintain an atmosphere of cheerfulness and courage for the sake of the sisters.

From Baltimore Father David sought to organize the community by removing Elizabeth Seton from office and replacing her with Rose White who had been his friend and protégée. Again Elizabeth sought help from the archbishop. Carroll, though in the same city and within walking distance of the men involved, pushed the matter back and attempted to make Dubois the target for Elizabeth's frustrations. Reassuring her that he would shelve the proposal until Mr. David had finished his visitation and made a report, he veered her persistence toward the Mountain.

"Mr. Dubois," he begged off, "has without doubt earlier information than me of the views of messrs. DuBourg or David."[44]

This was not so. Elizabeth's subsequent letters to Carroll show that Dubois was as confused as she was and that the two had by this time reached a level of commiseration just short of friendship. Repeating her accounts of the dissension caused in the new community, she would add that she had written "by the request of Mr. Dubois who has witnessed much more than I can ever tell you."[45]

The gentle John Cheverus who had ministered to New England's Indians and won the liking of even the grimmest Puritans arrived in Emmitsburg in November 1810, newly consecrated as Bishop of Boston. It was a first encounter between him and Mrs. Seton, who had met only by mail, and as well a joyous reunion between the two former schoolmates. When the day came for him to leave, Dubois hurried an almost boyish note to Elizabeth urging her to detain his friend. "Exert all your insinuating eloquence," he pleaded, "It will have a good effect if it has half the influence which it has on your devoted, etc."[46]

Cheverus, a saintly enough man to feel kin to sanctity, wrote afterward of his visit to "the holy mountain."[47] He was the first to acknowledge that something extraordinary was beginning to happen there. He also continued to nudge Elizabeth to realize that her surest ally in maintaining the independence of the new community was his old schoolmate. Telling her that he agreed with Dubois that the sisters should remain free of Sulpician plans to place the new sisterhood under the management of French Daughters of Charity, he gave advice for the best source for strategy.

"Have another conversation with the Rev. Mr. Dubois on the subject, then do with simplicity what he will prescribe or even wish."[48]

Elizabeth's subsequent admission to the archbishop, that she wrote "at the request of Mr. Dubois" was probably a result of this push from Cheverus.

In May 1811 Father David left for the mission fields of Kentucky with Bishop Benedict Flaget. For several months thereafter no one replaced him as a superior for the sisters' community.

DuBourg returned from Martinique where he had sojourned for his health. He resumed his interest in the community, but Elizabeth was now wary of him. To a friend she wrote that she was "so worn out now that it is almost a matter of indifference how it goes."[49] She still felt a reserve toward Dubois, but she was becoming more and more dependent on him for daily advice. Acknowledging Carroll's objection that the man was already over-burdened by work she nonetheless compared him as a potential Superior with the romantic but unreliable friend who was so much closer to her in temperament:

"Rev. Mr. Dubois, an economist and full of details dictated by habits of prudence—Rev. Mr. DuBourg, all liberality and schemes from a long custom of expending. In Spirituals, also, the difference is equally marked and their sentiments reflected from their habits. It is easy for you to con-clude that between the two my situation would be truly pitiable . . ."

Pitiable or not, her decision finally rested upon the man who did not touch her heart but who was durable and who fit more easily into diocesan structures than the religious community of men in Baltimore. "Rev. Mr. Dubois, on one point," she told the Archbishop, "has always had my preference as a superior—he always and invariably recommends me to refer constantly to you."[50]

It seems never to have occurred to any of the men involved during this interim that the women might have directed themselves and written their own rule. The emigré Sulpicians might have been reminded that women in religious life could boast a far better performance record than their male counterparts during the French Revolution. The latter disbanded in great numbers at the first invitation given by the government and before danger was involved. A very high percentage of women religious remained true to their vows even after the Revolution turned into the Terror.

The men who busied themselves with establishing this first American sisterhood were merely reflective of their contemporaries in treating women like children. The women themselves, including Elizabeth Seton, never seemed to conclude that they might be fully self-directed; it was their role to listen to the men.

At last the job as superior of the sisters' community and pulling order from the shambles of the previous two years was given to Dubois. So too was the copy of the rules of the Daughters of Charity just brought from France by Bishop Flaget. These rules had been written in the early seven-teenth century by one saint, Vincent de Paul, for another saint, Louise de Marillac. Now it was as if history was to be replayed in the personalities of John Dubois and Elizabeth Seton.

Vincent de Paul, ordained like Dubois at a younger than canonical age, served in Paris during the youth of his priesthood. Tutoring in homes of the wealthy, he eventually grew in his ministry while serving the needs of poor country people. Only in his middle years did he develop greatness of purpose. He took over a school, the College des Bons Enfants, educated men for the priesthood of service to the needy, and was, at this time, proposed as a spiritual director for Louise de Marillac. A well born widow and mother, determined to serve God in a life of religion, she was at first loath to accept his direction. He was too concerned with mundane details, too down to earth, and not at all mystical. He taught his students to avoid florid preaching and insisted that they would do more for Christ by sticking to what he called "The little method"—direct, straightforward, clear exposition of the Gospel. His motto was "Leave God for God," meaning that the pleasure of spending a life in quiet mystical prayer sometimes had to be sacrificed so that God's suffering poor could be cared for. Nevertheless even if Louise was reluctant at first, the joining together of these two souls brought about immediate results in the phenomenal growth of the religious order they founded: The Daughters of Charity.

John Dubois had begun his priesthood at the Petites Maisons, the same Paris insane asylum administered a century earlier by Vincent and Louise. There he had lived Vincent's rule with the sisters while serving his apprenticeship in the priesthood, caring for the very poorest of God's poor. Now with Vincent's rule in his hands he was filled with an almost Pentecostal inner flame. Having already followed for so long in the Saint's footsteps, he had the opportunity to become the Vincent de Paul for the United States. It was a turning point of resolution. Never again would he be referred to as the "agent of Mr. DuBourg." Never again would the aspiring group of sisters already in his care be left adrift while men far away nitpicked about the directions in which they should move. He determined to organize them into a great religious order and build that order with institutions throughout the United States. Contrary to Elizabeth Seton's belief that he would bow constantly to higher authority, he grew immediately into an assertive and bold authority of his own. He would henceforth haggle with bishops, making sure that his sisters were organized exactly according to his rule as he established them in orphanages, schools and infirmaries within their dioceses. His great life's work had begun, and like Vincent de Paul he would always combine grand visions with an almost obsessive concern for small detail.

He sat down and in his own hand wrote fifty-three pages of rules for the sisters, adapting those of Vincent de Paul to fit the situations and needs of the still young country. In these he was exacting both with the sisters in general and with Elizabeth Seton as their superior. Yet, at the same time, she knew that she never had a stronger champion. If she was reserved toward him, she nevertheless trusted him implicitly as an honest and strong man. She wrote to the archbishop that her deepest concerns were "known to him as to God."[51]

These deepest concerns involved her position as a mother. She was willing to abandon her place in the community if this was threatened. Dubois understood and sympathized. Within a week's time of receiving the rules, Carroll wrote to Elizabeth that he agreed with her new superior that special consideration had to be given "on account of your dear children." Assuring her that "Mr. Dubois has been very explicit in communicating, I believe, whatever it was proper for me to know," he accepted the rules with "the alterations suggested to and by him . . ."

The archbishop congratulated her on having moved, with this new constitution and with Dubois as director, beyond a tempest wherein her life had been tossed about by well-meaning but impractical men.

"It will be like freeing you from a state in which it was difficult to walk straight as you had no certain way in which to proceed."[52]

Elizabeth Seton went on record as being grateful to Dubois for emerging as a strong leader.

"Long may Our Lord spare him to the community," she wrote, "for who could ever be found to unwind the ball as he does and stop to pick out every knot."[53]

Long afterward, one of the first sisters who outlived her, and who knew both her and Dubois well, commented drily:

"This was not to the spirit of our mother, though she lent herself to it."[54]

The only element yet missing was some way to bridge the great difference of personality which kept his and Elizabeth Seton's spirits from working in harmony. That element arrived that summer in the person of Simon Bruté.

27

St. Elizabeth Ann Bayley Seton (1774–1821) arrived at Emmitsburg with sickly relatives in the spring of 1809. Father Dubois was not ready for them, but moved out of his own house to give them shelter. It took several years for Mother Seton to adjust to Dubois' workmanlike habits and appreciate his ability to act as a spiritual as well as physical guardian.

28

Above, *the exterior of the "old Stone House" at St. Joseph's, Emmitsburg, where Mother Seton and the first Sisters stayed 1809–1810. It was a cramped temporary shelter, and not a healthy environment. Below, a room inside the now restored home.*

29

30

The Common Room at the "old stone house." The
women left this house in February 1810, when
the new "White House" was ready at St. Joseph's.

While she was at Baltimore,
Mrs. Seton stayed at this
house on Paca Street, attached
to the Sulpician's St. Mary's
Seminary. Father Dubois was
part of the Sulpician Society
of priests from 1807 to 1826.

31

32

*John Dubois is likened as an American St. Vincent de Paul. St. Vincent
(1581?–1660) above, had founded the Daughters of Charity in France with
St. Louise de Marillac (1591–1660) shown below. Dubois' experience,
career and character closely parallel those of St. Vincent.*

33

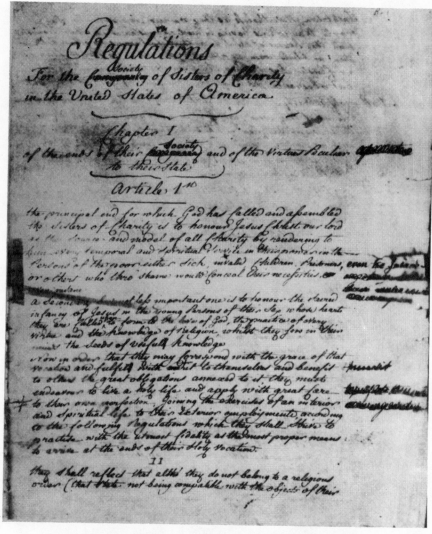

34

Once John Dubois became the Superior of the Sisters of Charity, he wrote
their first set of regulations. Above is the first page of the rules written in
his hand in 1811, which were adapted from the rule of the Daughters
of Charity. Dubois had been chaplain to the Daughters
at their insane asylum in Paris.

35

Charlotte Melmouth (1749–1823) is shown above, *as a young actress. She stayed some time at Emmitsburg, and John Dubois attempted to draw her into the Sisterhood at St. Joseph's.* Below, *Bishop John Cheverus (1768–1836) another French emigré, was warmly welcomed by Dubois at "the Mountain." He was the first to acknowledge that something extraordinary was beginning to happen there.*

36

CHAPTER 7

You Remind Me of Nothing Else But God

The United States was primitive, mission land. French missionaries looked backward to France and many, such as DuBourg and Cheverus, eventually returned home. Those working in America continued to be touched by affairs back home.

One of the Baltimore seminarians sent from time to time to help at the Mountain was a Breton, Joseph Picot de Clorivière, who had been involved in the 1800 Christmas Eve bomb plot to assassinate Napoleon. Clorivière had escaped, but one of the fleeing conspirators was treated for wounds by a young Breton doctor. The doctor, though innocent, was arrested and sentenced to exile. His fellow medical students unsuccessfully petitioned the government on his behalf. One of these, another Breton, Simon Bruté, later entered the seminary in 1803 after completing his medical degree and was assigned to serve at the Mass of Napoleon's uncle, Cardinal Fesch. Taking advantage of the Emperor's presence on one occasion, he tried to give him a written plea for the exiled doctor. When Napoleon swept past him he attempted vainly, and dangerously, to throw the missive in front of him as he departed.

In 1810, a priest of two years, Bruté arrived in the United States to give his life to the missions. Falling into contact, then friendship with Clorivière, he would thereafter complain that people "confounded" the two of them

59

because of their close backgrounds, thinking that he, himself, had actually been involved in the bomb plot.[1]

Bruté was a tall, thin man whose promiment bones and hollow cheeks would have made him seem older than his years but for the large, light blue eyes which dominated his expression and made him appear almost a child.

Assigned to the seminary at Baltimore he visited Emmitsburg in the summer of 1811, entering the scene during the final disputes over who was to be Elizabeth Seton's superior. Elizabeth, by this time, had developed a reserved respect for John Dubois. Her references to him never approached the realms wherein she heaped adjective after adjective of praise upon him as she did upon those whom she considered her spiritual kin. But, interestingly (as she would describe to her old Protestant friends), it was Dubois who worried less about her spiritual campaigns than about the security of her living situation.

"Our mountain pastor," she assured one, "is a polished, simple, truly holy man. He says Mass for us at sunrise all the year round; if anyone has a trouble it is carried to him, they receive consolation, and it is buried in silence."[2]

Such masculine silence contrasted totally with the flamboyance of the directors she would have wanted at hand. Nonetheless this man had filled an enormous gap in the lives of her fatherless children.

"[He] dotes on William and Richard," she granted. "He has the former in his study, with fire night and day, because he has been at times threatened with a cough."[3]

Then Simon Bruté arrived. He was as colorful and flamboyant as DuBourg, Babade, or Cooper. He was mystical, and he wore this mysticism on the outside of his innocent personality. Elizabeth set out to teach him the language of the United States and was immediately smitten with him. Though a genius, he was struggling as he would for the rest of his days, "to learn practically my English."[4]

He was less than five years her junior, but she began referring to him as if he were not only a child but her son. She expressed amazement to Archbishop Carroll that he was doing "much more than it could possibly be supposed so young a man could venture on."[5]

She hinted to Carroll that Dubois might be happier if he could be freed of the sisterhood and its disputes as to whom should be superior.

"Poor Mr. Dubois is so discouraged," she wrote, "He will do all he can without displeasing you; to quit all, even the direction."

In the same letter she pointed to Bruté as someone who might be the one to fill her spiritual needs.

"Sometimes," she confessed, "I am tempted to tell him all."[6]

Elizabeth was not the only one who was taken with Bruté. Dubois began almost immediately to call him "little brother" and his affection was as immediately returned. So very different in temperament; the one blunt, domineering and practical, the other artistic, imaginative and mystical, they shared a deep spirituality and basic selflessness. A mutual dependency developed from which both men were to benefit enormously.

In the peaceful atmosphere of the Mountain they could share their experiences of the French Revolution in which they had both suffered so much. Dubois, elder by fifteen years could tell Bruté firsthand stories of the personalities of his schoolmates Desmoulins and Robespierre. Bruté, twelve years of age when Dubois fled in 1791, could tell his older brother of the martyrdom Dubois had narrowly escaped.*

"It would be impossible for others to put themselves mind and heart into our own place," he shared, "and realize what was the habitual condition of Catholics at that time."[7]

The guillotine in Rennes, his native city, "stood permanently erected upon the public square, quite bloody and sometimes with heads exposed upon it."[8]

"During the progress of the persecution the greater number of the priests had been either guillotined or shot or transported to the penal colonies."[9]

"The letter of the law was most express," he remembered: "the priest and those who harbour him to be put to death within twenty-four hours after being seized."[10]

For two years Bruté's widowed mother, a strong woman who ran a printer's shop, hid two old priests in their apartments "with all that awful and anxious privacy which their own safety and our own prescribed."[11]

Bruté's married sister, living outside Rennes, was forced to give hospitality to gendarmes returning with two captured priests. The leader of the party, "a man of frightful aspect," expressed his grudging admiration for the younger of the two:

"We had given him up," he announced, "But we were gaining on the old one when lo! he turned back and came to help him cross the brook and all the time he kept covering the old man with his body against the fire of our guns. It was a remarkable and affecting scene."

"Yet," said Bruté, "as soon as they had got some refreshments they hurried on with their prisoners to the tribunal and from the tribunal they went the same day to the scaffold."[12]

Closer to home, friends of Mrs. Bruté harbored a priest. One day his presence was found out and he fled to the neighboring countryside.

"All of us were in the greatest anxiety and passed a sleepless night . . ." Bruté recalled, "The least noise in the street startled us."

The man was caught. Bruté went to his trial.

---

*Conscious of history Bruté also recorded, in his own hand while at the Mountain, the reminiscences which he now forced himself to relive.

"After the sentence of death had been passed it was found that the executioner, contrary to his usual custom, was absent," Bruté said.

Angry when he arrived, he handled the elderly man "with great brutality and affected hurry . . . rudely cutting off his hair and cutting away the collar of his shirt to leave his neck bare for the axe, tying his hands behind his back, and then throwing his coat loosely over his shoulder." The executioner "had wounded him in the neck and the blood was running down his breast." Yet the adolescent boy watching felt that the man being led to the scaffold "looked that moment as he used to look when following the processions of the people of his parish on the solemn festivals of the Church."[13]

The boy did not witness the actual execution; nor did he witness any others.

"I myself never had the courage to follow the victims to the scaffold,"[14] he confessed.

One day five priests were discovered. As they passed under the windows of the Brutés home, a soldier turned to one of the priests, Mr. Pourier, and said:

"Look there; take a look at Madame Guillotine."

The priest took no notice of him. The gendarme, offended, no doubt, at his composure and disregard of his order, immediately struck him a severe blow in the face, saying:

"Will you not look there when I tell you? You will soon be there yourself."

"I see it," answered Mr. Pourier quietly.[15]

One of the others was not so docile. At the tribunal he stepped forward to the judge, a former schoolmate, and reminded him that he himself would someday have to appear before God.

"The Judge turned pale and appeared much agitated but called upon the gendarmes to silence him. They were guillotined, the five of them, the same day."[16]

As another priest, bound together with the peasant who had hidden him, was marched through the streets on the way to death, he loudly and clearly sang his own *Libera Me Domine.*

"His black hair floating upon his shoulders, his beard long unshaven, the very hat upon his head, are present to my vivid recollections," Bruté said.

The boy ran from the house and followed, "agitated and partially frightened with the usual terror which rested on my heart." He followed close upon their footsteps across the square but stopped before they reached the public walk.

"I dared not follow them and be present. I had hardly reached our house when I heard the report of the guns simultaneously, as if but one, and their victims were in eternity."

Entering his home he started to relate the incident to his mother. She broke in to assure him:

"We know it all. We were praying for them."

"I remember my mother's look at that moment," he said "with a mangled look of sorrow and firmness—and that immediately afterwards all the family went about their ordinary family affairs as if nothing particular had happened and so it was for death was a daily tale."[17] Another trial involved a seventy-year-old priest and three sisters who had hidden him:

"It is as vivid in my mind as if I were still there, boy as I then was, standing behind and leaning upon the seat of the holy confessor with nothing but the railing of the tribunal between us—my poor heart beating so violently all the time."

When the sentence was passed, one of the sisters in turn angrily passed judgment upon the Revolution.

"Barbarous people," she exclaimed, "amongst what savage nations has hospitality ever been made a crime punishable with death?"

"The one who sat next to her pulled gently at her dress (I can see her now) as if urging her to stop."

The executioner immediately applied the handcuffs "securing them so tight I remember the priest gave signs of uneasiness and looked at the man as if entreating him not to screw them so tight."

The four were taken from the court to the scaffold.[18]

Not all the captured were recalled with admiration. Bruté recalled the trial of one who "gave evidence that he was much attached to life, making explanations and apologies which were strikingly in contrast with the spirit usually exhibited by his brother priests . . . I remember we were disappointed at what seemed a degree of weakness."

Afterwards, however, this man redeemed himself by approaching the scaffold "with firmness and dignity."[19]

The spirit which took hold in the soul of the fatherless boy was that exemplified by the priest who was brought into the square at Rennes in a cart. Across his lap lay the body of a farmer stabbed in the stomach when he had tried to protect his pastor.

"Where a short time before he would have received so many marks of respect," a mob now gathered about and made cruel jokes. A Daughter of Charity gave Mrs. Bruté a copy of the priest's last testament to his parishioners, written in a cell before his execution. Young Bruté kept it as if it were meant for himself.

"I pray for those who are about to put me to death," the pastor wrote, "I pardon from the bottom of my heart those who caused me to be arrested. I know them but I will not name them. If hereafter you find out who they were, remember that it is my injunction that you do them no harm."[20]

Bruté's interest in Mrs. Seton's American sisterhood, drawing its rule from the French Daughters of Charity, would have been heightened by the relation he had had with that order during the Terror.

The Daughters of Charity were allowed to remain in existence for a time because they served the hospitals and prisons where "so difficult was it to find anyone to replace them."[21] Finally they were disbanded. One ancient religious, a simple homely woman named Sister Magdalen, had spent the entirety of her adult life serving the incarcerated.

Many of her fellow religious were imprisoned. "It would have been no hardship, however, to Sister Magdalen to be shut up in prison, so they turned her out on the world . . ."

Mrs. Bruté took her in.

"She came and stood before my mother in the parlor, looking at her and sighing a little but saying nothing. She had not been accustomed to talk except to her prisoners. In the evening she told my mother that it was the first day for forty years, except for retreats, that she had missed visiting the prison and that she had never passed a day which seemed so long and tired her so much as this the first day of idleness."[22]

As the Terror abated, captured priests were no longer killed but imprisoned. Bruté became their contact with the outside world, slipping into the prison "disguised as a baker's boy and carrying a big bread basket on my head."[23]

In 1796 at the age of seventeen he entered the study of medicine. Still, he maintained his role as a comforter to the incarcerated clergy.

Assuring Bruté, "I find great consolation in your friendship," one priest secreted a letter to him, adding a caution with the reminder:

"In our present imprisonment it is forbidden us to speak or write to anyone." He wanted Simon to seek information. A rumor had reached the inmates that they might soon be released.

"When there is a fixed limit to sufferings," the priest assured the young man, "they can be endured with patience."[24]

Eventually the captives were liberated. Napoleon Bonaparte shrewdly saw the political advantages in restoring Catholicism to the people. In 1803, having completed his degree as a medical doctor, Simon Bruté had turned aside from a career in medicine and entered one of the newly reopened seminaries—coincidentally that of St. Sulpice attached to the parish where John Dubois had served in Paris. Now, in 1811, he was with this man attempting "to learn practically English," so that he might serve the mission land in the United States.

Bruté returned to the seminary in Baltimore for the academic year of 1811–1812 but he felt badly for the burden placed upon Dubois. He wrote to Emery in Paris telling him that more missionaries were needed, citing especially "the abandonment" of men such as "the worthy Father Dubois who, unaided maintains with undefatigable activities of the entire establishment of Emmitsburg."[25]

In fact there was another priest at Emmitsburg, Father Charles Duhamel, an old veteran of service in French Guiana, the Island of Santa Cruz and, for a number of years the town of Hagerstown, Md. Arriving in 1810, he spent the last eight years of his life with Dubois and is referred to by all as being a kindly, somewhat rustic individual. But he was beyond his years of active service, and he was only able to be a sacramental help to Dubois, principally at the town church.

Dubois, by this time weighed under with debts, pleaded with the Sulpicians in Baltimore that he had "all the spiritual and temporal care of two important institutions, not only to conduct but also to establish on a solid basis."[26]

Most students were in arrears paying tuition, and many bartered with flour, grain or whatever might be needed by the school. The father of one boy, recorded Dubois, "has engaged to send us a mare worth $125 to pay for one year."

He noted another sort of arrangement: "There are two other boys who have been paid by giving us a negro apiece, one for three years and the other for five."[27]

The result of this mess was that a financially strapped Dubois shifted debts from pillar to post: "keeping my cash for him who demanded it and leaving those who can wait . . . buying of those who know my situation whatever I could in order to get it cheaper than I could from a stranger of whom I could not ask credit."[28]

Such was the mystical world of John Dubois. Small wonder that Elizabeth Seton found him so little to her liking. In a sense he did too much for her. Though she had to beg for her children's expenses (usually supplied by the generous Filicchis), Dubois lifted most temporal concerns from her shoulders from the day he moved out of his cabin for her, until the day she died. Perhaps, if he had let the responsibility of it all fall upon her and then had offered to lift it, she would have appreciated him more.

He was, however, too much a gentleman to have thought of this. He felt helpless enough attempting to alleviate the personal burdens which weighed upon her. In the fall of 1811 her children Anina and William, sixteen and fifteen years of age, became seriously ill. William recovered but Anina sank steadily, a victim of the Seton family's vulnerability to tuberculosis.

At Christmas time Bruté was sent to the Mountain by the Sulpicians to inspect the books and to grant Dubois' petition for a sizeable financial loan; this given with the understanding that he was to begin charging the students retail instead of the wholesale price for goods as he had been doing. The visit was providential, for Bruté was able to comfort Elizabeth Seton where Dubois had been unable. Rather than be jealous, Dubois asked that Bruté might move to the Mountain, as once he had asked for Babade. Archbishop Carroll, along with the Sulpicians, refused the request.

"It is of the first importance to have a person of Mr. Bruté's talents, to say nothing of his other qualities at the seminary," wrote Carroll to Dubois. Nonetheless he commiserated:

"I am far from being insensible of the weight of the burden on your shoulders and am sorry that I cannot lighten it; but I do recommend to your brethren to devise the earliest means of doing something for you."[29]

At the end of January Dubois annointed Anina. He was about to begin a retreat wherein he was to direct that the sisters live according to the newly accepted rule a year before vows were actually taken by the fledgling community. Two days before this he had formally received Mrs. Seton's teenage daughter into the sisterhood. Even in this he was locked out of a spiritual proximity wherein Babade and Bruté would have been made welcome. After Dubois left, the dying girl whispered to her mother as if it were not for him to know:

"I could not but be amused to hear Mr. Dubois say so much about consecration, having been accustomed long before my illness to perform this act . . ."[30]

Bruté, who was to become famous for thinking nothing of walking back and forth the fifty miles between Emmitsburg and Baltimore, returned to check on Anina. Providentially, he was with her when she died in mid-March.

Elizabeth had endured the deaths of her two sisters-in-law with a strong faith, but the death of her eldest child left her "expecting to lose my senses." She became momentarily "uncertain of reunion" in eternity and wrote morbidly of the horror she felt when on one occasion she saw a large rattlesnake stretched out on Anina's grave.[31]

One evening in May, after returning to his room from Vespers and Benediction, John Dubois poured his own heart out in a letter to Bruté. He was tired, lonely, and felt very much the rejection he continually received at St. Joseph's convent. Realizing that "it needs a saint of the first caliber—a St. Francis de Sales" to be the spiritual director of potential saints he decided: "I am only an ugly little wretch."

In nothing else he had written or was to write did John Dubois reveal so much of his inner feelings; about himself, about Bruté whom he called "my dear little brother," and about Elizabeth Seton.

Seeing a polarity of personality traits in his new brother which Mother Seton, too, would observe, he warned Bruté against "introversion" and at the same time against his tendency to become "too affectionate, too personal . . . whenever there is the danger that the heart may become too attached."

"But this apart," he wrote, "why should we two not love one another? As for yourself you remind me of nothing else but God whom I love together with you and through you."

Having been brushed aside by those who saw Bruté as a fellow member of an elite band of mystics, Dubois could not believe that this beautiful man, so unlike the others, did indeed return his affection:

"As for myself, poor miserable sinner, I have nothing but my wretchedness to draw you to me," he confessed, ". . . do keep on writing to me. It is my only consolation. This cannot displease our Good Master since it draws me to Him even more than to you."

Every other priest Elizabeth Seton knew had dealt with her personally only for a short period of time, or had directed her from a long distance by letters. John Dubois had known her now on a day-to-day basis for three years. His observations were from a unique vantage point. He warned Bruté:

> As for Mother, do not flatter her. This is, I fear the one evil
> that has been done to her—there must be none of that. I
> fear that the terrible trial she suffered at the death of Anina
> was intended to put an end or to curb the exaggerated
> pleasure she took in praising her; to banish the excessive fear
> she felt lest her daughter say or do something too human
> when in the presence of others. The excuse was her fear of
> scandal, but I am afraid there was something else besides
> that. A hundred times I wanted to probe this wound; it is only
> lately that I dared to touch it. Besides I must be careful
> lest I do harm while trying to do good. I almost fear that I
> used flattery in order to conquer her. God grant that you may
> one day come to know this soul. What material. But
> like gold brocade rich and heavy indeed, how hard to
> handle. For these many years she has been flattered too much.
> As for myself, poor wretch, what can I do?

He did not directly say that Bruté was the man with enough spiritual stature for the job, but after encouraging him to continue his correspondence with St. Joseph's, he pointedly shared his worry for the future.

> The more I reflect on it, the more I feel I should give up
> the office of director. What a task it is, great God! But when
> I seek for someone on whom to lay my eyes I do not
> know where to find him . . . I fear to cause confusion by
> refusing the burden. I fear still more that my shoulders are not
> equal to the task.

It was late when Dubois finished his long letter and he was tired. He finished it by saying:

"My heart alone still has strength when it speaks to you for it loves you. Would to God that it be just as sure to love God, for the sake of God, for the sake of God alone and forever."

Anticipation of sleep perhaps moved his mind to drowsiness. Dubois forgot that he hadn't directly told Bruté he should assume spiritual direction of Elizabeth Seton. Thinking of the state of depression she was in from Anina's death and its probable causes he warned Bruté: "Do not touch this chord as I do now—that could drive the poor mother to despair— I merely offer you a thread by which to find your way out of the labyrinth should you explore it."[32]

In the summer of 1812 the bad times caused by the Embargo turned to worse when Congress, in June, declared war on England. Maryland, with its dependence on shipping geared itself for the worst, and Baltimore began by inflicting the worst upon itself with violent July riots between factions opposing and supporting the war. Dubois had long since turned his back on the follies of whatever governments might do. He waged his own campaign to have Bruté assigned to direct the sisters at St. Joseph.

The Sulpicians were becoming tired of Dubois' persistence in airing his needs—even if these were needs they had heaped upon him. They never considered that he might honestly feel himself inadequate to what he saw as an extremely delicate work of spirituality. They only heard—with impatience—that Dubois wanted help running the fast-growing school of which he was the only master. Help came from DuBourg, for the moment nearby at Harent's farm. As the first superior of the women's order, he claimed responsibility for its destiny and wrote to John Tessier, the superior in Baltimore, that Bruté should be sent to the Mountain, taking a backhanded slap at his persistent and practical-minded successor while doing so.

"I have given him my reasons in detail," DuBourg informed Bruté, "none of which I have imparted to Rev. J. Dubois. You perceive very well that I love you because nothing could please you more."[33]

The angriest man in Baltimore over John Dubois' victory was Archbishop Carroll.

"You have at length yielded to Mr. Dubois' perservering importunity," he declared, "by granting him not merely an assistant whom indeed may be necessary, but by granting to him the Rev. Mr. Bruté."

And this: "to fill the office of a director of some devout women."

Carroll insisted that he was "far from meaning to deprecate" such a task; "But a holy priest having the spirit of prayer and acquainted with sound principles of divinity is competent to that employment."

Blind to the possibility that Dubois might have wanted Bruté for the good of the sisters rather than for his own expediency, he objected: "Mr. Dubois will substitute him on every occasion of inconvenience to attend at the sisterhood . . . Insensibly the sisters will multiply their prayers and entreaties to confer with him . . . If the archbishop or other superiors deny the indulgence discontent will ensue. Mr. Bruté himself from the purest of motives may become their advocate."[34]

No doubt Archbishop Carroll was remembering the torrent of pleas and arguments which had buffeted him for two years while the sisters fought for or against Babade, DuBourg, and then David. With two such different personalities as Dubois and Bruté it was not unreasonable to fear that conflicts would once again arise.

In September at the beginning of the school year, Simon Bruté, who lived his life blown by the winds of whim and the Spirit, left Baltimore to join John Dubois, a man who drew strength from adherence to hard work within a structured schedule. Dubois probably waited for him to arrive by one of the regular public coaches. Bruté probably walked.

37

Rev. Simon Bruté de Rémur (1779–1839), the man whom John Dubois affectionately called "little brother." Although of opposite temperaments, they proved to be complementary. Besides aiding in the work of the college, Bruté and Dubois developed a mutual dependency, from which both benefited enormously.

38

As a child in Paris, Father Bruté witnessed scenes such as this where the Catholic clergy was regularly hunted down and led to execution. Bruté had firsthand experience of the terrors in France just after Dubois had escaped in 1791.

CHAPTER 8

The Little Bonaparte

The students at Mount Saint Mary's lived in primitive dormitories, and washed themselves, even in the dead of winter, in an outdoors trough. They helped work the plantation, cultivated their own gardens and kept their own chickens. Wild animals, including bobcats, abounded in the woods. Much living was done off the land and the boys were allowed to have guns. It was rough living. Yet, that first generation of students who lived with Dubois as a father would always recall the Mountain as if it had been created to be a child's dream of Paradise. The son of William Seton wrote that his father reminisced of the Mountain as a place "filled with an atmosphere of reasonable, practical, and joyous piety." It was a place of "enlightened religion" which afterward he seemed "never to have found in any part of the world."[1]

This enlightenment at Emmitsburg quickly attracted the public. While the Sulpicians protested loudly that he had made the place into an ordinary college, Dubois simply expanded the policy which he had always held, and accepted any boy who wanted an education. In his own hand a number of students are listed in the roll books of the first decade as "vocation unknown." One student in 1812, the year the United States went to war with Great Britain, was judged by Dubois as having "entered here to escape the necessity of military service."[2]

One reason for the immediate popularity of the Emmitsburg schools was that the public saw not only the raw physical atmosphere, but the highly cultured background of those in charge of the enterprise. Elizabeth Seton's social status was unquestionably a draw to Catholics who were not quite accepted by the upper-class Protestant society of which she had been a child. Dubois for all his workhorse occupations had an Old World grace about him, a genteel courtesy which was evident in all of his correspondence.

"There is no great variety of meats and vegetables now," he wrote in one typical letter to General and Mrs. Robert Harper who were planning to visit their children, "but the milk diet of the cottage and the coarse diet of the seminary will be seasoned with a hearty welcome."[3]

Bruté's learning as a medical doctor was as impressive as his personality. He and Dubois were known to have lived within the personal orbit of men who had changed the world: Louis XVI, Robespierre, Lafayette, Monroe, and Napoleon. Prominent families such as the Carrolls and Harpers sent their children. Elizabeth Patterson Bonaparte, relegated to a footnote in history after Napoleon and Rome annulled her marriage to his younger brother, sent her son Jerome to the Mountain. He remained there in the care of these cultured Frenchmen while his fey mother set out on a life-long quest to find a niche in European society. Trying every possible connection she would write back to Dubois wondering if he knew the Abbé Tonnellier of the Royal Society of Navarre as the latter had been once acquainted with a John Dubois. Others were more realistic in their dependence upon him. Sister Rose White made a will stating that should she die, John Dubois was to be given the guardianship of her son.

He had become a benevolent dictator in a world which he decided was absolutely his own, and he ruled absolutely over the lives of others within that world. The one group of people whom he owned outright were his slaves. He supervised their religious education and personal lives as well as their work. On one occasion he freed a woman as she married. He stipulated that her children were to remain bound to him until they were twenty-one. At the age of eighteen the boys were to start drawing wages and the money was to be kept by their mother until they were freed. The girls could be freed earlier than twenty-one "if meeting with a suitable match approved by their mother."[4]

Archbishop Carroll insisted that old Father Duhamel be called pastor of the Church in Emmitsburg; Dubois fashioned for himself the unofficial title "First Pastor" and ultimately ruled parish affairs from his Mountain. In this capacity he was as absolute with his parishioners as he was with his slaves. He refused to allow any power to fall into the hands of lay trustees even though this was becoming a common practice in American Catholic churches. He allowed pews to be rented at the Mountain chapel, but forbade it in the actual parish church in town. It was, he told his parishioners, a practice which was "an appeal to pride and made the frequentation of the Church less free."[5]

The decision meant that he would have to do with less money. So did his otherworldly attitude towards stipends, which he listed as "Nothing for baptisms, nothing for burials, and although it is decreed that the priest should have two dollars for a marriage the two dollars are not always paid."[6]

The Archbishop reacted strongly to Dubois' exercise of authority. When a man complained that Dubois had refused him sacramental absolution until he had fulfilled certain conditions, Carroll in angry response, sarcastically raised the "First pastor" of Emmitsburg into the hierarchy: "I am sorry that Bp. Dubois insisted . . . ," he began. Then he discovered that Dubois' admonishment had been properly pastoral. The archbishop backed down, "earnestly praying" the man "to comply with the conditions required by him, which contains no avowal or acknowledgement derogatory to your character."[7]

So too, if Dubois nettled parishioners with his stubbornness they knew from two decades of experience that he was dedicated to their own good. When someone claimed a section of Mountain property due to a surveying error, forty-three townspeople signed a subscription so that the land could be rebought for "an institution so useful to this neighborhood in every temporal and spiritual point." Another man died and left three thousand dollars to be divided between the sisters of St. Joseph and the Mountain because, as the will stated, "Dubois is the superior of both."[8]

The boys at the Mountain had their own way of getting back at their absolute superior—one given them by Dubois himself. He stuck to his rule that everyone from himself down to the smallest boy take a regular turn waiting on tables at mealtime. Whenever Dubois was on duty the boys arranged to keep him running repeatedly to the kitchen to get extras, a game which turned meals into an added recreation time. Someone at this time also notice a marked physical as well as temperamental likeness to Napoleon, and the president of the college was thereafter dubbed by his students: "The little Bonaparte."

The absolute rule of Dubois was balanced by the erratic presence of Bruté. Bruté's classes, like the letters he wrote, were brilliant but often impossible to follow. If fourth of July orators became famous for speaking armies of words in search of an idea, Bruté's presentations were armies of ideas in search of words. He was too brilliant to remain on one thought long enough to present it logically to students. It was always crowded out by other brilliant thoughts, some of which were at the other end of the universe from what had come before.

Bruté was as stubborn and as idiosyncratic as Dubois. Rather than confront his superior, Bruté would scratch out petulant notes in his own room and then deliver them all the way to Dubois' room next door.

He set about on a never-ending task to beautify the Mountain; planting gardens, finding springs, carving out pathways and creating grottoes. While doing so, this otherwise selfless man developed a fixation about his wheelbarrow. It was his wheelbarrow, his alone, and the Mountain experienced a calamity if anyone else ever touched it.

He was not fixed upon his personal comfort. He gave his coat away to a poor man and in doing so evoked the wrath of his practical boss.

"We are as poor as that man,"[9] Dubois bellowed. A sixteen-year-old seminarian had just died. Rather than let the tall Bruté get another coat, he made him wear that of the much smaller, deceased boy for several weeks.

Elizabeth Seton sought to calm Bruté after confrontations with Dubois, giving advice she often had to turn upon herself.

"You ought to know our Reverend Superior by this time and see that he is not to be pushed anywhere," she admonished, "and that your urging him cannot but keep him away. When anything essential happens I always inform him of it but if the thing is not essential his absence often hinders a fuss about nothing and suffers pets and little passions to drop in silence."[10]

It was good advice and Bruté used another occasion of confrontation to try a more blasé approach. Dubois once lent him a horse and a new gift saddle, with his name engraved into the pommel on a silver plate. A dripping wet horse returned later minus saddle and Bruté. Bruté followed, equally wet, and explained that instead of swimming the horse across a swollen creek he had tried to educate the animal to walk across a log which served as a bridge. He failed, rider and horse tumbling into the water. Dubois demanded to know what happened to the saddle.

"Alas, I know not," Bruté shrugged, "I watched it hurrying down the torrent and I could just see 'John Dubois,' 'John Dubois,' 'John Dubois,' bobbing up and down from one wave to another bidding me adieu."[11]

Even as they gave and took aggravations, the bond of their work drew them closer together. Listing the routine of a typical Sunday, Bruté noted that Dubois began with "his invariable meditation." He describes a morning crammed with Masses and confessions ("These six hours spent in that cold church"). The afternoon and evening were filled with Benediction, catechism and Latin classes. But in the middle of the day, as if it were an oasis of human pleasure for the two of them Bruté states simply: "Dinner; we talked."[12]

Elizabeth found it less easy to find common ground with Dubois, and admitted to Bruté that she found "little attraction for your brother's government."[13] She and Dubois were too much alike in one respect. They were both strong-willed, domineering persons, happiest when at the top of a pyramid ruling others.

Despite her avowal that she preferred to bypass rules ("Too happy I to break the knot and piece it again!"),[14] she was as authoritative in her own domain as Dubois was in his. Sisters and students lived under strong regulations at St. Joseph's and they were accountable to her. Physical punishment of the girls was allowed, and Mother Seton herself punished disobedience by having girls kneel in meditation. Girls who would not fit into the behavior pattern were expelled by her from the school. She could be sharp in reproving the sisters. One who commented that Mother Seton's pens were worn down received the rebuke:

"Well, my dear one, that is to atone for your waste of pens."[15]

Elizabeth's problem with Dubois, rightly or wrongly, was the Church's insistence that a man be ultimately in charge over women's religious orders. She could easily have handled a poetic weaker man like Babade. Dubois was a constant frustration to her.

Moreover, if he was mystically oriented he hid it. Bruté and she could share soul experiences which barely touched earth. Speaking of Scripture Bruté would impart to her:

"Sometimes I could almost weep all on a sudden with what only one of the most harmonious, tender sorrowful words does to me . . ."[16]

She in turn would praise him for words which she claimed came "from the hot press of the burning heart."[17]

Dubois had little place for such extreme emotionalism in his religion. Once when he carried Holy Communion up a stairway to a sick nun another sister bringing down chamber pots bumped into him. Afterwards she threw herself at his feet to beg pardon. Dubois laughed off such seriousness:

"What offense my child was offered," he asked. "The God of all charity met a sister of Charity performing an act of Charity. How could he be displeased?"[18]

Such behavior was too unvarnished for Elizabeth. She shared her displeasure with Babade and in return he chided her: "This feeling and antipathy for your superior is truly the old Adam. What consoles me is that the new Adam prevails and that you do your duty."[19]

This duty involved cooperation with Dubois in the rapid arrangements he was making to expand her religious order into a world which seemed to be falling apart. In August, 1814, the British entered Chesapeake Bay and attacked a poorly defended Washington. William Hickey, in that city, wrote his brother John at the Mountain: "Our own people burnt the Navy yard; the enemy, the capital and other public buildings." Congress deserted the city leaving the citizens "quite heartless." Living conditions were bad he reported: "Not much business of any kind going on, money is scarce, wood and all kinds of provisions very dear . . ."[20]In mid-September Baltimore was attacked. Volunteers left from Emmitsburg and Frederick to defend the city. Bruté was so agitated he went with them. Dubois carried on with his students as best he could. The war had stopped shipments of needed texts, food supplies and building materials. Even though the British were held back, the *Frederick Town Herald* declared bitterly that "All must now be convinced of the folly of declaring war in our unprepared condition," (The paper nevertheless allowed for the recent courage of Maryland's citizens and immediately after this angry article printed a new song in praise of the flag, written during the attack: " 'Defense of Fort McHenry,' F. S. Key Esq., formerly of this place—Tune: 'Anacreon in Heaven.' ")[21]

During all this Dubois continued to work on his own Vincent de Paul inspired vision to establish the Sisters of Charity throughout the United States. As superior he made all the arrangements with the local trustees and, two weeks after the British bombardment of Baltimore, the first daughter house was established at the orphanage in Philadelphia.

"It was not safe to go by the packets as the English were still in the Bay," Sister Rose White recorded. Instead they journeyed overland in a coach, escorted by Dubois.

"The good Superior accompanied us as far as Taneytown," Rose wrote, "giving us lessons of economy all the way."[22]

One can almost hear the sigh of endurance in the written words.

The next year, Bruté received orders that he was to go to France on Sulpician business. Upon his return he was to assume the presidency of the Baltimore seminary. It was decided that William Seton should accompany him across the Atlantic. He was eighteen now and had lived at the Mountain since he was twelve. Dubois pushed Elizabeth to let him make his way in the world. She entrusted him to Bruté that he might be deposited in Italy to work in the Filicchi's counting house. When the sailing vessel was delayed in its departure Elizabeth wavered, wanting to bring her child back home. Dubois held firm for the boy's sake.

"I find Mr. Dubois strongly bent on your pursuing the first intention . . . ," she wrote William sadly, "If it is your wish I will wish it too . . ."[23]

William realized that Dubois' forceful cutting of apron strings would drive a further wedge between these two who were the closest people to him in this world.

"Mother," he wrote back, both as an assurance and a directive, "all my love is centered in you, share it with Mr. Dubois."[24]

Both she and Dubois were heartsick after the departure.

"Your brother cried out to me what he had lost in his brother," Elizabeth wrote to Bruté, "and could hardly restrain his tears at my louder cry."[25]

Still, she was unable to reach out to console him, nor would she allow him into her own heart's feelings as she would have allowed Bruté or Babade.

She had promised to keep a journal so that Bruté would know what was happening at the Mountain. A composite of her entries about Dubois draws a portrait of that mixture of extremes in him which paralleled the personality of Vincent de Paul: the energetic, all-consuming pursuit of a grand vision—a pursuit which often involved more energy than she could bear—and the equal concern for everyday small details:

"... Your brother hardly takes time to breathe ..."[26]

"... Mrs. Oliver, (so rich you remember) is crazy and they apply to us to receive and take care of her. A precious beginning of our hospital as he offers any money [sic]. You may suppose how many plans of a building through the zealous brain of your brother [sic]. 'I will, I WILL, I WILL,' while I, with hands crossed on Mary's picture, and the crucifix under the shawl, bow and assent, and smile, and expect it may be in Spain ..."

"... Poor Superior! Often he will not dine because his head is so suffering, and no sleep. He said laughing, 'You see my haircut; I met the barber in the woods, and I sat down on a stone to let him do it there. There is no time at home.' Often I remind him of how you would suffer to know how little he spares himself, but you may as well speak to the moon ..."[27]

"... I would tell you something about his affairs, but they seem to me all comprised in his cautious, equal, daily grace almost miraculous. A moment of vexation on receiving Mr. Bertrand's bill to Mrs. Seton, but I laughed him out of the important affair. To tell you how gay and cheerful he is, it is impossible ..."[28]

"... Your brother's very soul dancing at a new thought of moving old Peter's house to the side of Mr. Duhamel's house and planting three old sisters there (maybe I shall go at last): I propose, I intend, I will ..."[29]

"... Your brother is delighted with a First Communion he gave little Hughes (Daniel Hughes' child) on her death bed last night. As soon as he brought in Our Lord she put up her hands and cried 'Oh my God I thank you.' He had his deacon Dedier and sub [deacon] Elder and is gay as can be planning and laying out future. 'What will I do.' He lives in futurity, and I in the past, until the World of Realities ..."[30]

Because they had such a different view of realities she could be left cold by his earnest efforts in a pulpit:

"... Now in retreat. The Superior in his element. Almost I laughed out at his opening, telling the children to be as many little stumps, no "chunks" of fire put together; one he said, if left alone, would soon go out. My eye fell on an old black stump in the corner, and a big inward sigh to the live coal far away which used to give it blaze in a moment ..."[31]

Still she could not move the stump out of the corner and near the less colorful flame of Dubois.

Without Bruté he felt very much alone:

"Not one soul, Mother, on whom I can rely to see a class well kept, much less to give spiritual instruction, Mr. Hickey pure as an angel, but _____"[32]

He didn't finish. He would ever be slow in passing harsh personal judgment, and John Hickey was newly ordained. He was the first "child" of the Mountain. Dubois had known him as a youngster in Frederick and had seen him through most of his education. But at best he was a petulant soul, geared to seeking the easiest path for himself while critical of the work done by others. He was sent as a replacement for Bruté and immediately complained to Baltimore that the work was too much for him. Father Tessier answered that he had written to Dubois asking him "to take upon himself what he may see you could not do of the various parts which were performed by Mr. Bruté."

"But I must also tell you my dear young friend," he added, "that you are too diffident on yourself. You are able to do more than you imagine . . . You see how many things Mr. Dubois is able to do on account of the same good and courageous will . . . Learn from him how to behave yourself. You cannot have a better model . . ."[33]

If the forceful personality of John Dubois overpowered Hickey, so too did the equally forceful personality of Mother Seton. She noted that after morning Mass he was constantly "so embarrassed with the three minutes I stand by his table in the morning, I believe it is the plague of his life."

The plague descended upon his head full force when he earned from her a wrath which might be directed to many priests in any age.

"Gave our Rev. J. Hickey a scolding he will remember," she wrote. "The congregation so crowded yesterday and so many strangers to whom he gave a sermon so evidently lazy, and answered this morning:

"I didn't trouble myself much about it, Ma'am."

"Oh Sir! that awakens my anger. Do you remember a priest holds the honor of God on his lips? Do you not trouble yourself to spread his fire he wishes so much enkindled? If you will not study and prepare while young, what when you are old? There is a Mother's lesson!"

"But, prayer _____ "

"Yes, prayer and preparation too."[34]

Dubois, then, agreed to preach twice for every one time for Hickey that the young man might have ample time to prepare.

Richard Seton turned eighteen in 1816. His mother, still class conscious, blocked his acceptance of a job in Mr. Elder's Emmitsburg grocery. Though she grieved at his "childish, thoughtless disposition,"[35] she still held that the simple life was not to be for her sons. She used her connections to place him in a Baltimore counting house. He quickly got himself into trouble there. Keeping fast company, he squandered whatever money his mother could give him and even the small amounts his younger sister Catherine earned teaching music while in the same city.

Like any prodigal still riding high, Richard had no desire to face a stern father figure. On a late summer visit home, he avoided a final confrontation with Dubois, spending his last night in town rather than at the Mountain, his home of seven years. When he stopped at St. Joseph's in the morning he noticed Dubois coming down the road, saw storm clouds of scolding, and "taking leave coldly" of his mother he dove into the carriage before Dubois could get to him.[36]

During that same season real sorrow came with the death of the youngest Seton child, fourteen-year-old Rebecca. Several years earlier she had fallen on ice and the injury to her hip had turned into a tumor. After a long, painful decline she herself asked Dubois if she might be annointed. Going against the pastoral practice of the day which held this off until almost the moment of death he decided:

"Although I saw no immediate danger I thought she should receive this last sacrament with better dispositions by being now sensible."

After he had heard her confession Rebecca asked him:

"Father, is there any harm to hope that I will go to heaven as soon as I am dead?"

"No, my child," he assured her, "if this hope is grounded not in any confidence you have in your own merits but in the mercy of God and the merits of our Jesus."[37]

When, at last, the end drew near he promised the girl he would not leave her bedside, and he remained until four in the morning when she died. His own deep admiration for Elizabeth Seton was expressed to Bruté:

"The Mother is a miracle of divine favor . . ." he wrote, "She held the child in her arms without dropping a tear all the time of her agony and even eight minutes after she died. Mulierum Fortem."[38]

He wrote to William in Leghorn and, to console the young man, filled its pages with accounts of improvements at the Mountain.

"I tell you all that, my dearest friend," he concluded, "because it has been the spot of your infancy and that it naturally calls to mind many sweet remembrances."[39]

It did, and William returned a loving letter to the father who had raised him from "infancy." Richard too, though he was to do little to mend his ways, wrote:

"I now see too well that what you used to tell me in time of spiritual reading—that these were the happiest days we would ever spend—has turned out to be too true."[40]

He then unburdened himself to Dubois about his loss of childhood innocence "for I can't find as good a friend on earth to tell it to."[41] He still sought a simple life. A Quaker offered him a position running a country store and farm beyond Gettysburg. He told his mother:

"I leave it all to you and dear Mr. Dubois. If you two like it, Amen."[42]

Elizabeth refused to let him choose this path. She still set her sights towards high society. William too had returned home in failure. The Filicchis, in embarrassment, let him go after he refused to apply himself. Now though she realized that Richard "like his brother . . . shows no remarkable talents,"[43] she packed him off to the patient Filicchis, hoping that Leghorn might provide the opportunities for success which he had tossed aside in Baltimore. Had he been allowed to pursue his perennial request to work in a grocery store he might have avoided the tragedy that his short life was to become.

Catherine Seton, born with the century in 1800, was the only surviving Seton girl. Quiet and reserved, she became closer to Dubois than anyone in the family, and as time would tell, the most like him in her sense of practical Christianity. After the loss of her two sisters Dubois deepened his role as her mentor:

"When you come again to the Mountain," he wrote, "you will pick out of my library what may suit you. Meanwhile I send you the dreadful *Expedition to Russia*. See what ambition can undergo for this world. Oh if we could do half of it for heaven, how rich we would be."[44]

The two exchanged gifts as well as books. She would embroider him a stole. He in return would send her a preserved pineapple, orange and two green apples, playfully advising her:

"In the choice, believe me, take the smallest."[45]

The network of Dubois' responsibilities spread. He had opened a convent orphanage in New York as well as in Philadelphia and he checked upon the sisters in person as best he could. Years later an elderly nun, Sister Martha Daddisman, reminisced about her relationship with her superior. Dubois had converted and baptized her conditionally as a child:

"I used to walk along by him and catch his hand. He was in Frederick then."

As a nun she was only eighteen when assigned to the Philadelphia orphanage and she spent her first week there in homesick tears. One day when they were expecting an official visitation, the doorbell rang.

"I said, 'I bet you anything that's Father Dubois' and I just put down the bowl of coffee I had in my hand right there in the hall and turned and opened the door. Sure enough it was Father and I threw my arms around his neck and he cried out:

'Oh, you Martha, don't you do that!'

and the way he scolded me and dear, there was a whole lot of Reverend gentlemen and seminarians at his back. My but he scolded me for it good."

However she added:

"It all passed off nicely as a good joke."[46]

Bruté was a fish out of water as President of the Baltimore college. The first three days there he was so heartsick he could not even bring himself to say Mass. He was only a figurehead in the position. The Sulpicians knew him for a scatterbrained genius and kept him away from practical affairs. He complained that he had so little touch with finances that he was made to give alms to beggars through the office of the procurator. For two years he was separated from Emmitsburg by this assignment and he and Dubois—so often at odds when together—pined to be reunited. They still shared their lives as best they could.

"I must follow the example of my brother and write at odd moments or

I cannot write at all," Dubois apologized. He confessed failures in his own priestly life. Once, when he had been pulled away from teaching for a sick call to a man who was "not so ill as they had represented him . . . I murmured a little at having been interrupted."

"I was well punished for it, for on the 15th they called me hurriedly to assist good Samuel Green, who, they said was very ill. I went quickly that time without complaining, and I returned at about 2 o'clock in the morning to endeavor to get a little sleep in order to keep up the next day . . ."

"'. . . I think nothing too much, but I do it ill," he wrote, "My heart is dry how can it lead others? Our Jesus has pity on me however—He had done good without me."[47]

Bruté wrote to the Sulpicians in Paris summing up the "executive occupations" of Dubois and his need for assistance. He turned his page sideways and labelled six columns: Seminary, sisters, Parish, teaching, spiritual and correspondence and made this his plea that Dubois needed him, exclaiming:

"Dieu seul connait le travail de cet excellent homme."[48]

At Christmastime 1817, Dubois cared for the bedridden Father Duhamel while he assumed his sacramental duties. The old priest died on February sixth. Four days later Bruté forestalled any attempt to replace Duhamel with anyone else. He deserted his college post and reassigned himself to Emmitsburg. It was willful disobedience on his part, and equal disobedience on Dubois' part for encouraging him.

"Mr. Dubois does not have the faintest idea of the spirit of St. Sulpice . . ." decided Ambrose Maréchal, a Sulpician who had been appointed the new Archbishop of Baltimore, "and Mr. Bruté is hardly more of a Sulpician than Mr. Dubois."[49]

On top of all this a letter arrived from the Superior General of the Sulpicians in Paris based upon the information given to him by Bruté. He praised Dubois' school in glowing terms and added the hope that it would never "degenerate into a college."[50]

The French fathers of Baltimore almost choked on this.

"Certainly," spat Tessier, "that would have been difficult for it was a college already."[51] Angrily, they took steps to end this degeneracy which now rankled them. Hickey, already expert at reporting complaints to his superiors, received a letter from Father Tessier in Baltimore. Needing an information leak, the latter knew he need only turn the young man on to get everything he wanted.

"I do not want you to speak of it to Rev. Mr. Dubois, who is rather vexed when applied to about temporal or pecuniary affairs," he wrote, "but you will privately write to me what you know of all the expenses that are made beside the usual current expenses . . ."[52]

While Hickey sneaked about gathering his data, Dubois wrote the young man a routine note. It showed both his unsuspecting affection for the Judas at his side, and his lifelong tendency to slip in and out of his native tongue:

"Cher Frere et Cher Fils," he began, "Aperant avoir l'occasion de notre ami Mr. Hughes, J'en profiterai pour vous faire—Pshaw! What am I about. I am writing French to a staunch American. It won't do."

After routine business he finished saying: "I would be most willing to go on in my scribble, but my incessant cough won't let me and this greasy paper plagues me too much."[53]

His greasy young confrère, who had let Dubois lift so much work off his own shoulders told Tessier that in his judgment the Mountain's debts might easily be paid "if our present Superior would retire and you would give us another more active."[54]

Even in the midst of a fight, this raised Tessier's eyebrows. "He surely means for the preparatory seminary," he said, "for Father Dubois does not lack activity otherwise."[55] He was also gentlemanly enough to remind Hickey that Dubois was still a bigger man than he was:

"He knows how to direct you," he admonished, "If he be a little hard sometimes, you may be sure that it will prove to your greater good."[56]

When the Sulpicians then suggested that the Mountain school be closed for financial reasons, Dubois in response drew up figures to show that it would cost more money to close the place than to keep it open.

A second attack by the fathers of Baltimore unleased a barrage of complaints about Elizabeth Seton's religious order. It was not the Sulpicians' business to maintain convents. They were a society dedicated to training men for the priesthood. The community of nuns had been all along an aberration brought about by the "grand enterprises" of William DuBourg. Now it had become "the Benjamin" in Dubois' eye and he gave it "the most precious part of his time."

"As soon as a Sulpician arrives at Emmitsburg to work at the preparatory seminary," Tessier claimed, "he finds himself transformed into Curé or vicaire of Emmitsburg and the chapel of ease which the college provides; and as long as Fathers Dubois and Bruté would be there, there would be no remedy for the evil."[57]

"Evil" indeed they felt it to be for the atmosphere of a seminary. They asserted that the nearness of a girls' school had resulted in the loss of several young men to the priesthood.

The townspeople of Emmitsburg rallied once again behind Dubois. As they had done once before they came forward, this time with eight thousand dollars, as Elizabeth Seton wrote, "to buy the seminary for him if he chose—if only he would not leave them."[58]

Dubois spilled an ocean of ink fighting the decision to close. He appealed to Paris to overrule the Baltimore priests. He wrote Archbishop Maréchal that the demise of the Mountain school would be "fatal to the interests of Saint Sulpice and to religion."[59]

Maréchal, remembered by one of the first sisters as a small ladylike man, overly emotional in public ("My father thought he should be more manly and control himself better.")[60] fielded the arguments from both sides, cryptically jotting his opinions on the back of their letters. Dubois' entrées in his long fight to preserve his school earned such notations as: "Petitions, complaints as usual," . . . "Evasive," . . . "Plans, schemes, etc" . . . "ab irato" . . . Bruté contributed an impassioned stream-of-consciousness epistle which won the label: "wild."[61]

Elizabeth Seton had a great deal at stake. Only the possible loss of Dubois made her appreciate his presence. She tried to ingratiate herself with Maréchal using the approach which had been so successful with Archbishop Carroll.

"An eternity of happy years to my dear and venerated father," she began, ". . . at beads this morning, coming to the mystery of our dear Savior loaded with his cross, a momentary imagination represented you to my soul so loaded and weighed under yours you have received from the Church that I would have died for you with joy to ease you."

Maréchal flipped it over and wrote:

"Pious chat."[62]

Another attempt he labelled: "of no importance."

Perhaps it was well for all that he was so bland a man, for he wanted no fuss or scandal. The battle between the two institutions would continue for another decade, but this round was settled in a compromise blessed by France and the Archbishop. The Mountain school remained open, run independently of Baltimore's administration. Dubois assumed all debts including the ruinous Elder annuity and was formally given back title to the land he had bought and upon which he had planned to retire long before he had been pulled into the affable world of William Valentine DuBourg.

39

The "White House" on the grounds of St. Joseph's at Emmitsburg. Father Dubois built this residence for the Sisters of Charity, and said the first high mass there when it opened in February 1810.

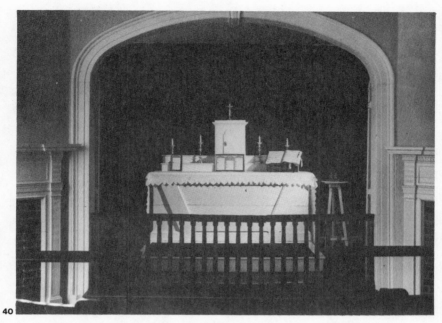

40

Above, *the altar and chapel in the "White House";* below, *a classroom*

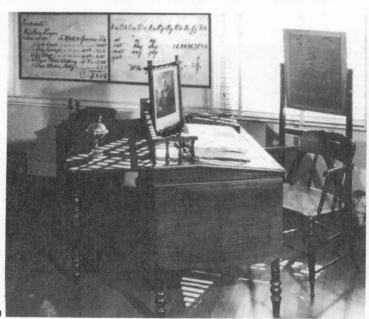

41

Archbishop Ambrose Maréchal
(1769–1828) of Baltimore

42

Because of a shortage of personnel and a dispute over the use of Mount
St. Mary's as a major Seminary and secular college, neither the
Archbishop of Baltimore nor Father Tessier (below) *were avid sup-*
porters of Dubois' "Mountain College."

Father John Mary Tessier, S.S.
(1758–1810) Dubois' Sul-
pician Superior in Baltimore

43

44

Four of Mother Seton's children: William (1796–1868) and Richard (1798–1823) above; and Anina (1795–1812) and Rebecca (1802–1816) below. Especially to the Seton boys, Dubois acted as surrogate father while they were in his school at Emmitsburg. Two days before Anina died Father Dubois received her into the sisterhood; and when Rebecca's end was near, he promised he would not leave her bedside, remaining until she died at four in the morning.

45

Sister Martha Daddisman (1797–1889), one of the earliest Sisters of Charity, who reminisced about her experiences with Father Dubois. She is shown above in the habit of the Daughters of Charity (USA) after the Emmitsburg Sisters affiliated with the French branch in 1850.

46

Father John Hickey (1789–1869), shown here in old age, was the first priest ordained at "the Mountain." He once was given a scolding by Mother Seton for not preparing his sermons properly.

47

CHAPTER 9

She Did But Follow My Express Prescriptions

Heavy emotional and physical stress was laid upon Dubois during 1818. He fought for his seminary's existence not only in writings but by repeatedly rushing to Baltimore to confront his adversaries in person. All the while he was plagued by catarrh and a persistent wracking cough. In May when the twenty-two-year-old William Seton, now in the Navy, hit his mother with one of his too frequent requests for money, she did not have so much as a five dollar bill in the house. She apologized, moreover, that another immediate resource was cut off because "Mr. Dubois is sick in Baltimore."[1]

In the midst of all these pressures the flighty Bruté decided that he was called to the missions in China. A scandalized Mother Seton slapped him down with the scolding:

"Surely you would not leave your brother now."[2]

Had he left, Dubois would have been thoroughly deserted. In retaliation for his victory in keeping open his school, the Sulpicians had recalled to Baltimore John Hickey and another priest just assigned.

Elizabeth Seton was very near death from tuberculosis. Bruté, chastened into remaining on the scene, was a proper spiritual director for this strongly mystical soul. In matters of the world she continued to rely upon Dubois. William, still heedless of his mother's suffering, nagged at her from Boston to use family connections to get him reassigned to a ship leaving port sooner than the one he was on. She responded:

"I have been bled in both arms for a slight attack of the breast and I got Mr. Dubois to write the very hour I received your letter."[3]

She might have compared Dubois' support with that given her by her long admired "patriarch" Babade. Dubois, ill himself, travelled to Baltimore and arranged that Catherine would live with the Harper family after graduating from St. Joseph's; an arrangement which brought great peace of mind to her mother. Babade, living in that same city, looked out from inside the moat of his religious community and wrote Elizabeth Seton:

"I would like very much to see you before you die, but I foresee that the Superior will not allow me to go to Emmitsburg in the present state of things." [i.e., the difficulties with the Mountain school].

He did, however, promise her:

"As soon as I hear of your death I will say Mass for the repose of your dear soul."[4]

Elizabeth Seton's illness and his own, along with the Mountain's survival, were not all that weighed upon Dubois. He received a letter from a nephew in France. Dubois' own mother had been in the care of a community of nuns, but her mind had become more and more deranged. The sisters decided that their house was not calculated to care for the addled and evicted her. The family placed her in a pension house where they paid for her care.

At such a point an ordinary man might have quit the whole business. Dubois had not seen his aged mother in over a quarter of a century. Bruté had returned to France and visited his own mother—in fact had stopped in Paris to visit Dubois' mother. Many of his fellow refugees of the revolution were giving up the missions and returning home. Babade who could not travel fifty miles to visit Mother Seton soon travelled eastward across the Atlantic. Dubois could return from the missions and live in a comfortable parish in Paris. He could even return to where he had begun his ministry at the huge Church of Saint Sulpice, so extreme in grandeur compared with all the little wooden churches he had built with his own hands. He could care for his own mother instead of caring for Mother Seton who seemed to appreciate him so little.

It was ironic. While he was building up the United States' first religious community, another religious community was turning his mother out because they were not acclimated to deal with the senile.

Robespierre and God had cast him into the missions; it was not a field he had chosen for himself. But now he was consecrated wholly to the Church in America; consecrated to teaching boys who would become America's first native hierarchy, consecrated to building America's first sisterhood. The only time he would ever return to France would be years in the future, long after it would avail him personal satisfaction; and then it would be on a thankless trek to beg for his mission diocese.

In the fall Archbishop Maréchal replaced the priests withdrawn by the Sulpicians with the newly ordained Samuel Sutherland Cooper whose money had placed Elizabeth Seton with Dubois at Emmitsburg. Elizabeth Seton, enjoying a temporary respite from her battle with tuberculosis, was overjoyed. Despite the man's eccentricities she saw him not only as the "founder of our house"[5] but as a spiritual kin to Bruté and herself. One of the early sisters remembered him as "an uncommonly ugly man. Uncommonly ugly. Had red hair, wore a wig I believe, and had all his teeth taken out. Someone asked him if it was for penance and he said 'No.' He denied it."[6] (This, to counter the legend that he had smashed them out after a youthful love affair.)

The decade since he had met Mrs. Seton had been chaotic for Cooper. In the seminary he had been attacked by "a violent sickness in which he suffered a madness and derangement of mind for the space of eight or ten days."[7]

He had left and wandered to Philadelphia where his family attempted to get back the money he had sunk in the Catholic Church, notably the thousands of dollars invested in Emmitsburg. In this instance Dubois went after Cooper to find out what the man was about and to insure the security of the sisters' home.

Having captained his own ship for years to Europe and India, Cooper sought his escape in travel. He eventually returned from Rome, Italy, in his right mind and resumed his studies.

Dubois, receiving him as a new priest, assigned him to the care of the Emmitsburg parish. He lasted less than a year and in that time created a furor over his decision to combat drunkenness with public penances. The new pastor declared that those guilty of such public scandal should "sit in some particular place in the Church and that their names should be mentioned from the pulpit . . ."[8]

As he announced this at a Sunday Mass, one man beat him to a recitation of a local who's who by getting up and stomping out. Already labelled, the man led an easily organized whiskey rebellion.

Dubois tried to hold Cooper back, but to no avail. Bent on enforcing moderation, he refused to be moderate. After months of yelling back and forth, the town's grog shops were still going strong and the parishioners were still throwing their empties at the pastor. Cooper, frustrated when people refused to follow his leadership while he refused to follow the leadership of Dubois, quit and went back to Baltimore.

His subsequent career was frenzied and tragic. The next year he went to Augusta, Georgia, and for three years lived a polemical existence arguing wildly against Protestant preachers and using defenses of Catholicism which bordered on the superstitious. He returned to Philadelphia in 1822 and soon left on a pilgrimage to the Holy Land. Home in the States within the year he failed to find his niche in the Church, moving from Richmond to Philadelphia to Wilmington, Delaware. There, his mind cracking again, he became involved in a scandalous love affair with a young girl and fled to France.

". . . What an example, what warning," wrote a young priest ordained from the Mountain, John Hughes, "She was a Protestant school girl of fourteen—he near sixty. A challenge was sent and refused . . . It makes me stupid and sick to think about it."[9]

This tortured man found peace at last under the care of the kindly John Cheverus who left America and became Archbishop then Cardinal at Bordeaux. Cooper attended Cheverus at his death in 1836, then lived on for another seven years. The once wealthy Protestant sea captain who had financed the beginning of the Sisters of Charity died at the age of seventy-six leaving an estate of eighty dollars.

Elizabeth Seton often accepted funds from her wealthy friends. Wanting to keep her sons in the society to which they had been born she let them become financially dependent upon others. Even the generous Filippo Filicchi in Leghorn, surprised by the unsought arrival of William, scolded her "for having sent here your son without previous leave."[10] To gain William an officer's berth in the Navy, she worked connections as high as the vice-presidency of the United States.

Yet several months after she had recovered from her brush with death, after Dubois had eased her mind by arranging for her daughter's adoption by the Harpers, he asked her to request of the Filichis that they send for his altar, urns which he wanted, not to beg, but buy.

Embarrassed, Mother Seton wrote to her wealthy friends:

"I cannot refuse to make the request as I cannot make him sensible how disagreeable such commissions are. However, as he has the money to remit your order he cannot see the pain of making the request."[11]

Elizabeth's frustration with Dubois' constant master planning was evidenced when, perhaps unconsciously, she sang the praises of two priests present at Emmitsburg when, in fact, there were three.

"I glance a fearful look at you and Mr. Cooper and say secretly, if I was one or the other . . ." She wrote to Bruté, "Oh! If I was light and life as you are, I would shout like a mad man alone to my God and roar and groan and sigh and be silent altogether till I had baptized a thousand and snatched these poor victims from hell."

She asked herself the rhetorical question:

"Why does not your zeal make its flame through your own little hemisphere?"

In so doing she pinpointed the reason for her exclusion of Dubois. He was the wall of her hemisphere. Neither Bruté nor Cooper was placed as an authority over her and even if they had been they lacked authoritative personalities. Dubois, stubborn and thorough as she was herself, stood present as a reminder that a masculine Church took the free spirit she brought to it and limited it with regulations. She answered her own question:

"True—but rules, prudence, subjections, opinions, etc. dreadful walls to a burning soul wild as mine, and somebody's.—For me I am like a fiery horse I had when a girl which they tried to break by making him drag a heavy cart, and the poor beast was so humbled that he could never more be inspired by whips or caresses and wasted a skeleton until he died. But you and Mr. Cooper might waste to skeletons to some purpose and after wasting be sent still living to the glories of the kingdom."[12]

"Were I a man," she once wrote, "The whole world itself would not be enough for me."[13] Were she a man, this larger-than-life woman entrapped in nineteenth-century prejudices could have led instead of being led. It was her absolute devotion to the Eucharist which had brought her into Roman Catholicism. As a man, she could have been a priest. She could have made her own decisions in life and enforced them the way she wished. The structure of the Church dictated that women religious be ruled by a man. The man at hand was Dubois.

It was this natural, no doubt unconscious, resentment of Dubois which kept him out of her pantheon of "venerated patriarchs." She took to referring to him as "The Pope," an interesting contrast to the "little Bonaparte" title given him by the students. Even in the last letter she was ever to write, on October 21, 1820, she reported to the sisters in Philadelphia that Dubois had made an unexpected visit to the infirmary and interrupted idle chatter. He asked if silence was not to be observed. As a result he wrote "In large Letters"—"Silence here at all times as below when not in recreation—at meals."

"You never saw such a change as that made,"[14] observed Elizabeth.

Change and growth had become the work of Dubois' life. In 1819 he had planned to put up a schoolhouse for the sisters, but an economic crash brought the United States so low that Mother Seton feared "our house may be empty next year."[15]

By the summer of 1820, however, Dubois was ready to move ahead. As before Elizabeth resisted new construction.

"The building is a bad business," she told Bruté, "but our endless obligations to the superior, the very formation of the house all his—what can we say now? I would rather trust Our God to draw us out of the danger than dare oppose or aggravate him in our relative position."[16]

She might better have taken a tack from Sister Anne Gruber who cooked at the Mountain. Unlike Mother, who fretted over each incursion made by Dubois, she drew the lines of authority once and saw that he respected it. With his usual flair for intervention he made the mistake of entering her domain once too often, lifting pot tops to test and advise upon what she was doing.

Silently she took off her apron and held it out to him. He stopped mid-recipe, stared at her for a moment until the threatened offer registered in his consciousness. Clapping a hand to his head he retreated exclaiming:

"Mon Dieu! Non! Non!"[17]

After that the kitchen was totally hers. In contrast, Elizabeth Seton suffered silently—too silently. Dubois, well meaning and determined to expand the work of the order had seen her get sick and well again many times. He did not stop to think, in the warmth of a Maryland summer that she needed absolute rest if she was to live much longer. As the building grew he called her one day to give advice to the carpenters. She had to climb a pile of boards and stand in the wind. She became ill—again. This time her steady decline brought her to her death bed.

For months she lingered. Both Bruté and Dubois kept close by. Dubois, aware that it was Bruté who was closer to Mother, allowed him to direct her soul toward Eternity. On January 2, 1821, Dubois annointed her with the final sacrament. Standing next to her bed, he turned and spoke on her behalf to the assembled sisters.

"Mother, being too weak gives me charge to recommend to you at this sacred moment in her place; first to be united together as true Sisters of Charity; secondly to stand most faithfully by the rules; thirdly, she requests that I ask you pardon of all the scandals she may have given you. I obey her desire."

As if he were a father softening the self-judgment of a scrupulous child, Dubois softened this idea of scandal, which she had directed him to say. He added:

"You know she gave none by the indulgences she was allowed—she means particularly in what she had to eat, or other allowances for her situation, in which she did but follow my express prescriptions and those of the physician."[18]

She died early in the morning of January fourth. Her social position, her conversion and strong witness to Catholicism had made her well known throughout the United States. In time she would be canonized a saint. Like another mystical saint, Louise de Marillac, who had been reluctant to accept the direction of the ruggedly practical Saint Vincent de Paul, she had only reluctantly accepted the guiding hand of her superior John Dubois. Yet, like Vincent de Paul his rugged day-to-day practicality embodied his own great visions. Unlike the poetic and chimerical men who had dreamed of grand enterprises with her but left her adrift without strong support,

Dubois worked to give structure to visions. Without him Elizabeth Seton might never have been known to history, and the work which she had begun might never have taken hold after her death.

After her death John Dubois still had much more work to do.

48

Father Bruté has left us several sketches of important events in his life. Above is his rendering of the death of Mother Seton, at which he was present on January 4, 1821.

49

At left, *Rev. Samuel Sutherland Cooper (c1769–1843) gave the Sisters of Charity money to buy their first property at Emmitsburg. When he was pastor there, he balked at Dubois' control and caused unrest.*

CHAPTER 10

The Lord Gave and
the Lord Hath Taken Away

Shortly before Elizabeth Seton died, her ofttimes prodigal son Richard lost his job with the Filicchis. Landing in Virginia, he promptly got in trouble with the law over an unpaid bill and cried out to Emmitsburg for help. Safely home in December, the twenty-two-year-old announced that he was following his brother to sea and left again, oblivious to the seriousness of his mother's illness. She died two weeks after his departure.

Dubois realized that his "well meaning but too indulgent mother was rather averse to his associating with coarse vulgar sailors," but he disappointedly allowed that the young man had already been "much injured by vicious, immoral and irreligious company."

"His candour is very questionable," he observed sadly, concluding, ". . . I see less than ever what can be done with him."[1]

The boy never had a chance to prove himself as an adult. Two years after this, the young sailor went ashore in Liberia and while there cared for an Episcopalian priest sick with typhoid. Back on board ship he, too, came down with the disease and died, June 26, 1823. He was buried at sea.

Dubois had more effective parental influence over Catherine. After her mother's death she hesitated to leave the convent in which she had lived most of her life. Dubois pushed her away from Emmitsburg and away from himself with a selfless love that was as obvious as it was wise:

"Your aunt will expect you," he insisted, "Mrs. Harper will claim your promise, Dear Ann will do the same. Changing your plan now would lead all those good people into the belief that you had been influenced, per- suaded to remain at St. Joseph's. Yourself one day might form to yourself a false picture of the world and regret a shadow because you would think it a reality."[2]

And so the young woman was sent out to judge for herself a world of which she had seen too little. Her familial relationship with St. Joseph's ended; her familial relationship with Dubois remained until she attended him at his death.*

When Mother Seton's obituary appeared in New York papers, an ac- quaintance of Dubois from that city encouraged him to write her biography. He toyed with this idea, but as usual he was too engulfed by practical projects to enter into one which required reflective work. Most immediately he had to find her replacement. One might conjecture what would have happened had Elizabeth Seton lived into old age. Shortly after the for- mation of the sisterhood she had gone into combat when Father David sought to replace her with Sister Rose White. Each time an election had come up she had been kept in office. Would she continually have held on to power as if the order were her own possession? Whatever might have been, her death meant that the order had to pass from being Mother Seton's sisterhood, and into its own strength as a community. The me- chanics of the transition fell upon Dubois. In January 1821, even as he informed the mission houses of Mother Seton's demise, he gave directions about the election of a new head. Each sister in every mission was to send to him two names on a sheet of paper which was not to be seen by the local superior. The result brought about the election of Sister Rose White who would have been placed in office a decade earlier if Father David had had his way.

When Dubois had presented John Carroll with the rules for the Amer- ican Sisters of Charity, the Archbishop had opined that a good century

---

*Catherine Seton proved herself to be very much the spiritual child of John Dubois. After he pushed her into the world, she travelled extensively in Europe, then shared life and society with her well-married brother William, who worried her by his lack of care for religion. After Dubois died, for reasons now buried by both religious communities, she was discouraged from entering the order her mother founded and became the first postulant in the Sisters of Mercy brought from Ireland by Bishop John Hughes. She lived to the age of ninety-one, to the last undiminished in a delightful sense of humor which made her especially loved in her community. Dubois' Vincent de Paul philosophy was not lost on her. For the greater part of her life as a sister she made New York's prisoners her special children. Week in and week out without fail over the span of decades, she walked jail tiers, going from cell to cell, be- friending and giving comfort to the inmates.

and more would pass before the sparsely populated United States would have need of sisters caring for the impoverished sick—the prime mission of the order in France. Rather, he suggested, the work of the American sisters should be in the field of education.

Dubois disagreed. With his Vincent de Paul vision of service, he began almost immediately to establish orphanages in major American cities. Shortly after Mother Seton's death, he negotiated to place the sisters in an infirmary for the poor in Baltimore. In his arrangements with the trustees, he paralleled Saint Vincent's painstaking concern for detail in planning daily work; for structuring the spiritual life of the sisters; and for strictly holding to the vow of poverty. In his arrangements with the trustees he asked for a one hundred dollar annual allowance per sister, but added: "Should this sum be too much the surplus will be returned." The sisters were to teach catechism and care for the poor, distributing food and clothing "either at their house or in prison." They were to work in the infirmary which was to be established, and were to seek out needy sick people in their homes where, as Dubois instructed, "they will prepare those dangerously ill for a good death, lay them out when dead and provide means for a respectable funeral."

With such apostolates, the order over which he was Superior came even closer to being like the one he had been chaplain to in France.

"Now they feel that they are true Sisters of Charity," he exulted.[3]

Dubois could rest his reputation upon decades of service to the poor. But he was always a realist. He discovered that the sisters were giving money, allotted to St. Joseph's schools, to a shiftless Emmitsburg family who regularly knocked on the convent door for handouts. He ordered a stop to this, noting that the physically able family simply chose to beg rather than work.

Later he heard that the sisters, in sending the family off, passed the responsibility on to Dubois as being the refuser. Offended, he educated the nuns to the difference between acting as an individual and vowing to live in a community. They were free to give away the "scant resources" of St. Joseph's if they voted as a group to do so. As matters stood it was their rule and not he, as superior, which forbade them financial largesse. He himself regretted "the pleasure so dear to me when I was a private priest of giving away all I had of my own."

"One of the most painful circumstances of the vow of poverty is to have nothing to give . . . ," he told them, "It is easy for people to be liberal about what does not belong to them, and I might very conveniently for my vanity acquire the reputation of a very charitable man by giving away what does not belong to me though it should finally ruin our two establishments."

For religious who are truly poor themselves, he told them, "It is with their persons and exertions and not their money that they are to relieve the poor."[4]

Dubois was absolutely firm about the schedule for prayer and meditation. No matter how involved the sisters were with their apostolates they were to be present for prayers, which he insisted, "far from interfering with their duties . . . will on the contrary enable them to fulfill their functions with greater facility."[5]

He also forbade the use of the title "Mother" for the head of the order. Elizabeth Seton had struck this title for herself. Dubois, saying that he had never heard it when he was chaplain to the Order in France, decided that it would cause confusion for an elected official with a limited term. It was a reform which lasted only for the next five years that he was in authority. As soon as he was gone the nuns readopted the title.[6]

Niceties about titles were the least of Dubois' problems as Superior to a religious order of women. If it was their frustration within the framework imposed by the Church to have to deal with a man placed in charge over them, it was Dubois' frustration, as a man, to have to deal with personal problems which arose between the individual women who vowed to live as sisters. He would never be allowed the luxury of pretending, as the world at large would pretend, that men or women who entered the religious life abandoned their temperaments. Occasionally he was called upon to pry apart clashing personalities.

On one occasion when entering the Mountain infirmary he expressed shock "to see it so extremely dirty." The two sisters in charge, Johanna and Magdalenna, fell to arguing as to who was to blame. Sister Magdalenna said that Sister Johanna refused to get her an assistant. Sister Johanna retorted that she had told Sister Perpetua not to help because Sister Magdalenna would "kill her with work." Dubois stood between them as the accusations flew back and forth.

"I was then at a loss what to say," he confessed.

Finally he ventured to suggest that perhaps Sister Magdalenna really wouldn't kill Sister Perpetua with work.

"Then I am a liar," declared Sister Johanna. Thereupon, related Dubois, "she flew into a passion out of the room and went off without asking my leave."

Later to Rose White, Dubois concluded in embarrassment that Sister Johanna "wants to meddle with everything, do everything, does it badly; prevents by her interference others from doing their duty."

Charitably he added:

"I do not wish her to know I wish her to be removed, poor soul. She means well but she cannot master her temper."[7] It was, at times, a thoroughly uncomfortable job for someone so balanced and sturdy as Dubois.

There was great spirit at the Mountain, and if early students remembered it as being like a "manual training school" such memories were filled with affection. Archbishop Maréchal reluctantly allowed Dubois to keep major seminarians to serve as teachers, a development which turned the Mountain school into a major, as well as a minor, seminary and college.

This duplication of everything the Sulpicians had done in Baltimore only heightened their resentment, and their efforts during the 1820s to see Dubois' school closed. Yet, it was more than duplication; it was one-upsmanship. An official Sulpician inspection from France in that decade noted of the Baltimore school that "few of the former students returned affection for the seminary or returned voluntarily to visit there."[8] In contrast to this, the archives of Mount St. Mary's soon spilled over with letters written with love from former students to Dubois. A newly ordained priest, George Elder, returned home to his "native forests" of Kentucky. He had grown into manhood in Emmitsburg and when he arrived his family did not recognize him even after he stood by the fire. He wrote Dubois a picturesque letter describing his journey by stagecoach to Pittsburgh ("that city of smoke") and thence by the new wonder of the age, the steamboat, down the Ohio River. Recording his emotions along with scenic descriptions of the western wilderness he told his father of eight years: "I set out from the Mountain with no eagerness whatever. Sorrow for the friends I left behind left no room for joy at the idea of visiting my family."[9]

The general feeling was more than just one of affection. There was a sense that the Mountain seminary would have far-reaching effects on the American Church. The boys joked with one another that they were studying not so much to be priests but bishops. Oftentimes they were right.

Some of these future bishops played intimate roles in Dubois' last years. John Purcell and John Hughes were born in Ireland as were so many Mountain students. Purcell, a gentle scholarly youth arrived from County Cork equipped with a classical education, and for two years supported himself by tutoring on the Eastern Shore of Maryland. In 1820 he was accepted at the Mountain where, both as seminarian and teacher, his presence was immediately valued. Hughes, rawboned and toughened by hatred for England's tyranny, arrived from Northern Ireland with little formal education. He worked as a laborer digging roadways and building bridges in the vicinity of Emmitsburg. Determined to be a priest he sought entry into Mount St. Mary's. Dubois saw little possibility in him and turned him down repeatedly. Finally, toward the end of 1819 he gave in and hired the young man as an overseer for the slaves, agreeing to lodge and instruct him by way of payment. He proved his intelligence to Dubois and in the fall of 1820, at the same time as Purcell, he was accepted as a full student. While Purcell was exalted as a student-professor, Hughes was, at first, assigned to keep order in study halls. Purcell was genteel and well liked. Hughes was argumentative and taciturn; Dubois had to remove him from the office of prefect after he gave a heavy beating to a boy. Purcell was eventually sent by Dubois to finish his studies in Paris. Hughes began to give vent to his muscular approach to theology by arguing, while still a seminarian, with anti-Catholic polemicists in newspapers. Oddly enough in the frontier atmosphere of Mount St. Mary's the two young men, so unalike, became strong and permanent friends.*

Dubois travelled to New York frequently to check on the sisters stationed there and, during one summer recess, he took a group of Mountain students on a tour of the Hudson River, the partially completed Erie Canal, and the falls at Niagara. In New York City he was brought a twelve-year-old boy named John McCloskey who had studied at the school of Dubois' friend Charlotte Melmouth. By way of an entrance test Dubois sat down with the boy, handed him his breviary, and asked him to translate. Pleased with the results, he brought the future Cardinal back to the Mountain as a student.

The priestly staff at the Mountain once again included the whining informer John Hickey. In 1820 he had nearly died, and a worried Dubois had offered to send a gig to Baltimore that he might be brought home to recover. He did come and immediately began complaining again to Baltimore that Dubois ruled like an absolute monarch. He was, of course, quite right. The little Bonaparte's gift for ruling would have been overbearing to all had it not been mixed with so much humor and affection. An alumnus recalled that it was Dubois' custom to announce a winter's holiday the first day that the ice was strong enough for skating. One morning the students judged that it was cold enough and sent three of the smallest boys to head off Dubois as he came out of the sacristy after morning Mass. Dubois refused the request, telling them that the ice was too thin. One of the petitioners, Robert Harper, "sprang up into Mr. Dubois' arms exclaiming 'Oh Please, Mr. Dubois!' and the two slipped and rolled together in the snow. A burst of laughter followed as they struggled to their feet." Dubois laughed with them, turned to John Hughes and declared:

"Well, you may send down to the creek and if the ice will bear let them go skating today."[10]

It bore. A holiday was declared. Robert Harper who had toppled Dubois was the grandson of Charles Carroll, soon to be the last surviving signer of the Declaration of Independence. Little wonder that with such stories as this told around the family table, Carroll was fond of Dubois and, in a lighthearted missive, the elderly patriarch told the priest that he knew he

---

*Later, as priests on the nominating block for the episcopacy, a mixup in names would send Purcell as bishop to Cincinnati when by intention the pioneer outpost was intended for Hughes—who not long thereafter was fitted with a miter and sent to New York. In his later years, inept as a businessman, Purcell would be disgraced by the crash of a bank he and his brother organized to help his financially struggling diocese. In the 1860s the self-made Hughes, a trusted friend of Secretary of State William Seward, would be sent to convince the Catholic powers of Europe of the rightness of the Union cause in the Civil War.

would "excuse the playfulness of this note" because of "your uniform cheerfulness."[11]

Another alumnus, who had first arrived at the Mountain in the 1820s as a child, wrote, in later life, a picture of Dubois which captured both this cheerfulness and his absolute authority:

"Sometime after my arrival, in passing over the upper terrace, I was amazed to see Father Dubois playing marbles with some of the smallest boys of the seminary, and one audacious little fellow scarcely freed from his baby list, stoutly arguing with the old gentleman over the fairness of a shot. Father Dubois appeared to be amused. I stood by to watch the game. Just then the quarter bell rang and such a change of countenance I never beheld before or since. That face, that a moment ago was wreathed in hilarious smiles, now dropped into an aspect of the sternest gravity that could be imagined. It chilled me. With index finger extended to the building, he ordered the young gentlemen to hurry to their class rooms without delay. They hurried."[12]

Dubois formed boys to strength by showing strength himself. One evening he was called to attend a dying person twenty miles away. He rode out on horseback and was gone all night. Returning before morning prayers, he took his place in chapel and then fell into a faint. Carried out to fresh air, he was revived whereupon he went back in and began prayers.

In 1823 Dubois decided it was time to put up an edifice worthy of the school's ever-growing reputation. He began work on a five-story stone building which in design looked not unlike Louis Le Grand.

Characteristically, Dubois plunged headlong into the project. He butted into everyone's work, especially the architects, directing them even in such details as the type of carved design which should top the porch columns. No one, it seems, was safe from his orders.

Nor could anything sidetrack him while he was engulfed in his task. While he was building, the Marquis de Lafayette went through Frederick on a triumphant tour of the land whose independence he had fought for half a century earlier. It was commonly known that Dubois had left France with a letter of introduction from the Marquis, and prior to the celebrated guest's arrival Dubois received an inquiry from people in Gettysburg wondering about the visitor's itinerary. Dubois kept aloof from the festivities. One student, Michael Egan, wrote apologetically to Catherine Seton that it was "impracticable for Mr. Dubois to go to see him or invite him here—he expects to have that occasion in the spring."[13]

Frederick was three hours away by horseback. Dubois had, two decades earlier, readily served that community along with Emmitsburg. There would have been no difficulty had he really wanted to see Lafayette again.

Most likely the occasion raked up ugly memories of the revolution. Dubois' mother had died the year before. The last time he had seen her was in the spring of 1791 when the Civil Constitution had been enforced against priests in France. Lafayette's popularity courting indecisiveness at that time had helped open the floodgates which brought on the Terror. The man was irreligious. If Madame Lafayette still lived and was with her husband on the tour Dubois would certainly have gone to see her for the sake of affection and gratitude. She had been his loyal parishioner. She had supported the priests in their defiance of the oath. Her vacuously polite husband had written his letter only because of his wife's devotion to her religion. Even now in the United States Lafayette dined with anti-Catholic masons and attended Protestant services rather than Catholic. Dubois kept at work, quarrying stones from his Mountain to erect the new building.

In late winter Bruté left again for France, taking John Purcell to finish his studies at St. Sulpice. Bruté's mother had died shortly after Mrs. Dubois and he wanted to set family affairs in order. Purcell, in Paris, wrote sadly to a friend at the Mountain that this had already been taken care of for Dubois. A nephew had declared that Dubois was dead "and so possessed himself of all his property."

This injustice, not so much of money for that could not have been much, but of claiming a man to be dead who served so selflessly in the missions, weighed heavily upon Purcell.

"Everything I see reminds me of him," he wrote, "A new building makes me think of our own. A tree is magnified into our mountain woods, and a venerable priest whose life has been all for God and who [bears]* troubles in his old age makes me think of our father with respect and gratitude."[14]

On Pentecost Sunday, June 6, 1824, John Dubois could reflect on how the Holy Spirit had filled his own hard work. His institutions were flourishing; filled with young men and women to be sent forth to serve the immigrant church of the United States. His new stone building was all but completed; the lower floors were occupied and classes were being held there. He could go to bed on this feast of Pentecost well satisfied with what God had worked through him.

Around midnight that night, Sister Helena in the infirmary awoke as Sister Félicité returned from checking on a sick boy. Looking out her window, she noticed an orange glow emanating from the cupola of the new building. It snapped her into full consciousness. She saw one of the slaves crossing the yard.

"Clem," she yelled, "call fire."[15]

The two sisters raised the alarm while flames burst from the cupola. The students piled out of the dormitories. One young man raced up the stairs carrying two buckets of water, hopefully enough to check the still-localized flames. In clumsy haste he tripped and fell, spilling the water. After that the fire was beyond control. Valuables were thrown from the

---

*Word obliterated in original letter.

building. An art teacher carried a large mixing stone to a window, dropped it, and in horror watched it fall towards a boy who ran underneath. It missed him by inches. Hot ashes from the tall structure fell to the college's other buildings. The students formed bucket brigades and heaved water on blankets stretched upon the roofs.

By dawn the exhausted community stood and stared at a smoking shell of ruin. Calmly, drawing his strength not from his life of hard setbacks and harder work but from his deep faith in God, Dubois quietly told his children:

"The Lord gave and the Lord hath taken away. Blessed be the name of the Lord."

The sisters prevailed upon him to come into the convent to rest. Only inside, away from the boys who needed his strength, did his strength break. He crumpled into a chair and sat with tears streaming down his face.

Afterwards, his composure regained, he walked about the grounds a short distance in front of the smoldering ruin. Suddenly, with Napoleonic decisiveness he announced:

"I will place the new building here. I have all along felt that it was a mistake to build on the upper terrace."[16]

50

Mount St. Mary's College, Emmitsburg, Maryland as it appeared about the time when John Dubois left in 1826. The large building in the center is "Dubois Hall" completed in that year after the first major building was destroyed by fire.

MOUNT ST. MARY'S SEMINARY.

We have not in this number room to give all that we could wish upon the subject of this Institution, and therefore must content ourselves with copying from a newspaper the following afflicting articles :

" It is with deep regret we have to record the destruction by Fire, on Sunday night, the 6th inst. of the new and spacious edifice intended for the accommodation of the students of Mount St. Mary's Seminary, near Emmitsburg. And what renders the loss still more to be lamented is, that the fire has been communicated by some fiend in human form!

The building, we learn, was 95 feet long by 50 deep, of stone and three stories high, and would ave been completed in a few weeks at an expenditure little short of $16,000. When first discovered, about 11 o'clock at night, the flames had made little progress and were found to issue from between the roof and ceiling of the garret, a part where accident could not have carried the fire. Besides there had been no fire used in the building for several weeks, and no person was permitted to carry even a lighted segar in or near the premises. Being destitute of either engines or hose all attemps to check the progress of the flames were soon found unavailing, and it was only by vigourous and unremitted exertions, for several hours, tha they were able to preserve the old buildings which stood contiguous. As these remain uninjured the students in the different departments will continue their studies without interruption.

Considering the confusion incident to such a scene and the great number of youth at the Seminary, it must be considered fortunate that they have all escaped uninjured. Two or three individuals, not connected with the Institution, have suffered from accidents, one of whom it was at first apprehended had been very seriously injured, but we understand is now better and likely to recover.

By the proceedings given below, which have been communicated for insertion, it will be seen that an appeal is about to be made to the Public in behalf of the Seminary. We sincerely hope this appeal may be met with a spirit of liberality, and that the worthy founder and principal of th!s excellent school will yet have the gratification to see this darling of his declining years prosperous, flourishing and useful."

CONFLAGRATION.

Of Mount St. Mary's Seminary,

Frederick County, Maryland.

The President of Mount St. Mary's Seminary, begs to present his humble supplications to his friends and the public in general, in the distressing situation to which the malevolent and successful attempt of a midnight incendiary has reduced the institution under his care. It is well known to the public, that the aforesaid seminary has subsisted for more than fourteen years. The exertions of the President and his associates, and their distinguished zeal in its erection, are equally known. The rapid decay of such buildings, as their scanty means permitted them to raise at first, and the increasing number of pupils, made it necessary to erect a more permanent and spacious edifice. To this purpose they devoted the hard savings of fourteen years. But at the moment w n they expected to enjoy the fruits of th r sacrifices and exertions, some evil m ded person, whose guilty design, cannot be ailed in question, has reduced it to ruins, and thereby frustrated all their expectations. Every effort was made to avert this calamity, but in vain. All that could be done was to prevent the old buildings from being involved in one common ruin. Under such circumstances, the President of Mount St. Mary's Seminary and his associates cast themselves on the generosity and patriotism of their friends and fellow citizens—upon which depends the future prosperity of an establishment whose object has always been, and shall ever be to diffuse the light of science through the United States.

At a general meeting of the Students of Mount St. Mary's Seminary, held on Tuesday the 8th inst. for the purpose of returning their heart-felt thanks to the assistants at the late awful conflagration of the new College lately erected, and for the passing of such resolutions as appear expedient under the present afflicting circumstances :—

Rev. JOHN M'GERRY was called to the Chair, and Rev. MICHAEL EGAN appointed Secretary.

The following resolutions vere proposed and unanimously adopted :—

Resolved, That we view with feelings of sorrow and indignation, the work of many years of persevering philanthrophy, now prostrate by the hand of an incendiary, and that we warmly sympathise with our venerable President in his present severe affliction ; and further, that our hearts are filled with the most lively gratitude towards him for his past affectionate and tender regard for our welfare, and that we will make every possible exertion to prove to him our remembrance of his conduct towards us

Resolved, That we address a letter of condolence and sympathy to the Rev. JOHN DUBOIS, and that we therein assure him of our unshaken attachment to the interests and welfare of Mount St. Mary's Seminary.

Resolved, That we are intimately convinced, that the late destructive fire has been occasioned by some daring and malicious incendiary, and that we offer a reward of Two Hundred Dollars for the conviction of the wretch, who has thus endeavoured to blast the most flattering prospects of this useful establishment.

Resolved, That we feel deeply penetra-

51

ted with gratitude towards the inhabitants of Emmittsburg and vicinity, for their active exertions in endeavouring to stop the progress of the flames, and for the generous disposition which they manifest for the interests and success of this Institution.

Resolved, That a copy of these resolutions be sent for publication to the Editors of the respective newspapers, who are hereby respectfully requested to insert them in their respetive papers.

Resolved, That the thanks of this meeting be voted to the Chairman and Secretary.

After which the meeting adjourned.

J. F. M'GERRY, *Chairman.*
MICHAEL D. B. EGAN, *Sec'y.*

LETTER TO THE PRESIDENT.

Reverend and fond President,

The duty of condolence which is now feelingly imposed on us by gratitude and sympathy, is one of so painful a description that we hardly know, in what manner to discharge it. The ruins of your new and splendid edifice stand before us ; your generous and fervent anticipations have been heartlessly frustrated by the desperate hand of an incendiary ; the fair prospect which arose to your fancy is darkened, on a sudden ; and an universal gloom has been spread around these once bright and happy mountains. Such a scene, so dreary, so unexpected, has awakened, in our breasts, all the mingled feelings of horror and compassion. We weep to behold your virtuous exertions towards the dissemination of morality and of education, so foully, so basely requited ; but the fortitude and courage which you have displayed amidst the wreck of your fondest hopes, have cheered our bosoms in a great degree, and supported them in their despondency. Religion alone, which commands us never to yield, in the hour of adversity, to the feelings of nature, could have inspired you with such virtuous resignation : and never more, than at such a period, can we discern the truly good man from the dissembler. We had often before, in trying circumstances, had reason to admire your magnanimity, but never half so much as on that fatal night, which saw your noble edifice reduced to a heap of ashes. But heaven cannot desert the good, nor look with disregard, on the misfortunes of its friends. When it permitted your virtue to be proved, it seems to have had some other end in view, which time alone will be able to disclose : and if the zeal of the public go on increasing as it has begun, instead of suffering any loss from this malicious event, your Institution will arise, with greater lustre, from its ruins, and excite more interest, and awaken more affection than if it had been permitted to answer all your former expectations. This thought encourages every feeling heart, and surely yours Reverend Sir, must feel invigorated by it—your cause is a good-

one—a noble one—a popular one. Our fellow-citizens know how to participate in the distresses of the promoters of their country's interest ; and no individual, they must feel convinced, has contributed more successfully to them than yourself. Receive then, respected President, the sincere feelings of us all—be assured, that we will not be wanting, in any thing, that may be beneficial to our beloved Institution We love her more in her calamities than in her prosperity—we feel still more attached to her in her ruins, than in the proudest hour of her magnificence, and present you this artless effusion of our feelings as a pledge of our attachment, an assurance of esteem, a mark of the tenderest sympathy, and the most unaffected condolence.

We are, Reverend Sir,
Your most affectionate, &c. &c.
(Signed by 115 *Students.)*

ANSWER OF THE PRESIDENT.

My beloved friends,

I receive daily so many proofs of your affectionate and virtuous dispositions, that the expression of your sympathy, in this heavy trial of mine, has not surprised me. It could add nothing to my affection and regard for you ; but I must confess it has given a new vigour to my mind. I would be ashamed to betray any weakness and discouragement, when you, whose tender years it is my duty to guide, shew me such an example, not only of resignation to the Divine will, but of presence of mind in seeking a remedy to the present calamity— instead of giving way to despondency or idle lamentations. You rely on the public sympathy, on this trying occasion : I have the same confidence in it. But I must candidly acknowledge, that worn out by so many years of laborious exertions, I would have recoiled at those required in this circumstance, if you had not volunteered your services with so much zeal. May the consciousness of having so effectually contributed to the consolidation of an establishment intended for the public good, be one day the comfort of your declining years. May it meet, hereafter, from the Author of all good, with that reward, which alone can satisfy virtuous hearts. Had you expressed your sentiments to me, as usual, in the confidence of verbal communication, I would have answered you in the same manner : But since through delicacy for my present feelings, you chose to do it by writing, I adopt the same mode of communication in my answer, with the more pleasure, as your letter will remain with me as a precious monument of the goodness of your hearts, and mine may be preserved by you as a testimony of the deep sense I entertain of your worth.

Most affectionately, I remain,
Your devoted friend & common Father,
JOHN DUBOIS

Article taken from the U.S. Catholic Miscellany *of June 24, 1824*

52

*Bishop John Baptist Purcell (1800–1883) of Cincinnati.
A "Mountain" student, and protégé of John Dubois,
Purcell remained close to Dubois in his old age. Below, an
1834 woodcut of the motherhouse of the Sisters of
Charity of St. Joseph, Emmitsburg.*

53

CHAPTER 11

Should You Send Old M. Dubois to New York

After the fire—rumored to have been set by a workman hoping to prolong employment—Dubois sent volunteers from the older students to solicit funds from the public, as another building took its place.

To their astonishment, they found people eager to give. The nationally distributed *United States Gazette* had reported the conflagration and in doing so lavished praise upon Dubois' accomplishments at Emmitsburg. The generosity of the American public was aroused. Letters sent between students that summer—one addressed appropriately to "Brother beggar"— listed sizeable amounts collected from the great Maryland families and from simple people who had received decades of service from Dubois.

"The Mayor of this city received us with incredible politeness," wrote one young mendicant arriving in Baltimore, "and has promised to do anything in his power for us all."[1]

As if to reassure them that they still had something to complain about, Dubois cheerfully opened their correspondence before sending it on to them.

"I knew there was nothing but which interested all," he assured one violated correspondee, "and my Egan, as well as my Purcell, has no secret from me."[2]

If they did, they learned not to commit it to paper.

The sisters, without consulting Dubois, voted to give him what money they could and appealed over his head to the archbishop for permission to do so. Deeply touched, Dubois gently acknowledged that their gift hurt his pride.

"It was my wish to serve our sisters gratuitously,"[3] he said.

After all the collecting, Dubois was still financially strapped. The Sulpicians, backed by the Superior General in France and by Archbishop Maréchal, took advantage of this to again insist that Dubois reduce the Mountain to a minor seminary. When both he and Bruté flatly refused, they were officially drummed out of the Society of St. Sulpice.

Totally cast upon his own, his back to the wall, Dubois searched about for alternatives. He pleaded, unsuccessfully, all along the Atlantic seaboard hoping that one of the bishops would adopt and support his establishment as a diocesan seminary.

He thought of starting his own religious order.

"I am getting old, I must assure myself successors," he wrote, ". . . The sad experience which I have had from the moment of my union with a foreign society induces me to prefer to form one entirely American for the reasons specified above."[4]

It was a reasonable enough thought. He had, after all, successfully organized the first women's religious order in the United States. Why not, like Vincent de Paul who founded the Lazarists in France, start an order of men who would go forth from his Mountain to serve the Church in the United States?

However, with creditors, to say nothing of the Sulpicians and the archbishop on his back, he let it be known that he was also considering more drastic and negative solutions. The least of these was to sell the Mountain to the Sisters of Charity and clear out. A horrified student body and even more horrified Bruté watched as he also sounded out secular and even Protestant groups interested in a ready made college. Did he mean it? It seems in character, given the passion with which he always defended the Mountain and his desire to have good priests for "the Benjamin" of his eye, the sisterhood, that he meant very much to send out alarums to a public which had already poured out its hearts and pocketbooks to him after the fire. To have closed the Mountain would have gone against every ounce of energy and spirit which he expended in almost twenty years of time. In any event Bruté believed him and, reduced almost to irrationality in sentence structure, he lent his slight weight to move Maréchal.

". . . Should you send away old M. Dubois to New York," he pleaded, "he could not carry the house and you could give it to the Sisters or sell it to the government for a barrack or a military school, which some had the impudence or nonsense to suggest to M. Dubois. Alas! Have I lived to see young cadets?"[5]

Rumors of what might become of the Mountain were not the only rumors flying about. Ironically, the set back of the fire had given John Dubois a good deal of national attention. People—especially churchmen—began to take stock of his accomplishments. Though he had never shown an iota of ambition for the episcopacy, talk became ever more insistent that Rome intended to send "old M. Dubois to New York" as its bishop.

American Catholics were embroiled in bitter internal strife; for the first several decades after the American Revolution most Catholic laymen had run their churches in the absence of a local hierarchy. As bishops took over dioceses throughout the United States, laymen were openly reluctant to hand over authority. Moreover, Irish and French factions were forming lines of battle to gain hierarchical control of the immigrant Church.

As the Irish population grew, so did their resentment of the French clergy. The priests who had fled the French Revolution had proven themselves heroic missionaries, but the Irish who had escaped the tyranny of Britain had no desire to live under any other kind of foreign domination. A network quickly developed between the Irish in America and the Irish in religious orders who held sway at the court of Rome.

Irishman John Connolly, a Dominican friar sent from Rome as New York's first resident Bishop,* wrote in 1818:

"If bishops continue to prefer priests from the continent to those of Ireland it will harm the Church. The Catholic population consists chiefly of Irishmen; they build the churches and expect priests who understand them."[6]

On the other side of the ethnic fence, Archbishop Maréchal bitterly complained to the Propaganda Fide (the department of the Roman Curia charged with the administration of the missionary activity of the Church) that he would only accept Irish priests with reluctance and claimed that eight out of ten of them turned against the Church and were not able to live in peace with missionaries of other backgrounds. As he watched the Irish lobby grow in power, Maréchal wrote to a friend in Rome that it was essential that the Archbishop of Baltimore be given the exclusive right of presenting candidates to the American sees.

"It is the only way to terminate the intrigues of Irish priests," he pleaded, "and the highly improper interposition of Irish bishops."[7]

Father William Taylor, a convert from Protestantism, lived his life seemingly angry at everyone. In Rome to complain about affairs in New York under Bishop Connolly, he wrote Maréchal:

---

*He was the second Bishop named for New York. The first, Luke Concanen, an Irishman and Dominican living in Rome, died en route to America.

"I could not describe to your grace the censurable and unchristian conduct of the Irish friars here."[8]

To Cheverus he insisted:

"I should not be surprised if the under agents here, by their mismanagement detached whole countries from the communion of the Holy See."[9]

Such mismanagement was the last thing the Church in the United States
needed. In Philadelphia, wandering friars who had come to seek their fortunes in the New World rallied factions of laymen to themselves and fought
for control of wealthy congregations. Seeing the situation through the eyes
of the Irish lobby, Rome's response was to assign to Philadelphia an iras-
cible, self-willed seventy-year-old Irish Bishop, Henry Conwell. Shortly
after his arival, this cantankerous old man took to fighting with his priests
in the press and in the public law courts. Factions of laity took to fighting
in the streets.

A saddened young alumnus wrote to Dubois from Philadelphia that the
idyllic life he had known at school had not prepared him for such scandal.

"I often picture to myself the Mountain Church during the festivals as a
paradise on earth. So much devotion, such love of God. O how happy you
must all be—one heart to govern all; Not as we are here. All the evil passions of our nature are raised . . ."[10]

New York's situation was not much better. Bishop Connolly attempted
to wrest power from Church trustees and found himself fighting Father
William Taylor along with them. Again both sides rushed to Rome demanding "a canonical scrutiny" of Connolly's administration.[11] Unsuccessful, Taylor returned and was suspended by his Bishop. A fruitless attempt to reconcile the two men was made by Father John Power, a handsome Irishman with fair blue eyes and dark curly hair. Power had arrived
in New York in 1818. Intelligent and popular, he was ambitious and
courted public favor. As early as 1820 John Dubois had learned to dis-
count Power's objectivity with regards college applicants:

"Mr. Power is too lavish of his recommendations," he observed, and,
on pretext that he doesn't want to give pain, recommends anybody."[12]

When Bishop Connolly died in 1825, Power moved boldly to win the
episcopacy. Within a week after New York's first funeral of a Catholic
bishop—an event The New York Gazette and General Advertiser found to
be a "novel exhibition"[13]—Power sent testimonials about himself to Rome.
The capable John England, bishop of Charleston and publisher of the U.S.
Catholic Miscellany, stoutly and insistently took up the cause of his close
friend and fellow Irishman. Other support was rallied. On St. Patrick's
Day the clergy of New York set off a petition that Power be named bishop.
Upon close scrutiny the petition was less impressive than at first glance.
Signed by only two priests, Reverends J. Conroy and Thomas Levins, it
claimed to represent the views of three additional priests too far in distance
to be consulted. A petition was sent from the Trustees of St. Peter's church

on Power's behalf. Interestingly a petition was signed by twenty-one members of the French and Spanish populace.

Even without the animosity of the Irish, the accidental control of the United States' hierarchy by Frenchmen was coming to an end. No great numbers of French immigrants had come to the United States. With regard to clergy it had served primarily as a haven for a couple of dozen emigré priests who had then remained to put the American Church in order. Their day was done. They were aging and some, like Cheverus, were returning to take sees in France. Nonetheless, the Irish clergy who showed up in the States were an unproven lot. Oftentimes they left home owing to conflicts with ecclesiastical authority, and they very often proved themselves scoundrels. The short list of real choices for the episcopacy among priests in the United States left room for the mention of a Frenchman even by one of the Irish newcomers. Conwell, thrown into battle in the city of brotherly love, took note of the famed, idyllic community at Emmitsburg. When Cheverus' departure left the See of Boston vacant, Dubois' name was sent by Conwell to the Propaganda Fide as his third choice for that office. It was enough to start Rome asking about Dubois' credentials. A small rumor that he might be appointed crept back to the States and prompted one man to write him:

"Are you going to put on Bishop Cheverus' shoes? So it is reported here. That, however, leads to a still more important question. Who will put on yours? They will pinch the feet of any ordinary man who although he may have two sound legs will not travel along so well as you do with your lame one."[14]

When New York became vacant—even under the barrage of recommendations sent on behalf of, and mostly by, John Power—the name of John Dubois was repeated. He was never anybody's first choice; he was generally listed as a third possibility. This was where Maréchal put him—after Rev. T. Gillow, the vicar general of Trinidad, and Benedict Fenwick, the president of Georgetown, who was subsequently appointed to Boston.

DuBourg, backed by Flaget and David, wanted New York and Boston combined into one diocese, owing, so DuBourg said to "the comparatively small number of Catholic congregations in both territories." Moreover, he decided, one bishop might easily serve the two city centers as it was "easy to travel from the one to the other in a couple of days." Though Flaget and David put Dubois on their list after Fenwick, DuBourg ignored him. Power was listed, but DuBourg's first choice was "unhesitatingly" for Fenwick. As "a native American," he could be a "mediator of peace" for the Church at New York, "distracted as it is by foreign parties."[15]

All influences weighed, once Fenwick was named for Boston it looked like an easy race for Power.

Acting as the diocese's administrator, Power added one further insurance and suggested that Propaganda Fide ask the opinion of Father Anthony Kohlmann.

Kohlmann, a Jesuit living in Rome, had served in New York for a number of years, and, but for his superior's adamant opposition might easily have been named to the See himself. A dedicated, spiritual man, Kohlmann, while in New York, had been involved in a criminal case which ended up in history books. Called as a witness after he returned stolen goods given him by a penitent, he refused to testify on the grounds that the matter involved priestly confidence. Much rhetoric was expended before the courts decided that he was not bound to divulge his source, and a legal precedent was set. Kohlmann had started two projects, both unsuccessful. A convent of Ursuline nuns was brought from Ireland but, failing to gain novices, they returned. A college, run by Jesuits folded after four years, and the grounds upon which it stood, well out in the country, remained unused by the Church for another half century. It would later be the site of Saint Patrick's Cathedral.

Even with these failures Kohlmann wrote that three things were needed to help the growth of the Church in New York: "A Catholic college for young men, a nunnery for the education of young ladies, and an orphanage conducted by nuns."[16]

John Power, who did so much to aid the orphanage run in the city by the Emmitsburg Sisters of Charity, reasoned that he had fostered one of the works seen as a need by Kohlmann. A nod from him could be the deciding factor. Propaganda Fide, then, as Power suggested, asked Kohlmann for his opinion. On December 5, 1825, and again on March 31, 1826, the one-time missionary to New York sent and then repeated to Propaganda Fide his recommendation for the See of New York: John Dubois—the man in the United States who had successfully started the three things which Kohlmann felt were needed for the health of a diocese in the United States. On April 24th the Congregation unanimously presented its report and on April 30, 1826 Pope Leo XII named John Dubois Bishop of New York. But for the tactics of John Power, Dubois might have been left to finish his days as President of Mount Saint Mary's.

If news travelled slowly in that era, rumors flew with the wind, and rumor confirmed Dubois as Bishop before the fact was out. As early as February, 1826, the notion that Dubois might be named Bishop evoked an angry article in the *National Advocate*.

"Who formed the congregation of New York," the paper demanded, "Irishmen or Frenchmen? Why should a Frenchman govern an Irish congregation? ... The French junta of Baltimore have seized on the fruits of Irish labor. Will Irishmen permit it?"[17]

They would not, if an appropriately surnamed priest, Father Savage had his way. Writing from Albany, New York, to a friend he spat:

"We have for a bishop a Frenchman who, I think would be, if he dare, a restless little despot. A man with very little learning and less brains has been appointed at the instance of the French party for the most prominent and most respectable See in America . . ."

As if in answer to the *National Advocate's* question he opined:

". . . If the Irish be faithful to each other there is no fear . . ."[18]

To his credit, in fact making sure that credit was widely given to him as he acted, John Power demanded that the *National Advocate* cease its attacks. He was still playing a game of power politics and he had more to gain by rising above the mob than joining it. Others, friendly to Dubois assessed the situation. A New York Mountain seminarian noted:

". . . the majority from what I could see are opposed to him. This I attribute to their not being acquainted with him, and a little prudence on the part of Mr. Dubois will, I have no doubt, reconcile all parties . . ."[19]

A layman, writing from the city told Dubois: "Some of the Reverend gentlemen could hardly believe the news . . ."

He implored that Dubois "not make any appointment until after your arrival in their city, which will give you the opportunity of making yourself perfectly acquainted with many circumstances you ought to know."[20]

The most prophetic letter came from a young nun, Sister Elizabeth, at the orphanage, who warned:

"I fear so much if you do come to this place that you will find much less happiness than you may now imagine awaits you . . . As far as I know many are more like wild people than anything else at the idea of having a French bishop. If I mistake not it is quite a task for Revd. Mr. Power to keep them from bursting into an open revolt . . . My dear Father, will you allow me to beg you not to let your mind be known with whatever changes or arrangements you may contemplate making in case you do accept the bishopric here . . . believe me my dear Father, the less you say or put in the power of anyone to say the better . . . May I tell you I think you will do well to invite Revd. Mr. Power on to your consecration. When I see you I will give you my reasons for saying this . . ."

As if to shed a ray of sunshine into the stormy picture she had painted, Sister Elizabeth added that Sister Agnes had rejoiced, "if you come to be our bishop she will be willing to stay here fifty years."[21]

"If you come . . ." He was still free to turn away from the task which was offered along with so many dire warnings. There would be a number of priests in the American Church who would make a career out of turning down episcopal sees. Dubois wavered. In August he wrote:

"Having been appointed by the Holy See Bishop of New York, it is probable I will resign the presidency of this house into other hands, although

I have not taken a determination to accept or refuse, it is probable I will be under the necessity of accepting."[22]

Some pleaded with him not to go:

"I am not without fearful apprehensions that it will lead to the dissolution of your rising and celebrated college," wrote one, "in you Reverend and dear sir, the parents of all pupils have most unbounded confidence."[23]

The weight of his decision was visible to others. A seminarian observed:

"This nomination has caused considerable confusion here, as being entirely unexpected by any belonging to this place, and it has affected the old gentleman so that he does not appear to be the same person as formerly."[24]

With almost comic irony, Archbishop Maréchal suddenly realized the importance of Dubois' establishments and cried out to Propaganda Fide that his departure for New York would cause the ruination of the Mountain seminary. As Dubois began to pull up stakes, Maréchal came quickly to an accommodation—Mount St. Mary's would be considered a "petit séminaire," but, for at least the next five years, courses could be taught to major seminarians who were on hand as instructors for the younger students. Dubois' establishment at Emmitsburg would survive. With his house— his many houses—in order, the sixty-two-year-old Dubois accepted the responsibility of the hostile See of New York. To please the Irishmen who had ranged themselves in advance as his enemies, he used a shamrock for the design of his episcopal shield.

On October 5th, his beloved brother Bruté, the students of both colleges, the professors and the sisters, along with the townspeople of Emmitsburg gathered to say goodbye as he climbed into a coach for Baltimore. It is unfortunate that the development of photography was still a decade away. Here, at a most dramatic moment, stood together the next three occupants of the See of New York. John Hughes, leaving for his own ordination to the priesthood, accompanied Dubois, and the sixteen-year-old John McCloskey was one of the boys seeing them off. The lifespans of these three succeeding bishops of New York would be an indication of the immense growth of the immigrant church within the coming decades. Dubois was assuming leadership of a sparsely populated diocese which Bishop William DuBourg adjudged not worthy of being a see; Hughes would rule as an archbishop with suffragan bishops beneath him; McCloskey would become the first cardinal of the United States.

The journey to Baltimore had to have been somewhat uncomfortable for the two men so different in age and personality. The taciturn Hughes seemed never to have forgiven Dubois for making him work his entry into the seminary as a slave oversee. Just the year before, his Irish temper had caused him to explode at Dubois over a couple of trivial incidents. One of the nuns had made a cassock for Hughes only after making cassocks for others who had requested after him. When he finally received his, he judged it to be inferior to the others. Then Dubois had refused Hughes permission to buy specially made shoes for an ailment in one of his feet. Hughes so shocked his elderly superior with the force of his temper tantrum that, later, the belligerent young seminarian apologized that his anger "wore in your estimation a far more malicious aspect than was ever intended by me." Defensive even in apology, Hughes wore his continuing resentment on the outside.

"I could not help looking on myself as something of a step-child, in a family," he said, "when I saw myself denied of that which was granted to others in similar circumstances."[25]

If Hughes was determined to think of himself a stepchild, Dubois who larded-out heavy-handed, Gallic affection to everyone in his domain, seemed incapable of understanding what the term stepchild should mean. His children were his children. At Frederick he instructed Hughes to dash off a note telling someone at the Mountain to send his copy of *The Imitation of Christ* which he had neglected to pack for his retreat. ("You will find it in his room,"[26] Hughes wrote, forgetting that Dubois no longer had a room at Emmitsburg.) When they parted, each to enter into prayerful solitude, Dubois wrote a letter of paternal advice to Hughes, whom he called his "ever dear child," hoping that they might "reunite one day where we can no more be separated."[27]

Those words would someday taste of gall in Dubois' memory.

It was an autumn which abounded with ironies. The same issue of the *U.S. Catholic Miscellany* which carried the news that Dubois would accept the bishopric of New York, also carried the news that DuBourg was quitting his post as bishop of New Orleans to return home to France. Describing the United States as "a country where the chief ecclesiastic is obliged to perform the same function as the youngest missionary," the man of grand ideas laid forth his apologia for resignation:

"I did flatter myself to be able from Europe, to render that mission more important services."[28]

Meanwhile Dubois, forgetting any acrimony which might have crept into his fights with the Sulpicians, placed himself under their spiritual direction for a retreat, and prepared to assume the missionary responsibilities which DuBourg had just rejected.

His consecration on the twenty-sixth of October was symbolically eventful of a turning point in his life's fortunes. For decades he had been surrounded by people who loved him. He was now to enter an arena where he would be an object of constant derision. Baltimore's Cathedral was "unusually crowded" according to the *U.S. Catholic Miscellany* and its reporter observed "some of the most respectable citizens in the Union."[29]

The sole survivor of the Declaration of Independence Charles Carroll, who
so appreciated Dubois' sense of humor, presented him with his episcopal
cross and ring. The new bishop was surrounded by his Mountain children
and, childlike himself, he used his new episcopal prerogative to promise
them all a day off from school "for me who refused them so many."[30]

Amidst this celebration of love, Reverend William Taylor entered the
pulpit to preach the homily. Dubois had followed the advice of friends from
New York and had prudently invited this priest and John Power to take
prominent parts in the celebration. The angry Taylor, suffering from a
severe cold, hacked and coughed his way through an ugly hour wherein he
vented his anger. The New York *Truth Teller,* a Catholic and Irish paper
begun by John Power the year before, reported that Taylor, with "fearless
intrepidity" described "the present state of the Roman Catholic Religion
in this Country."

As reported in the columns of *The Truth Teller,* either written or edited
by John Power, Taylor "wished that his words would resound under the
dome of the Vatican, and, after complimenting the congregation of New
York:

"He alluded to the disastrous consequences which resulted to religion
from injudicious appointments to the Episcopal office—talked of ecclesiastical intrigue and of 'bats hanging together in a drowsy cluster.' He prayed
that some heavenly light may break in on them and expressed a hope that
the flapping of leather wings consequent on their dispersion may yet be
harmony to the ears of the pious, practical and contemplative Christian."[31]

And so John Dubois, a twilight appointee of the French "bats hanging
together," a reminder of the courtly and genteel men who served the young
Republic in the post revolutionary age, headed north to assume control of
an immigrant Church, which was becoming a fiercely nationalistic, Irish
immigrant Church.

54

View of Broadway and City Hall in New York City as John Dubois would have known it in the 1820s. (Original watercolor by Baron Klinckowstrom.)

55

DOMESTIC.

NEW-YORK.—The Bishop arrived safe here on the 23d ult. after a very severe and dangerous passage. He speaks in very high terms of the conduct of Capt. Thorp, of the Commodore Perry—of his judgment and activity during the hard gales that they experienced, and of his very kind attention towards himself.

We find that the administration of the Diocess of New-York, by the very Rev. Mr. Power, has met with universal approbation—this is indeed what we expected. His exertions to establish a *Catholic Orphan Asylum* have been very successful ; he has also, as far as in his power provided Catholic Congregations with Pastors, where there were none previously located. Though we are ready to bow with respect to whatever appointment Rome may make to the see of New-York, yet we know of no Clergyman on the American Mission more worthy of this Bishoprick or more likely to advance the best interests of Religion in that large and important Diocess.

Above, *Bishop John England (1786–1842) of Charleston was a strong supporter of his friend Rev. John Power. His newspaper, the* U.S. Catholic Miscellany (left), *carried his opinion that Power should be made bishop of N.Y.*

56

57

58

Above, *Father John Power (1792–1849) promoted himself to be the next bishop of N.Y. in 1825. Instead, the post was given to John Dubois. At* right, *Old St. Patrick's Cathedral in New York City.*

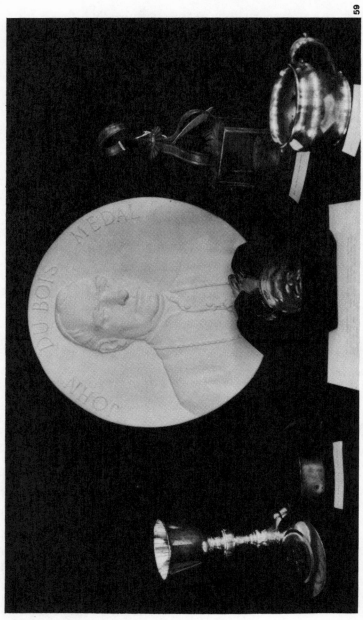

59

Personal artifacts associated with Father John Dubois, preserved in the Archives of Mount St. Mary's, Emmitsburg: in background center: plaster cast for the John Dubois Medal (MSM); from far left across: his travelling chalice which unscrews into three parts and fits inside one piece; his snuff boxes; cruet used at Loudon Co., Va. while guest of James Madison; small lantern; and silver cup used by him.

CHAPTER 12

If I Had Help . . .

New York City fell all over itself growing up from the toe of Manhattan. Though in 1807 a street commission had declared: "It is improbable that for centuries to come the grounds north of Harlem Flat will be covered with houses,"[1] by the mid-twenties an astounded Lafayette, on his triumphant tour, looked upon a boom town so different from what he had known and exclaimed:

"Do you think Broadway will reach Albany?"[2]

The northward movement of the native citizenry was largely a desire to escape from the wretched refuse of Ireland's teeming shores, who were fast changing the city. Once fashionable neighborhoods degenerated into crowded slums, and former owners abandoned both houses and churches to the newcomers. There was a tendency to react at one and the same time to both the Irish nationality and the Roman Catholic religion of the slum dwellers, thereby creating a problem for established groups of earlier Catholic immigrants such as the French. As soon as John Dubois arrived in New York, he took note of the conversions of his own countrymen to the more socially respectable French Episcopal Church and asked the Sulpicians for a French-speaking priest for these people. He did not get one. A French national parish would never become a reality until his Irish successor would manage to establish one in 1841. In the meantime the

Catholic Church in New York, even with its French bishop, began very much to take on the image as it did all throughout the United States, of being an Irish National religion.

The Irish were, in general, an impoverished lot. Those with no means at all piled into such historically notorious hell holes as the Five Points district. The pioneer-spirited followed jobs inland. The construction of the Erie Canal created the strong Irish character of the towns and cities that lined its route.

Escaping the inhuman laws of Great Britain, these immigrants were in every sense a displaced people. Pathetic advertisements filled pages of the decades' newspapers. One typical ad for "Steerage Passage from Sligo to New York" made its appeal "to persons wishing to send for their friends."[3]

Other notices reflected the situation of separated families trying to find one another in a vast new land.

> Information wanted: Manus Dogherty, formerly of the
> Windmill, Newry, Ireland is supposed to be residing in
> the State of New York or Canada. His two sons Michael and
> Thomas have lately arrived in Albany where they now
> reside. Any information respecting their father will be
> thankfully received by them.[4]

It is little wonder that these liberty seeking immigrants resented the hostile reception given them by native citizens when the Constitution of the United States had lured them with bright promise of equality. Natural leaders among them rose up to defend their less able compatriots. The Reverends John Power and Thomas Levins sponsored *The Truth Teller,* a Catholic newspaper far more Irish than it was religious. In retaliation against such ads as "Irish People need not apply, nor any one that will not rise before six o'clock" the paper effectively began listing these employers so that the ever growing Irish community could in turn boycott such places of business. The year before John Dubois' arrival, a significant complaint was voiced in *The Truth Teller* against a native Catholic who, in *The New York Statesmen,* made a distinction between American born and Irish priests—terming the latter "foreigners." Calling this "an uncharitable and unchristian act wholly unworthy a Catholic" *The Truth Teller* declared that such distinctions "only mark the weakness of the minds who urge them," adding a scold: "as if the birth place of a person could either give or take away talent."[5]

When Dubois was forced upon them, this plea became an ironic prophecy turned upon those who had made it. Some efforts, at first, were made to do the right thing by the new "foreign" bishop. The *U.S. Catholic Miscellany* caught the local papers when these wrote that Dubois had lived seventeen years in America, and made the correction that his career in the States spanned a full thirty-five years. And, added the paper, linking the new Bishop to the recent hosannas New York had sung to another French-man: "His introductory letters were given by General Lafayette."[6] An editor of an Albany paper whose father had printed anti-Catholic books and who in his childhood had witnessed the pope burned in effigy on Guy Fawkes Day in Newburgh credited Frenchmen with having erased such bigotry in the early days of the nation.

"The Catholic King of France took part with the Protestant rebels of America," he wrote, "He sent his Catholic armies to fight our battles. We found that Frenchmen were not our natural enemies for they came to be-friend us in our struggle for freedom."[7]

Nonetheless, prior to Dubois' arrival, the seeds of dissension were deeply planted. When a Maryland man praised Dubois' character in a letter to *The Truth Teller* the paper coldly noted:

> The writer having left his name with us we feel it our
> duty as impartial editors to give it insertion, premising that
> we ourselves do not presume to pass any opinion upon
> the motives of the article alluded to.[8]

Cantankerous old Bishop Conwell, who took his religious battles to the civil law courts and worked full time alienating all parties in Philadelphia, gossiped that he would soon have company in misery. To Maréchal he reported:

"I had learned there had been debates in New York whether or not Mr. Dubois should be received or admitted into any church of the city."

His sources added that the new bishop would be received but that after-wards they would "give him trouble, as a person intruded upon them by undue influence."[9]

The formal reception took place in early November. As noted by *The Truth Teller*, as Dubois was installed in his Cathedral, John Power "re-signed into the Bishop's hands the important trust he had filled with honour to himself and to the satisfaction of the Catholics of New York." Dubois then addressed himself particularly to the Irish, reminded them of what they had suffered for the sake of religion under Britain's laws and pleaded that there "be one heart and one soul" between bishop, priests and laity. By living as such he declared "The Catholics of New York might almost work miracles."[10]

In the weeks that followed he tried to bring miracles into reality and doggedly insisted—perhaps to convince himself—that this unity existed.

"Reverend Mr. Taylor has been most wonderfully changed since we came here," he wrote back to the Mountain, "Although he's going and must go to France he has most humbly apologized for his imprudent speech in Baltimore and has given me here the most edifying example of respect and even affection. All parties appear to unite in giving me a welcome."[11]

Taylor's affection was, in truth, less than generous. He did not help

Dubois' position with the Cathedral congregation when he preached his farewell. *The Truth Teller* reported that "His hearers were moved to tears," as he promised that he would return if his aid was essential to the good of religion. But this, he allowed, could not be the case "while his respected friend Rev. T.C. Levins continued attached to their church."[12]

Dubois dove into his pastoral work. On the first day of January 1827 he ordained to the priesthood one of his mountaineers, Luke Berry, whom he had brought to New York. He would be the first of Dubois' children to serve with him; truly the bishop's man. He, and two other priests brought from Maryland were assigned exclusively to the instruction of the city's children. ("Ignorance is the bane of true religion and government," Dubois wrote in doing so.)[13]

He purchased Christ Church on Ann Street from the Episcopalians ("Making it the *Fourth* Roman Catholic Church in this city,"[14] warned the *New York Observer,* a paper soon to evolve into a strongly Nativist sheet.) With the same diplomacy he had always shown to Protestants, Dubois announced that he would retain the Church's "ancient name." When necessary alterations affected the cemetery, he put a notice in the papers saying that he wished to act in concert with the relatives of all the deceased "to devise the best means to dig the foundations without disturbing the ashes of the dead."[15] The only opposition he received came from Catholics who objected that Dubois did not properly place the deed of the church in the hands of trustees. It was his first real brush with this issue which was, at that time, tearing Catholicism apart in Philadelphia. Expressing surprise at the suggestion that people might think a Church could fall "into the hands of our heirs" or be taken over by creditors should the Bishop fall into debt, Dubois thanked those who did express confidence in his honesty and assured his new flock "You shall not be disappointed."[16]

As evidence that this first skirmish involved no anti-Irish feeling on his part, Dubois simultaneously alienated the French in this same parish vicinity. When they wanted to purchase their own "elegant Church," (as reported by a young priest to a Mountain friend:)

"They had regulations drawn up by which it should be governed. He rejected the whole for it was very evident their object was speculation." The result was that in Christ's Church "not ten pews have been taken by French families. They and the Bishop are two . . ."[17]

In charge of all this, Dubois placed as pastor Father Felix Varela, a Cuban refugee forced from his homeland because of his anti-government writings. A deeply spiritual man, he resembled Simon Bruté both physically and in his generous nature. His assignment in the midst of all these national sensitivities was an added irony. At this time he could speak only Spanish, and Dubois had to arrange for the city's other priests to take turns preaching for him.

The Bishop set out to introduce himself to the entire diocese in his first pastoral letter. In masterful prose he set forth his hopes, sought to placate those who would be his adversaries, and presented an apologia for his entire life's ministry.

"We are aware that our appointment to this See has been objected to by some whom we have not been acquainted with and who do not know us," he began, "They were probably influenced by the best, most patriotic, most generous motives."

His coming to New York had involved a separation from a place to which he had a "strong and natural attachment"; a school which he had built twice, "amidst all the difficulties of a new settlement and during the time of war, and again from its ashes after the late conflagration . . ." Because of this attachment he too might have joined those who objected to his appointment:

"So far from considering it a reward we view it as the last sacrifice which we can make to duty and religion. We did not come among you to seek our own interests or gratifications but to devote ourselves to your service."

He praised his predecessor Bishop Connolly who had accomplished "the difficult task of laying the foundation stone of the edifice," and John Power for serving as administrator during the two year interim: "He has done all but impossibilities."

On this point he bravely directed himself to those who felt that Power alone had deserved the bishopric and thought that the populace as a democracy had had the right to choose him.

"Estimable as he is," Dubois reasoned, "What must be the consequence of this principle once admitted? That any other, less estimable, in the same situation would have an exclusive right . . . Let them not talk of local services in a choice which interests the whole Catholic Church of America. The question is not whether the choice has been fixed on one who is worthy of it. Alas, We acknowledge our unworthiness."

He acknowledged it with an example which would be constantly pointed to by his foes—the heavy French flavor of his speech.

"No doubt if oratory were a necessary qualification for the episcopal office," he pleaded, "the appointment of one whose foreign accent is still perceptable might be objectionable."* He asked only that he might prove himself by his actions, and pointed "to those in the Church's history who though poor speakers redeemed this deficiency by other endearing qualifications."

Besides, if such an objection were valid, a pointed question might be asked in return.

---

*Ironically, at this time the Duke of Saxe Weimar Eisenach, travelling in the U.S., heard Bishop England speak and recorded: "Mr. England delivered a long sermon with a strong Irish accent of which I did not understand much except that he drew comparison between a republican state citizen and a good Catholic."[18]

"Who are those who object to our foreign birth? Are they not in the same sense foreigners themselves? For the question is not why an American had not been appointed but why was not an Irishman."

He personalized the objection:

"Did they suppose we would have less affection, feel less interest for the Irish who are the greatest number of our diocesans? . . . We appeal to those dear exiles of Ireland whom we took to our bosom and educated at Mount St. Mary's when they were fatherless and friendless."

He appealed as well to history:

"Were the apostles natives of the countries to which they were sent to preach the gospel? . . . Is Saint Patrick less the patron of Ireland for having been born in Gaul? In this city there are American, Irish, English, French, Spanish and German Catholics. Is each nation to have a bishop of its own? When formerly we watched over the couch of our sick American, Irish and German brethren; when for thirty-five years we rode nights and days to afford them the sweet comforts of religion, did they ever inquire where we were born? . . ."[19]

It was one thing for Dubois to write his well reasoned pleas for acceptance; quite another to get them before the public. Thomas Levins, stationed with his bishop, controlled the diocese's only newspaper along with John Power. They coolly refused to print the pastoral letter. Dubois, avoiding at all costs the scandalous sort of war which Conwell, in Philadelphia, carried on with his clergy and laity, remained quiet. He had been frozen out before, by no persons less than Mother Seton and her first sisters. As he had bided time and won over that community, so too, patience might win out in New York.

At winter's end a layman rebuked *The Truth Teller* for its attitude. He wrote the paper that during Bishop Connolly's administration "party feuds cramped and defeated every effort of that sainted man."

"The truly patriarchal letter of our worthy prelate," he insisted, "in justice, demands more attention from those for whose benefit it is promulgated than it seems to have received."

Oddly, *The Truth Teller* printed this indictment upon itself. Even more oddly it responded only by coldly stating:

"A few copies of this letter remain on hand and can be had at the office of *The Truth Teller,* or from Sextons of the various churches."[20]

In that same month the paper proudly reported that Levins, who held degrees in mathematics and science and had briefly taught at Georgetown, had been appointed to the board of visitors for the next yearly examination of the Cadets at West Point.

"Genius," proclaimed the paper, "here is rewarded."[21]

Perhaps Dubois was too busy to notice or care. Apologizing to those he loved at the Mountain for his lack of correspondence during that spring, the old man wrote:

"... I scarcely have time to take my meals and very little rest at night ... with a population of twenty-five thousand people and seven priests only to share in my labors ... As it is, I do not quit the confessional from Saturday morning to Sunday night except for my meals and the divine service ... I am so tired, by visiting the sick over this immense city, that it is out of the question for me to write in the night as I used to do at Mount St. Mary's. Everything would go well here if I had help ... Good Archbishop Cheverus sent me a neat vestment which is the more valuable to me as it was that of his saintly predecessor, the late Archbishop of Bordeaux. I am as poor as 'un rat d'eglise'—but thank God without debts."[22]

If one might tend to doubt this great amount of time listed as spent in the confessional, the fact is corroborated by Father Michael Egan. Dubois' young successor as President of the Mount visited New York and wrote home just after his arrival:

"The bishop was hearing confessions from 8 o'c in the morning and did not come in till half after nine—I got supper at 10 o'c after having scarcely eaten all day .. He has a great deal of drudgery to do—particularly missionary duties—yet I never saw him more active."[23]

One realm wherein he tried to remain non-active was that of lay trustee politics. This was a new world to him. The spring and early summer brought about trustee elections in several parishes. Various factions attempted to woo the Bishop.

"I tell them they must follow their consciences and be ruled by nobody,"[24] Dubois wrote.

In St. Peter's, one slate put the bishop's name on their ticket ("As if I approved of it which I was obliged to contradict.")[25] At St. Patrick's a party again used him against his wishes. As reported by a Mountain graduate, Father James Rooney, this attempt to remain impartial caused Dubois to be rejected by all:

"The bishop said there should not be any meddling with the people respecting their choice. His friends obediently did so, but the others acted with all their influence, and supported by a clergyman proved to others but not to him that he had a different people here to act with to those at the Mountain. I have been asked what sort of people were the Mountaineers who would be led by such a nonsensical talker as the bishop. He has not made a respectable acquaintance since he came here."[26]

In the midst of losing face politically, Dubois was further hurt from the scandals created by Thomas Sumter, a Mountain collegian staying with the Bishop while awaiting his mother to come from Charleston to meet him. He took to city life with a passion, openly visiting bawdy-houses. He chivalrously escorted the whores on walks along Broadway and to the city museums where he and they put on an exhibition of their own.

"This ruffian passed as the Bishop's young man when with those unfortunate women,"[27] spat a frustrated James Rooney.

The unfortunate bishop, unable to control him, tried to send Sumter home. He refused to go and told Dubois—who no longer had any real authority over him—that if he was evicted from the Cathedral rectory he would simply move to a boarding house. Fearing further scandal Dubois wrote Sumter's parents pleading with them to order the young man home.

Mrs. Sumter, ignoring the crisis at hand, responded that she needed to amass funds and wondered "what chance she would have by sending wines to New York."

Sidetracked, perhaps wanting her to get travelling expenses for her son, Dubois wrote back with his usual Gallican toleration:

"Brandy would probably fetch a better price."[28]

Thomas remained throughout the spring and early summer. He passed about a sarcastic piece written about the Bishop, and according to James Rooney, it turned out that he was merely the transcriber. Thomas Levins was the author. Rooney, furious at Dubois for allowing Sumter to walk all over him, wrote:

"He [Sumter] acts with him as the ex-friars do and gets on smoothly. Instead of the Episcopal palace a boarding house is the name given to the house."[29]

Yet Dubois was unable to return harm for harm.

"I do not know how to get rid of the poor fellow who was on many accounts very troublesome to me and refused to go to Carolina," he pleaded. "To turn him out of doors . . . would not remedy the evils, and rather, increase them."[30]

Instead, Dubois turned himself out of doors and left in July for a visitation of his vast diocese. It was to be a process of following widely scattered pin spots on a map to search out Catholics.

"In a territory which has an area of 30,352,000 acres I have but nine churches worthy of the name," he reported, "and these are from two to three hundred miles apart."[31]

At Albany he observed the behavior of John Savage (he certainly could not have known how the priest had slandered him in private correspondence to Ireland) and found the man so negligent to his duties he removed him. Better that the state capital should have no priest than one who made a mockery of the priesthood. He travelled westward along the Erie Canal, discovering "ten times as many Catholics as I expected."

"Seven hundred are found where I understand there were but fifty or sixty," he wrote, "eleven hundred where I was told to look for two hundred."[32]

In Rochester he had to cope with the situation advertised six months earlier in the newspapers by the trustees of the Catholic church: their pastor the Reverend John McCormick had "eloped with a young woman in violation of morality and of the obligations of his sacred office."[33]

Dubois' presence in the western part of the state might well have been observed by the angel Moroni and/or Joseph Smith. It was at exactly this moment, not far from Rochester, that Smith attested that he had received golden plates from an angel, from which he produced the Book of Mormon. On these golden plates the Romish Church and possibly even McCormick's affair was predicted long before the time of Christ ("I looked and beheld the whore of all the earth and she sat upon many waters, . . . 1 Nephi 14:11). Perhaps Dubois had Cheverus' hand-me-down "neat vestment" with him, for Joseph Smith put forth: "And the angel spake unto me saying: Behold the gold, and the silver and the silks and the scarlets and the fine-twined linen, and the precious clothing; and the harlots are the desires of this great and abominable Church" (1 Nephi 13:8).[34]

Oblivious as to whether or not he had passed into posterity in the Kingdom of the Saints, Dubois moved on to Buffalo. There, anticipating fifty or sixty Catholics he found almost eight hundred, many of them German-speaking. Despite this difficulty, Dubois heard their confessions.

"I accomplished it by means of interpreters," he wrote, "but in such a way that the interpreters themselves understood nothing about the confessions of these poor people. It was a method long ago forced on me by necessity in the missions when I would meet foreigners or Indians whose language I did not understand."[35]

He headed northeastward along the Canadian border, hearing continual pleas for priests who could speak two or three languages when he would have been happy to have any priests at all to send. He noted a special problem with the French who had moved over the border into New York. They refused to support the erection of churches "since they were accustomed to receive everything gratis in Canada where Church and clergy are supported by taxation."[36]

At St. Regis he was called to settle a dispute at an Indian settlement divided by the national border. Their church was in Canada. The United States Indians wanted their flag flown in front of the building along with the Union Jack. This issue had led to a serious division and a second church building had been proposed on New York's soil. In a rustic setting reminiscent of the scenes of his earlier missionary successes Dubois made the same plea for unity that he had been making since taking over his See. He used the example of a bundle of sticks. Bound together, he said, they are all but unbreakable, separated they are easily broken.

"I pointed out," he wrote, "that their conduct might afford the two governments a ready pretext to take possession of their land . . ."

His words touched his listeners' hearts. An elderly chieftain turned to him and confessed for the tribe, "Ah Father, we are no longer Christians, since we lack charity."

This was the sort of response he had been accustomed to for so long in Maryland and Virginia. After a year of having doors slammed in his face in Manhattan, he was once again among his own kind of people. He wrote:

"I celebrated Holy Mass the next day assisted by a dozen young Indians who made surplices for themselves out of blankets. The singing, which is practically the Gregorian Chant, although the words are Indian, was very touching . . . They learned it from the Jesuits who are still held in great veneration by them and they pass the chant along from generation to generation."[37]

He visited Quebec and at the convent of the Ursulines sought out Cecilia O'Conway. One of Mother Seton's first sisters, she had transferred to this more contemplative order and had wounded a very defensive Dubois by doing so. Now he burst into the convent sacristy calling out:

"Where is my child?" and embraced her "with all the affection of a father."

"You may well suppose how great a consolation this reconciliation was to me,"[38] she later wrote.

He returned to his less conciliatory children in New York. When he arrived in the city, placards were hung accusing him of having interfered in the recent trustee elections. He was also accused of mismanaging funds at Christ Church, deeded in his own name. In response he published the Church's accounts to give evidence that he had not stolen from his people.

One good thing happened to Dubois. In his absence his Pastoral letter had been circulated, in July of 1827, in a Catholic newspaper; not New York's, but Charleston's *U.S. Catholic Miscellany*. The public now had an opportunity to read not only Dubois' apologia but his astute observations on the social and religious conditions of New York. His worries were not about governmental structures or the finances of parishes but the state of the Faith. His greatest concern was that the continued neglect of public instruction had led to an "almost total neglect of frequenting the sacraments," and an "Ignorance of the truths of Religion." Many of the poorer classes worked on Sundays and missed Mass because of this. Yet, diplomatic as ever, he interjected:

"God forbid that we should attribute the last difficulties to the illiberality of their Protestant employers. They may be the natural consequences of the nature of their employment."

Other abuses resulted from an enthusiastic acceptance of the cultural habits of "our dissenting brethren." He singled out several which he found disturbing.

Marriages were often "attended with a levity, a coarseness of behavior to be reprobated even before a civil magistrate."

Baptisms, "from the remotest antiquity," a matter of bringing children "to Our Lord in His Holy temple," were, in New York, reduced to a "meeting of a few friends in a private room where refreshments are prepared."

The Catholic way of death was not so much a social adaptation borrowed from "dissenting brethren" as a time-honored Irish way of doing things. Scandalized, Dubois wrote:

"A wake is kept where frequent libations of liquor are used instead of Holy Water; idle conversations instead of the prayers formerly said; and would to God these wakes were not enkindling those passions which the sight of a corpse ought to smother . . . [many] betray on the road to the grave the excesses of the preceeding night."

Then, this man who viewed the world through the eyes of his spiritual mentor, St. Vincent, addressed himself to social ills.

"What a climax of miseries and sufferings did we not discover almost at our arrival in this city," he wrote, describing the immigrants. "They come in search of civil and religious liberty and they fall into the double slavery of poverty and of their own passions which deprive them of both."

Realistically labelling financial help as "necessarily too limited," he espoused a gradual building of workhouses and employment agencies, cautioning "we are far from calculating an immediate success."

He called for assistance not only for orphans but for the impoverished elderly, those "dreading a protracted existence which might exhaust their scanty resources before the grave had offered them a refuge." He called for the establishment of hostels:

"We speak from our own knowledge, having witnessed such an establishment in Europe, owing to the admirable zeal of St. Vincent de Paul, the founder of the Sisters of Charity. That establishment, from a low beginning, afforded an asylum to hundreds of unfortunate old people and has survived the wrecks of a revolution which spared nothing."[39]

These were the words of a man who had already proven his mettle, a man who saw that "Everything would go well here if I had help . . ." The Pastoral stands as an indictment against those Catholics—especially of the priests in the next decade who impeded Dubois' selfless ambitions for the Church with their own national and personal pride.

In January 1828, *The Truth Teller* explained to its readers the workings of a new "steam carriage" which could propel itself at the rate of ten miles an hour.

"At every stage," envisioned the paper, "instead of the old fashioned way of travelling by changing horses, they will stop for a supply of coal and water."[40]

Before such an age could come to be men would have to labor laying thousands of miles of roadbed and tracks. So, too, before the Church could effectively care for its immigrant members, servile labor was needed to build and put matters in order. For the first three years of his episcopacy, John Dubois alternated his time between caring for the great bulk of Catholics in New York City and visiting his scattered charges along the backwoods roads and waterways of his diocese. His life was one of inces-

sant movement. In the spring of 1828, shortly after he was in Baltimore
for the consecration of Archbishop James Whitfield, one priest noted that
Dubois was off to Canada "on a begging or borrowing mission."[41] He returned to Buffalo where a fellow emigré of the Revolution became his
benefactor. Stephen Louis Le Conteulx de Laumont had fled from France,
though his wife elected to accept the New Order in France. Remarrying in
the United States, he built up a fortune as a merchant and, but for two
years at the turn of the century when he was imprisoned in Quebec as a
French spy, he lived successfully. In Albany he helped erect the first
Catholic Church and now, in Buffalo, he repeated his gesture and gave
Dubois land on which to build. Dubois won the hearts of the city fathers.
As in Richmond, Virginia, nearly forty years before, he was invited to say
Mass in the city's courthouse, using the judges' bench as an altar. Some
eight hundred people gathered for the occasion, after which he agreed to
bless not only the new church grounds but a distant cemetery as well.
Dubois himself recorded a display of faith which he felt "afforded a won-
derful sight to the Protestant multitude present":

"Without any instructions from me, they arranged themselves four
abreast to march from there to the cemetery, which is about a mile and a
half away. Four old white-headed men began the rosary in German. The
French, English and Germans present recited the second part of the Pater
Noster and Ave Maria in their own language. Each side of the road was
lined with the inhabitants of the town drawn together by this ceremony . . .
Upon arriving at the cemetery these good Swiss sang the psalms and litanies
specified in the ritual for the blessing of the cemetery and it was after sun-
down when we separated."[42]

An encounter with another Frenchman in Manhattan gives evidence that
he remained in the city long enough to have a strong effect on some men's
lives. Mark Frenaye himself attested that he had "led a very rough life."
Imprisoned and nearly killed in the San Domingo uprising he had shown
his talent for making money in France, Philadelphia, Alabama, and Mexico.
In New York in 1828 he came under the influence of Dubois who brought
him back to a faith he had "neglected for twenty-six years." He became in
his own words "a new man no longer of the world."[43] He returned to Philadelphia where for the next several decades he placed his talents and fortune
in the service of the Church—and most immediately in the service of the
shrewd John Hughes who used Frenaye's extensive funds to pull the rug
out from under the feet of lay trustees. Ironically, Dubois, in dire straits,
never benefited materially from having brought Frenaye back to religion.

The schoolmaster who had himself been trained at Louis le Grand felt
most keenly the American Church's lack of schools as he journeyed about
his diocese. With a half-jealous eye he observed flourishing Protestant
schools.

"How sorry I have felt when passing near Princeton College . . ." he wrote, "to behold boys of from ten to fourteen years of age smoking cigars at the door of the hotels where they reside, and to find out that quite as little restraint was placed on their drinking propensities . . ."[44]

In September of 1828 a gift from heaven seemed to arrive. A group of religious brothers under the leadership of a James D. Boylan arrived from Ireland and offered their services to open both a pay school and a free school for the poor. Overjoyed, Dubois welcomed them with open arms. New York's lay trustees—who held the purse strings—held them off. The trustees insisted upon control not only over the property but over the religious society as well. This right to hire and fire would have left the brothers, as Dubois protested, "subject to the caprice of rulers who might dismiss them when they would become old and worn out by teaching."[45] Unable to operate under the religious security of the jurisdiction of the bishop, and with the trustees sitting through repeated meetings refusing to budge, the brothers left the work they had already undertaken and returned home.

Brokenhearted, Dubois still fought to realize "the object dearest to my heart"—a seminary "where we may train up a national clergy."[46] Already, the school he had begun in 1808 was filling the American Church with American priests, and soon these Mountain graduates would begin taking over the Church's hierarchy. Why couldn't New Yorkers see that such a seminary in their own diocese would help realize vocations to the priesthood? He had received an insufficient donation from the Propagation of the Faith for this purpose, but in the interim this money had to be used for pressing needs. A church in Newark ("a small town in New Jersey belonging to my diocese,"[47] explained Dubois) would have been lost in debt if he had not stepped in and given the money for that. Likewise, the Catholics in Albany needed help in replacing their first primitive Church building. It was as if he were sliding backwards trying to climb an ice mountain. In the city, Levins and Power continued to knock him down. The latter, who kept behind a veneer of respectability in public, placed responsibility on his cohort when writing to Bishop Conwell:

"Levins is hurling defiance at the Bishop; the latter is threatening suspension . . . The former has the people and is doing everything to lower Doctor Dubois whom you know is no favorite with the flock."[48]

Levins moved out of the Cathedral rectory and into his own dwelling. He complained to friends that he was at an age in life where he had to think of security, and while he preferred to act as a priest he could always go somewhere and teach the sciences.

In early winter an anonymous writer in the *U.S. Catholic Miscellany* scolded the American Bishops for failing to provide colonization policies for immigrants.

"I have found those who have not seen a priest for the space of four, six, thirteen and twenty-five years,"[49] he wrote.

Levins who lived comfortably in Manhattan society was not under fire in this accusation. Dubois, wearied from travelling incessantly, prevented by lay trustees from bringing in needed help, could only wonder in desperation what else he could humanly do.

A letter from his beloved brother at the Mountain evoked longings for the simple life he had left. Bruté happily reported "a bit of our country politics," telling Dubois that Andrew Jackson had swept all of Emmitsburg in the recent Presidential election. He told of improvements at the Mountain school and inadvertently sharpened Dubois' homesickness by referring to a refectory addition, extended "under your window."[50]

He grew ill. He never had given in to sickness and he refused to give in to it now.

"In spite of all I could say to him," wrote a faintly sympathetic Power, "he continued to pursue his own system of quackery for upwards of fifteen or sixteen days until he saw it would never do."[51]

For a month he lay in bed with an intermittent fever, too debilitated to walk across his room. The newspapers reported his illness and a worried Bruté wrote to John Hughes that he feared the worst owing to Dubois' age. Clinically, Power noted:

"I perceive that his mind is shattered."

Presuming that the Bishop was heading for death, Power went on to assess for the virulently healthy, diocese-destroying Conwell, the contribution of John Dubois and his fellow French missionaries:

"What are the advances made by religion? I say none . . . This Catholic Community in every sense is Irish. There are French here, but where is their faith? Even on their deathbeds they seldom seek the aid of a priest. Hence, I say, French priests are useless in this mission; useless in every part of North America, except in Louisiana and Canada."[52]

By March Dubois was regaining his strength. His "shattered" mind produced a long report to the Propaganda Fide in Rome, written in his own neatly flourished handwriting. Avoiding the sweeping generalizations of John Power, he complimented good Irish priests, but noted that bishops in Ireland were reluctant to let these go into the missions. Oftentimes, Dubois wrote, the Irish priests who left home without the blessing of their bishops were "vagabonds, without principles, without zeal, without talents" who did more harm to religion than good.

Dubois announced that he intended to travel to Europe to beg funds, and to Ireland in order to personally recruit "truly apostolic"[53] priests. As if to prove the point about less than apostolic priests Dubois then suspended an Irish priest, John Farnan, for showing up drunk at a Vespers service. It was Farnan's second suspension. Bishop Connolly had temporarily removed him from Utica in 1823 when he threatened to sue trustees in a dispute over salary. While suspended, he took to interrupting the services of his replacement. After Dubois suspended him, he set up his own "Independent Catholic Church," and sued *The Truth Teller* when it warned Catholics of his status.*

Dubois did everything he could to ingratiate himself to the Irish. He contributed money to the "Friends of Ireland in New York" and avowed: "my appointment to this diocese, composed in a great measure of exiles from Ireland, has rivetted my affection to them forever, not only here but in every part of the world."[54]

When the Catholic Emancipation Act was wrung from Britain in 1829 he ordered Te Deums to be sung throughout the diocese and a special collection to be taken up for the care of Irish orphans. All this was not enough for his enemies. Bishop Conwell had been called to Rome to give an accounting of his mismanaged Diocese. As if he were in a position to carry weight with Propaganda Fide, Levins and Power sent him a continual barrage of complaints about Dubois to pass on to the highest authorities. First, Power had to reestablish his own reputation. He had been assured by his informants "that my promotion to the See of New York was checked by a report which reached Propaganda that I struck a man in the graveyard of St. Patrick's." The fist fight had come about, he insisted, because the other man was drunk and had assaulted him. He had returned blows only in self defense.

"You, my lord, know my natural disposition," he pleaded, "and can safely tell them that I am not a person of bad temper or inclined to strife in any way. I love Peace." The peace lover then passed on the good news about Bishop Dubois.

"When you have the opportunity, tell them in Rome that the screws are loose in his head, which you yourself know to be a fact."[55]

Both Power and Levins avowed to Conwell that they were frightened of their Bishop. Dubois had asked Power to travel to Rome for the sake of the diocese.

"I will not go and fear much," he insisted, "He would do everything to oust me in my absence. He is all for Deluol and the rest of them."[56]

Levins felt that Dubois would certainly have moved against himself "were it not for the suspicions of serious happenings from an Irish congregation."

Yet, while they raised alarms about his wielding of power, they contradicted themselves by portraying him equally as an ineffectual leader without support.

"He is never visited by the respectable citizens of the city," sniffed Levins. Trusting in God that the next bishop would be an Irishman and

---

*For almost a full generation he maintained his independence and fed fuel to Nativists' charges against Romanism. In the late 1840s Bishop Hughes accepted him back into the Church and arranged for him to serve in Detroit where he died in 1849.

bring "an end to the French dynasty," Levins observed that Dubois "has been forty years in America and Cannot speak English correctly."[57]

Power seconded this with a claim which might have said as much about the congregation as it did about the bishop:

"Hundreds leave the Church," he insisted, "and actually go to the rum shops while he is speaking."[58]

Their claim about Dubois' accent was borne out by a source quite innocent of their own prejudices. The saintly Pierre Toussaint, a highly cultured hairdresser and ex-slave, was a man of great charities. From his own earnings, he supported his former owner, and gave continually, as well, to the poor of New York. At home he played the game of keeping a daily written correspondence with his beloved niece, Euphemie. In one of these notes she wrote:

"It is a great pity that the Bishop cannot speak English better for he made a beautiful sermon."[59]

Had her opinion been public it hardly would have been welcomed as support by these producers of *The Truth Teller*. If they resented the French emigrés who had come to America before them, they were none too loving of those who now occupied the only rung on the social ladder below them.

"The increasing insolence of the blacks in this city is a subject of universal complaint," the paper claimed. In a perverse example of two persecuted peoples persecuting a third, the Catholic *Truth Teller* reprinted and endorsed the Jewish Mordecai Noah's *New York Enquirer* which declared: "the free negroes of this city . . . are not free to share with us and mix with us in the enjoyments of social life."

"His caste is his colour, immutable and fixed," Noah pronounced, "Let him bear the bitter sentence as he can, unchanging and unchanged."[60]

Dubois' bigoted enemies would not have been pleased to know that the impeccably cultured Pierre Toussaint, quietly magnanimous in his widespread charitable works, both supported the Bishop and laid blame upon his Irish persecutors. In his preserved correspondence Toussaint's concern is evidenced in a response to him by a friend in Paris who reflected:

"Je vois toujours avec beaucoup de peine que le trouble continue toujours dans l'eglise de New York. J'attribue le peu de respect que ces malheureux— Irlandais ont pour la religion a leur ignorance."[61]

Unaware that they were earning the disdain of an educated and aristocratic black man, barred from mixing with them in the enjoyments of social life, Levins and Power plowed forward with their campaign. Levins told Conwell that all but three of the priests in the diocese were ignorant and that this was no worry to Dubois:

"For these ignorant men are his own choice. They have been educated at his own seminary."[62]

Somewhere in the midst of this dust storm of words was the real Dubois. Unaffected by the petty campaigns of his adversaries, he worked to build

up the American Church. In the same month as Levins' charge about ignorant priests from poor seminaries, and still weak from his brush with
death, he renewed his long term squabbling with Father Tessier at St.
Mary's in Baltimore. Significantly, when Dubois argued with someone—
as he had with Tessier for so many years—he charged at the issues, not
his opponent. Moreover, the issues about which he chose to argue hardly
reflect a man who accepted poor priestly formation:

"I heard with pain," he wrote to Tessier, "that the very useful custom
you had to make the young ecclesiastics preach in a room and give them
proper admonitions is suppressed in the seminary. I hope and beg you will
reestablish it . . . it compels them to lay up materials for that future ministry."[63]

In the fall of the year he planned to sail for Le Havre; just as the bishops
of the United States, after years of delay, arranged to meet at Baltimore.
Dubois felt he could get better help from Europe than from his equally
impoverished peers. He wrote his opinions for Whitfield and delegated
Power to represent him. The only slap he gave Power in return for his
continual animosity was to appoint the loyal Felix Varela as a co-vicar
general to run the diocese with Power until his return.

The night before he left Dubois shared his table with one of his Mountain
children, Irish-born William Quarter, whom he had just ordained to the
priesthood (and who would become, in 1844, the first bishop of Chicago).
It afforded him the opportunity to dwell for an evening in the happy realm
of his Mountain world. Quarter wrote to a friend at the school that Dubois
"made me frequently smile in secret whenever he entered deeply into conversation and dwelt upon some of his old favorite places, such as the garden,
farm, etc. He always spoke in the first person plural." When Quarter told
his old father to remember the school he had founded when he reached
Rome: "He made no answer but a smile beamed upon his cheek which
seemed to tell me he would not forget it."[64]

Strengthened by these memories of his past, he dealt again with the
present and future. On September 20, 1829, he boarded the packet ship
DeRhom and set sail upon the Atlantic he had last crossed in 1791. If the
reports of his disloyal subordinates had taken root in Rome, he would have
to convince the Pope that he was more than a crazy bumbler. There was
always the remote chance, however, that reports might precede him from
secular sources, for in the world at large the work of Dubois was well respected. One Protestant, Henry Barclay, had given him land for a church
in Saugerties at the time of his departure. On a darker note, the *New York
Observer* (owned by the family of Samuel F.B. Morse) worried about the
ever growing Roman Church in the United States: "In the City of New
York there are now three Churches including a Cathedral. The increase of
monastic establishment is also worthy of notice. Twenty years ago there
was nothing of this kind dreamed of above the thirty-second degree of

North latitude. Now there are Nunneries at Emmitsburg, Georgetown and Bardstown." This growth was more than just the result of immigration; it gave evidence of Catholics' "astonishing success in proselytizing."

"The grand and master means they have adopted" revealed the paper "is getting the education of youth into their hands."

All of the Catholic colleges were listed, but only one was so notable as to be described: "Mount St. Mary's in Emmitsburg where they have one hundred twenty students and thirty ecclesiastical students, chiefly American."[65]

Dubois the Frenchman was off to beg funds so that he might accomplish with his diocese what he had done for other areas filled with immigrant Catholics. He would make it "chiefly American."

60

Travel in the time of John Dubois was rarely easy. Above, a "Safety Coach" was
an improvement for long distances, but it lacked much comfort. In his days as
a missionary John Dubois also travelled by horseback, once owning two
horses, so he would not wear one out. Below, as Bishop of New York, Dubois
was able to use the Erie Canal for his frequent journeys to upstate New York.
Building the Canal also provided work for thousands of Irish immigrants who
came to America.

61

62

Bishop William Quarter (1806–1848), of Chicago, travelled with Bishop Dubois on one of his last missionary journeys in upstate New York. The young man marvelled at the Bishop's strength and vigor at age 73. Below, Pierre Toussaint (c1766–1853), former slave and philanthropist, supported the bishop against his Irish detractors.

63

CHAPTER 13

Home for Another Revolution

The backwoods of Maryland and the boom town of New York where pigs still scavenged the city streets had been home to John Dubois now for two-thirds of his life. His critics, however, were constant in pointing out that he had never really adapted to this New World home. His manners were of another culture. In early winter of 1829–30 Dubois once again walked about the exquisite city of his childhood. Louis le Grand, where he had been educated, had survived; the only school in Paris to remain open throughout every turn of the Revolution. Saint Sulpice, having been a theater, a banquet hall and a warehouse, was, like the similarly misused Notre Dame, returned to its ancient grandeur. A king, Charles X, once again sat on the French throne, and the Church was once again comfortably—too comfortably—married to the fortunes of the monarchy. The old man had come home to conditions remarkably the same as those France had known in his youth. It was frightening. Once again discontent was in the air; freedoms of speech and of the press were curtailed by a king who grew more unpopular with each passing day.

Dubois moved on to Lyon where he himself was royally received by the Association for the Propagation of the Faith. In Rome by late February, he was welcomed by the ailing and elderly Pius VIII who in 1808 had been imprisoned for his opposition to Napoleon. It was not the first visit

by an American bishop within that year's time. Bishop Conwell of Philadelphia had been summoned by the Pope to explain the poor handling of
his diocese. Realizing that the man's very presence was the ongoing cause
of much of the troubles there, the authorities had offered him a post almost
anywhere in Europe if only he would remain on the eastern side of the
Atlantic. Conwell's response was to disappear in the dead of night, leaving
word that he feared he would be detained forcibly. He resurfaced in Paris
where again the authorities sought to persuade him to stay. Again, performing his disappearance act, he set sail for America, travelling west at
the same time Dubois sailed eastward.

     This second American bishop made a vastly different impression upon
the Pope and upon Cardinal Bartolomeo Cappellari, head of the Congregation of Propaganda Fide. This time they encountered a man about whom
the only petty complaints they had received were the nationalistic resent-
ments of ambitious subordinates. Not only was his own long record of
achievements and hard work unblemished; his only concerns as he stood
before them were worries about what was needed for the good of his flock.
Dubois later recalled that he was received "most affectionately" by the
Pope and that Cardinal Cappellari became while he was in Rome "my
most particular friend."[1]

     He remained until midsummer, and DuBourg, now Bishop of Montauban,
conjectured in a letter to Bruté that such a prolonged visit was a good omen
"for the affairs of Dubois' diocese."[2] In July he returned to France and
was the guest of the Bishop of Chambrey when news from Paris froze him
in his tracks. Once again the city had exploded in revolution. Barricades
were thrown up in the streets. The revolutionary tricolor was again flown
from the spires of Notre Dame. The king fled. The Church which had
shared the blessings of the royalists now reaped the anger of the mob. The
house of the Archbishop of Paris was pillaged. At Montrouge priests were
beaten. Seminaries were searched for arms. In the confusion of the revolution some people again played the exact same roles they had played forty
years earlier. The noble La Tour du Pin family, who in the 1790s had
worked a dairy farm on the Hudson River, now was imprisoned for its
loyalty to the Bourbon dynasty. Lafayette, no more decisive an old man
than he had been a youth, was swept aloft as a living symbol of liberty by
the revolutionists. He vacillated, waiting for a stronger man to tell him
what to do. That stronger man was Talleyrand; the one-time crippled
seminarian who was a Parisian scandal when Dubois was a schoolboy;
one-time bishop of Autun; one-time exile in the United States, had survived,
chameleon-like each succeeding regime since 1794. Now he manipulated
to maintain a constitutional monarchy rather than have a republic headed
by Lafayette as President. Before France even realized what was happening, he set forth before the masses Prince Louis-Philippe who as a youth

had escaped to the United States during the first revolution. Easily convinced that this man was what France needed, old Lafayette stood on a balcony of the Hotel de Ville before the assembled populace and gave the new king a kiss as a sign of political benediction.

For Dubois it was like walking into a forty-year-old nightmare. He had returned home after a full lifetime in the missions to be engulfed by the same turmoil that had driven him from France as a young man. He turned and headed south to Italy, embarking at Genoa on a ship bound for England.

Ireland had held his strongest hopes when he first set out on his begging tour. If the American immigrants were predominantly Irish, perhaps the Irish bishops, realizing this, would allow him to borrow priests for his mission diocese. In October he arrived in Dublin and was formally welcomed at a Pontifical High Mass. His solicitations, over several months time, were fruitless. The poverty of the land was overwhelming. The bishops, in the wake of the Act of Emancipation were in a process of putting their own house in order—especially with regards to a real school system to replace the traditional 'hedge schools' in which the once outlawed Faith had been taught. Dubois diplomatically wrote that he understood the bishops' reluctance "to part with their ablest and most worthy clergymen."

"Catholicity," he observed, "freed from the shackles which an unjust policy had imposed upon it, is spreading more and more, and requires the assistance of all piety, genius, zeal and labor of its native clergy."[3]

One unfriendly observer of his visit was Father Vincent Harold, having returned from "the wrong side of the Atlantic" where he had added so greatly to the discord in Philadelphia. Writing to Thomas Levins in New York, he rejoiced that their native land was "at last assuming the appearance of a Catholic Country," and insisted that he had turned down an unlikely invitation from Dubois to return to the United States. The Bishop of New York was preaching for funds to begin a seminary to train native American clergy. This, Harold told Levins, "like all his castles, is of course, as yet in the air and likely to remain there."[4]

With little more than air in his pockets and with no priests to accompany him, Dubois left Ireland and travelled south in the winter of 1830–31. Pius VIII had quickly blessed the new government in France and in doing so stabilized conditions for the Church. Dubois was able once again to visit his native land and see for the last time in his life old friends; DuBourg, Cheverus—even Samuel Cooper, who, having destroyed his reputation as a priest in America, served quietly with Cheverus. When Pius VIII died that winter, a slow-moving conclave took almost fifty days to choose his successor. Dubois' "most particular friend" Cardinal Cappellari became Pope Gregory XVI. The Bishop of New York continued on a slow begging tour into Spain and Portugal. He always stopped wherever he found a community of Vincent de Paul's Sisters of Charity. As the man who had adapted the order's rules for the United States, he happily expressed that he always felt "perfectly at home with them."[5]

After almost two years in Europe he had gained little materially and had not recruited his hoped-for missionaries. On a personal level, however, he had been praised and hailed as a man who had accomplished much for the Church. He must have been tempted to remain, like Cheverus and DuBourg in France, where for the few years left to him he could receive adulation as a grand old man of the missions. Instead, he set sail for the second time in his life westward across the Atlantic. Even with the ugly opposition he knew he would face from his own clergy and laymen, he had great visions which he wanted to bring into reality. The primary goal he was determined upon now was the building of a seminary and college in New York to create a native priesthood.

"I am rather old to begin," he admitted, "but if I can only put the machinery in motion before I die, I shall leave all confidently in the hands of that Divine Goodness that has blessed my efforts far above my deserts."[6]

At right, *Cardinal Cappellari (1765–1846) was impressed by Bishop Dubois, and called him "my most particular friend." The Cardinal became Pope Gregory XVI in 1831.* Below, *while Dubois was in France in 1832 another violent revolution occurred in Paris.*

64

65

66

John Dubois (1764–1842) as he appeared as Bishop of New York. (Painting in Archbishop's House, New York.)

CHAPTER 14

Tried in This World—As by Fire

In 1830 the ailing ex-president James Monroe was brought to his daughter's house in New York a short distance from the Bishop's residence on Prince Street. He made only one public appearance, presiding over a giant rally in support of the July Revolution in France. He died on July 4, 1831. Had he been home, Dubois would only have had to walk a few steps to repay the hospitality Monroe had shown him so many years earlier. He would have disapproved of the founding father's revolutionary huzzahs, as he certainly had in 1791, but both men were true gentlemen of the old school. As they had managed to do once before, they could have steered free of their political and religious differences.

But the times were changing. Any vestiges of an era of good feelings were vanishing like smoke. Protestant America had never been comfortable with Catholicism and anti-Papist feelings had always surfaced sporadically. When Dubois, in Emmitsburg, began establishing the Sisters of Charity in neighboring towns, Father John McElroy reported back to him in 1825 a typical reaction:

"Dr. Schaeffer commenced on last Sunday and warned his pious flock of the great danger they were in by the female wolves lately arrived in Frederick."[1]

Yet, as long as their numbers were small, Catholics were tolerated. "In 1788, the Papish religion of the United States was almost entirely confined to the state of Maryland and a few scattered districts of Pennsylvania ..." chronicled the *New York Observer* at the beginning of the eighteen thirties. Now, after riots in Philadelphia between warring Catholic factions, and with the cities of the Eastern seaboard turning into immigrant dumping grounds, America was waking up to what it saw as a danger within its borders. The *Observer,* owned by the Morse family of telegraph fame, had evolved from a mildly Nativist paper into a fiery anti-Catholic sheet. Owing to the position the Morse name would hold in history the paper's puritan vision of a preferred American is worthy of record. At the onset of the Nativist era the Morses declared:

> The number of negroes imported from Africa in one
> hundred and fifty years was less than three hundred
> thousand—less than the number of Papists we are now
> importing every five years from Europe. We shall soon have
> more Papists in the North than they have slaves in
> the South. And who would not prefer two million slaves under
> the control of two thousands masters, owners of the soil
> and prompted by every consideration of duty and interest
> to promote the peace and prosperity of the country,
> to two million papists, under
> the control of two thousand priests—two thousand bachelors
> bound to the country by no tie of interest or affection—
> two thousand emissaries of a foreign prince.[2]

Inadvertently exploding these statistics, the New York *Sun* broke down the State's sixteen hundred and fifty clergymen by sect.

"The Presbyterians have 500," it listed, "the Baptists about 450, the Methodists about 400, the Episcopalians about 165, the Reformed Dutch rather more than 100; the remainder belonging to various other denominations."[3]

The forty-five unaccounted clergymen, included Jews, Lutherans, Unitarians, Mormons and, of course, Catholics. Not many issues later *The Sun* betrayed that it watched Catholics far more closely than to categorize it with "other denominations." Under a heading "The Richest clergy" the paper set forth a comic routine:

"Roger and Raikes were amusing themselves lately in a pungent contest of pun making.

'Now' said Raikes to Rogers, 'Can you tell me, Sam, why the Roman Catholic clergy are richer than the Protestant clergy?'

'Rogers,' cried Raikes, 'are they not mass-ing everyday of their lives?'

Rogers was so delighted that he threw a somerset and dashed his heels through a chimney glass."[4]

Nativist sentiments were not always maintained at this lofty level. Men whose hatred of Catholicism amounted to a passion came forward to propel the movement into the mainstream of the nation's consciousness. A Dutch Reformed minister, Rev. William Craig Brownlee earned lasting laurels in this respect. The Dictionary of American Biography would label him "one of the earliest of the Protestant clergy of America to take a firm anti-Catholic stand."[5] After his death in 1860 a memorial was published in which his fellow ministers gave him prime credit for having raised the alarums.

"A pioneer in the Catholic controversy," lauded one clergyman, "He was mainly instrumental in rousing the attention of the community to a system then regarded by him and now regarded by many as fraught with danger to our cherished liberties."[6]

Added another: "He went to work as calmly to batter down the walls of Romanism—which he regarded as baptized paganism—as he did to visit the sick or to preach the simple gospel to sinners."[7]

Short of neck, peering angrily at the world through heavy gold spectacles, Brownlee prophesied to America that Papist immigrants would destroy their native Puritan world—speaking as he did so with the heavy brogue of his native Scotland. After several years of doing this, Brownlee in 1830 launched *The Protestant* to inform wider audiences yet "that the hierarchy and total organization of Papal Rome are the grossest system of imposture, impiety and despotism under which the bodies and especially the minds of men ever groaned . . . [and] that it constitutes the mammoth anti-Christ of scripture."[8]

The ensuing tales about dungeons under Cathedrals (including St. Patrick's in New York) and sexual orgies in convents and rectories might have remained under store counters like pornography and never won the attention of respectable Americans if Catholics had continued to ignore such bile—as Dubois and his contemporaries had ignored it for decades past. The newer Catholics—Irishmen—were more temperamentally disposed to respond to attacks. Catholic reactions were couched at first in terms of polite shock. When Rev. Samuel Ely, writing in *The Philadelphian,* described ten new priests arriving in the country as "ecclesiastical adjutants in the cause of the man of sin" the *Franklin Repository* in Chambersburg responded:

"There is nothing of the spirit of the Gospel in such a paragraph as the above . . . but the very reverse."[9]

When a Catholic attempted to answer the seventy-three ministers who sponsored *The Protestant* in a letter to the New York *Courier and Enquirer,* the paper rejected it. Finally he printed it in the *U.S. Catholic Miscellany.*

"I had thought that the days of Religious discord and fanatical zeal had nearly terminated," he wrote, ". . . I am heartily sorry Reverend Sirs, that respect for yourselves, for your profession, and for your Catholic fellow citizens (now too numerous and respectable in this city to submit patiently to unprovoked insult) did not inspire you with caution."[10]

Others thought such slaps on the wrist too mild. Thomas Levins in *The Truth Teller* created a cast of lampooning characters called the Sheet Anchor brotherhood. From their pub at the Navy yard his fictional alter egos Barney McAlphin, Malachy MacArthur, and Corney O'Hanlon took to roasting Nativists. In 1830 Father John Hughes, using the pseudonym Cramner, sent a series of wildly anti-Catholic contributions to *The Protestant.* Thinking them authentic, the paper printed them for months, each one worse than the one before it in claims of what the Papists were doing in America. Only after Cramner was claimed as a heroic celebrity by the paper's sponsors did Hughes—still maintaining anonymity—expose the jest played upon their desire for scandal and label them "the clerical scum of the country."[11] When Brownlee and company accused Levins of perpetrating the hoax, he hotly denied it. He rightly guessed that Hughes was the author and angrily employed his "Sheet Anchor Brotherhood" to lampoon his fellow priest for having used lies to expose liars.

The atmosphere grew hotter. What might have been considered scurrilous language only a short while earlier now became the accepted mode of expression. When Andrew Jackson appointed Dubois' lawyer and friend Roger Brooke Taney as his attorney, the *Belfast Advocate* in Maine guessed that both the Pope and the president claimed personal infallibility and that the adherents of both were "equally blind and equally devoted." *The Protestant,* under the heading: "New Attorney General is a bigoted Papist," declared that "every sincere Papist is disqualified defacto from holding any office under a Protestant government."[12]

When New York's Father Charles Constantine Pise—a handsome fellow who wrote poetry and was popular with the ladies—was named to the token position of Chaplain to the U.S. Congress, the same paper was beside itself, vaguely warning:

"This defiance of Jehovah is pregnant with more evils and secures a deeper curse even than some other abominations of appalling magnitude."[13]

The Dutch Reformed minister George Dubois used the *Observer* to tell the tale of a Catholic girl given a copy of the Scriptures by Protestants. Her parents called in their priest who then "cursed the Bible."[14] New Yorkers were also told of a priest in New Jersey who annointed a sick man and told his wife that her spouse would die in two weeks. The man's death according to the *Observer* gave proof "that the priest according to custom, administered a slow poison that the wretched creature might not survive his Extreme Unction."[15]

Brownlee drew the line. Papists might kill their own, but America would keep its own people safe. When John Power told the seventy parsons of *The Protestant* that their pronouncements showed they "had not a leg to stand on," Brownlee translated this into a threat that Power "will burn the parsons as soon as he has power." He warned the Romish priests "that the blood of the first 'parson' whom they murder will leave Cain's indelible mark upon American popery and the first Protestant whom they will burn will kindle a fire that all the briny water of the Papal See will not extinguish."[16]

This volatile oratory was translated into action. In November 1831, St. Mary's Church on Grand Street was torched. According to the *Courier and Enquirer* the first persons who rushed in after the shot of 'fire' saw flames in a pew in the center aisle, and a second blaze growing in another part of the church. As men hurried to save sacred vessels they discovered that the tongue of the church bell had been muffled to prevent a call for help. A Catholic witness reported that the tabernacle had been broken into:

"The Blessed Sacrament was crumbled to atoms and thrown about the sanctuary."[17]

Two weeks later, John Dubois arrived from Europe. Standing in the ashes of this violence, he had to accustom himself to an ugly era of hatred which had grown into full force during his absence. He was well hardened by a lifetime of shocks, but his Mountain child Luke Berry, the first priest he had ordained, was not. He had dutifully served in Utica and New York and was pastor of St. Mary's Church when it was destroyed. Already bowed down under a litigation fought between the parish trustees and sexton, this disaster finished him. He died shortly after Dubois' arrival.

Brownlee observed the Bishop's return and threw down a gauntlet to draw him into battle alongside his priests. Daring to take on, as the *Observer* applauded, "four men led and shielded by 'infallibility' itself," the Scottish parson "publicly and formally" challenged "Bishop Dubois, Dr. Power, or Dr. Varela, or Dr. Levins to enter the lists in a series of letters . . . I offer to take them individually or as a body."[18]

The three, goaded priests together signed an acceptance. Dubois, as he had for a lifetime, ignored the chance to enter into public polemics. After his long absence he was absorbed in the care of his diocese. He was crushed not only by the death of Luke Berry but by an unexpected transfer of Sister Rose White from Dubois' New York orphanage. A clever John Hughes had used her health as a ploy to pull the able lady from Dubois' heavy missions and into the lighter tasks of his own orphanage.

"Tears came to my eyes when I heard you had been called to Philadelphia," a frustrated Dubois wrote to her, "Had I been there I would have opposed the measure with all my might."

He brushed off the reason given him.

"I am told that you are infirm, but we wanted your head here more than your hands."[19]

It was not the last time that John Hughes would push Dubois out of the way to reach an object he desired.

The Bishop issued some public statements he felt necessary. One, published and repeated in the press, was indicative of the concern for obscure detail which sometimes drove his subordinates, much like the subordinates of the detail-obsessed Vincent de Paul, to banging their heads against walls. Amidst all the great issues at hand he asked his "numerous correspondents to pay the postage of all letters which may be addressed to him."[20]

A more significant statement warned Catholic laborers working along the canal against bogus priests showing up to collect funds. A Spaniard doing so had collected several hundred dollars around Albany and Troy. Another collector was the suspended John Farnan bent upon setting up his own independent church.

As soon as the weather permitted, Dubois left on a visitation of his people. He ordained a priest in Albany, then headed westward, being able to travel, for the first time, the new railroad which connected that city to Schenectady. In some eighteen towns in the northern and western areas of the state he found new communities where—if he only had priests—he could have started parishes. He confirmed over one thousand people. At Oswego, midway through his mission tour he was confronted with the Asiatic cholera.

Throughout the year this dreaded disease, for which treatment was unknown, swept westward across the continent of Europe. It struck like a medieval plague, caused sudden vomiting and diarrhea, and killed its thousands of victims within a day, sometimes within an hour's time. The constant influx of sick and dirty immigrants caused America to hold its breath awaiting any signs that this curse of the old world might jump the Atlantic. In mid-June, it was learned that cholera had broken out in Quebec and Montreal. Irish immigrants finding travel easier within the British Empire often went to Canada and then traveled south by route of New York State's waterways. Attempts were made to stop the flow of traffic. With the disease breaking out heavily in Plattsburgh and Whitehall, Albany's city marshall, on the night of June 14th, went to the second lock of the northern canal and removed the operating cranks. He stopped three boats, but travellers on board jumped to the shore. Soon afterward a man was found dead on the railroad outside of Albany.

The epidemic hit full force within a week. In a panic people fled the cities. Being in the North, Dubois was swept up in the disease where it first appeared. He issued an immediate circular urging his clergy to renewed spiritual labors. As later reported by *The Truth Teller:* "There [in Oswego] and through the other congregations in those parts which in the present dearth of clergymen are unhappily destitute of priests the bishop was employed in administering the sacraments to the faithful as long as the pestilence existed in any degree amongst them." Not unlike St. Peter returning to face death with his people in Rome, Dubois made his way back to the great center of his diocese where his exhausted priests, along with his

Sisters of Charity, tended the hundreds of people dying each week throughout the course of the summer. He arrived in the second week of August,
and *The Truth Teller* welcomed him back not so much as bishop but as
another pair of helping hands to relieve the clergy whom it reported "are
generally worn out by either disease or fatigue."

Dubois, the paper said, assumed a share of the work with "that zeal
which has ever characterized him."[21]

By summer's end the horrible siege abated and city life gradually returned
to normal. It was a rarity for Dubois to have won public praise. In Emmitsburg a proud Bruté wrote to Bishop Rosati in St. Louis of his brother's
moment in the sun:

". . . You saw in *The Truth* that he was spoken about very honorably as
he should have been. Then in the *Catholic Press* of Hartford of the twenty-
third a letter from Troy spoke of his visit along the frontiers of New York
and Canada, having travelled himself several thousand miles, hearing confessions, not hours but whole days, etc."

Knowing of his brother's unpopularity before the epidemic, Bruté considered what might happen when Dubois' subordinate clergy reassumed
their routine hostility and added:

". . . I cite this [public praise] Msgr. because his absence at first will be
remarked in New York, although it was anterior to the Cholera."[22]

He was right. Power had served well enough during the beginning of
the crisis but had been removed from the ranks by an altogether different
illness—gout. Jealous as always of what Rome might think of him, he wrote
to Anthony Kohlmann:

"As to my being confined with gout whilst that poor old Bishop was
overpowered by fatigue attending on cholera, I have to say that I was taken
honourably out of the cholera field . . . Malice and ignorance I know would
attribute this disease to overindulgence. If so, Gregory the Great must
answer to the charges. I defy anyone to say of me that I am in any sense
of the word a sensualist."

Power, who would always feel that others had blackened his reputation
in Rome blackened himself by omitting the truth about his bishop.

"As to Doctor Dubois' attendence on the cholera in this city, it is false,"
he wrote, "He was not in the city during the scourge. It is not my business
to explain his absence."[23]

As soon as the cholera had spent itself, Nativism returned to plague the
immigrants. Again in February 1833 Brownlee challenged New York's
bishop and priests. Once again the priests, minus their bishop, responded.
This time they entertained the masses not in the public prints, but in lustily
cheered and booed oral debates. For a season they were the liveliest thea-
trics New York had to offer. This time Dubois published his disapproval
in a formal statement:

"It has always been a subject of regret to me that this mode of circulating the truth should be resorted to," he wrote. "It is calculated to give rise to angry feelings; illiberal language, and uncharitable reflections ... and I generally observed that both parties claimed equally the palm of victory."[24]

Those Catholics who were choosing to fight, however, might easily have felt that Dubois, as a Frenchman, stood naturally off the field in the current persecution. The Nativists were not just attacking immigrants in general but, almost always, Irish immigrants. The Irish would naturally resent that a paper such as the *Journal of Commerce* might declare that:

"Men who have been accustomed to be kept in order by bullets and bayonets may think it a great feat to rush through the streets in squads of fifty, or one hundred or five hundred brandishing their shillelahs and knocking down whoever chances to come in their way. But this only proves their unfitfulness for the degree of freedom they enjoy."[25]

Likewise *The Sun* would go out of its way to dramatize Irish incidents in police court:

"Magistrate:—What was you doing in the gutter Daniel?

Prisoner:—Keeping St. Patrick's Day, your honor. (laughter)

Magistrate:—In the gutter, eh?

Prisoner:—Can't your honor understand plain spakin? I mane I was keepin St. Patrick's Day before I got in the gutter. (laughter)

Magistrate:—Why Daniel, I thought that the people who celebrated St. Patrick's Day were sober people.

Prisoner:—Indade, Sir! Does your honor mean to say I'm not a sober people? (laughter)

Magistrate:—You may go home—but don't get intoxicated any more.

Och! Devil a bit; said Daniel as he went out of the office singing: 'St. Patrick was a gentleman and came from a decent people' "[26]

James Gordon Bennett, at the onset of a long career of rabble rousing, quickly saw the thorny point of division between Dubois and his clergy and presented two stories to the public in his *Herald*.

"Which of these anecdotes presents the true sentiments of the Bishop?" he asked in mock naiveté. The first:

"You must have a rich diocese in New York," said another clergyman to Bishop Dubois on board a steamboat going up the river.

"A rich diocese! Not at all, sir. I have nothing but some dirty, stinking, filthy Irish."

The second:

"When the good bishop was presented to General Jackson during his last visit to this city, he said, 'I have nothing to present to you Mr. President but the hearts of 40,000 poor Irish devoted to your cause.'

The President bowed to the ground."[27]

In June 1833, Jackson made a triumphant visit to New York and received a thunderous welcome from the city. Philip Hone, the ex-Mayor and diarist, observed that the president was "a gourmand of adulation,"[28] and as such he was carefully attentive to the gravitation of the immigrants to the democratic party. He received the Catholic bishop of these immigrants in a private visit. Afterward, in a twice passed quote, it was claimed that the President described John Dubois as "the most complete gentleman he had ever met with."[29]

The last account seems far more likely than the first two. As a product of Louis le Grand of the ancien régime, Dubois' manners had always opened doors among people who appreciated gentility. Ministering in the Hudson Valley, he had become friends with the Robert Livingstons and had helped them find a proper governess for their children. They had responded by donating land for a church and funds to help erect the building. When Robert's son Montgomery travelled to Italy, Dubois wrote in an introductory letter to Cardinal Weld that the Protestant Livingstons had "none of those low prejudices which are the low offsprings of ignorance and unacquaintance with the world" and hoped "that the kindness your eminence will show him will convince him that the Princes of the Catholic Church are not the uncharitable, prejudiced beings, which sectarians represent them to be."[30]

A Protestant clergyman, the Reverend Isaac Fidler from England, arrived in New York and called upon Dubois. He wrote that the Catholic Bishop was "a pleasant and intelligent man and has the cast of countenance very similar to what we often find in pictures of Cardinals and Popes."

In their long conversation the Bishop made "a somewhat curious remark"—most curious considering the debates raging at that time between Power, Levins, Varela and Brownlee. Dubois offered his opinion that "Protestants and Roman Catholics are approximating rapidly towards each other and that we shall all be Catholics in the end." It must have been offered in a most pleasant manner for Fidler agreed that a liberality of feeling could cause differences to disappear gradually. Dubois gave him an introductory letter to Dr. Wainwright in the city saying as he did that he had a "great respect for the Episcopal clergy."

He bid Fidler off "with a warm invitation to repeat my call whenever I could find an hour of leisure."

Later when Fidler mentioned Dubois' remark to a fellow minister it brought from the man a smile and the response:

"I hope all members of the Christian family may become true members of the Catholic faith, but not of the Roman Catholic."[31]

The point is that it brought a smile—and the friendly response. This was Dubois' method, rather than polemics. In the 1790s it had won him a banquet given him by Richmond's Protestant ministers. Had the new generation of Catholic spokesmen listened to the old Frenchman, worked at winning friendships and left anti-Catholic assailants alone in the ring swinging wildly at the air, the era of Nativism might have died a good deal sooner and easier than it did.

The young Irish priest John Purcell, preparing for his consecration as bishop of Cincinnati, was caught between those Irish who despised Dubois, and his love for the man who had taught him at the Mountain. Fortunately a wise man convinced him to place himself under Dubois' direction for his retreat.

"As he was your first Father, . . ." Bruté wrote, "[he] will I think comfort and excite your diffident and timid heart. Of his French notions you need not be afraid; the balance will soon be made by the country, its exigencies, etc., etc. alas."[32]

Power, in his steady stream of reports to Rome about Dubois began to include the theme that the bishop disparaged Rome in general and the Propaganda Fide in particular to any who cared to listen. Bishop John England, visiting New York, corroborated this for Power, writing to Father Paul Cullen at the Irish College in Rome that "with the great portion of his flock and the public at large Dr. Dubois is looked upon as worse than crazy." By contrast, Power "has risen five hundred feet in my estimation for his moderation and charity towards a man whose enmity he knows and whom with one word he could banish from the city."

He then gave damning witness against Dubois:

"I have learned with horror the statements that the Bishop made to persons here of the profligacy of Rome and the immorality and vice of the Propaganda."[33]

Considering the exalted position of John England in American church history it is difficult to charge a lie to him. It is, however, more difficult to believe his charges. It is not only that there is no other evidence of John Dubois having spoken as such; it would have been entirely uncharacteristic of him to do so. Even in the midst of his worst battles with the Sulpicians concerning the survival of Mount St. Mary's, he was always charitable both to and about his adversaries. It is unlikely that he would have disparaged Rome after having been so graciously received there. Even more, being so aware of the enmity of Power, who could "banish" him from New York "with one word" it is unlikely that he would have given him such ammunition. Finally, John England was passionately committed both to the advancement of his longtime friend John Power and to the end of French control of the American hierarchy.

The French and Irish factions clashed headlong at the Second Provincial Council of Baltimore in October 1833.

"Had there been more personal courtesy, fraternal charity and less bias, less anti-Irish feeling," wrote Francis P. Kenrick, coadjutor and acting bishop of Philadelphia, "the results of the council would have been more consolatory."[34]

The Irish already formed the greatest part of the Catholic population in the United States, and Irishmen dominated the priesthood. But in 1833 aged representatives of the early French missionaries still outnumbered the new faction among the hierarchy. Benedict Flaget was too ill to attend, but Dubois was joined by his compatriots John David, and Michael Portier of Mobile. Archbishop James Whitfield, reluctant to call the council and sullen about John England's insistence that he do so, was English but had been Maréchal's protégé. Likewise, Joseph Rosati of St. Louis, Italian, had been made bishop by DuBourg and was an intimate friend of Simon Bruté. Frederick Rese of Detroit was German. Only four of the bishops were Irish and one of them, Benedict Fenwick, was born in Maryland. Henry Conwell, whom Rome had stripped of authority, was represented by Bishop England's only full Irish ally, Francis P. Kenrick. John Purcell, born in Ireland, was a product of Mount St. Mary's and was devoted to Dubois. It is little wonder that not much was accomplished. The bishops refused to accept John England's proposal to set up a national seminary in Ireland in order to feed the American missions. Why should that country be able suddenly to produce vocations for the United States when John Dubois had just returned from there without a single priest responding to his pleas for help?

The Council for the most part restricted itself to setting up boundaries for dioceses, and the procedures for electing new bishops. Following the lead of Dubois' public statements, the bishops urged Catholics to ignore the rantings of Nativists and by their lives to prove their loyalty to Church and Country.

Stung by the reaction of the bishops to his own machinations, England later wrote:

"After the exhibition in October 1833 I fear to move in anything, for suspicion seems to attach to everything that I suggest and some of the most influential persons appear to thwart anything that I would propose. This has determined me to keep as far aloof as my sense of duty will permit."[35]

Protected in a group of his peers, Dubois was still vulnerable to the continual slander of his subordinates. As the Council met, a letter was on its way to Rome portraying Dubois as a failure in the realm of education.

"I do not know if they are aware of the manner in which he headed the college of Mt. St. Mary's," Power wrote to Cullen, "[It was] within an ace of falling into the hands of the Lutherans . . ."[36]

Rome would have gotten an opposite view from the American newspaper accounts of Dubois' return to Emmitsburg on his way to the Council in Baltimore. Protestants as well as Catholics in the town prepared to welcome him back, and the ladies in town made a cope as a gift for him. Church bells pealed to announce his arrival, and Bruté, like a gangling Pied Piper, led the college students out to greet him. One of the girls from St. Joseph's addressed him in French. Assisted by Bishop Kenrick and Father John Hughes, he said Mass and when he spoke he opened his heart to them:

"My dear children; for my dear children I must call you. Most of you

were raised under my eyes. Many of you I washed in the sacred waters of
Baptism . . . I thought my children that after having lived so long amongst
you I should have died among you. But such has not been the will of God."

He told them that "surrounded by pastors, under the care of loving
mothers," they were like the man in the gospel with many talents and that
God would expect them to daily increase in fervor. He compared for them
the desolate immigrants of New York where "even in our chief city fifty
thousand souls are depending for all kinds of spiritual aid upon twelve
priests" and that in the remote parts of his diocese thousands of souls were
only "occasionally visited" by priests "who must go a hundred miles or
more" to reach them.[37]

Dubois did not have to exaggerate when describing the forlorn state of
his diocese. He arrived back in New York just in time to learn a lesson
about the shaky prospect of buying secondhand churches. A weakened
wall cracked during services at Christ Church on Ann Street, creating a
scene of panic described—without much sympathy—by *The Truth Teller:*

> Crash followed upon crash. The windows were dashed to
> the ground in an instant by the terrified people endeavoring to
> make their escape. The greater part rushed towards the door,
> the half of which only being open, rendered their egress still
> more difficult. Those who could not get downstairs threw
> themselves from the upper windows incurring a risk nearly
> as great as that from which they were endeavoring to escape.
> One gentleman, a Spaniard, in his anxiety to succour a
> young lady in the body of the Church, actually leaped from
> the choir. Before, however, he had time to extricate himself
> from the pew into which he had fallen the lady was out
> of the reach of danger . . . A large fat man, after scampering
> over some ladies reached a side window, from which he
> endeavored to leap, but his coat being caught by the window,
> held him dangling in the air, to the terror of those underneath
> who dreaded the descent of this incubus of fat more than
> the roof of the Church.[38]

The problem all fell upon Dubois. Writing to Rose White that he had
baptized William Seton's firstborn son while Catherine Seton acted as
Godmother, he vented the frustation of a man called upon to create solutions without any materials to do so.

"Oh, if we had the means of building Churches enough," he wrote, "Our
five churches cannot contain half the population. We are going to build
one for the Germans. We are building one at Harlem and Yorkville near
the hospital. Another at Jersey City one mile from New York . . . I am
going to lay the first stone of the second wing of the asylum in Prince
Street."[40]

The New York Weekly Register and Catholic Diary calculated the number of Irish immigrants against the capacity of the city's churches and the number of Masses on Sunday.

"Say even that six thousand more than our hypothesis will attend the five," it reported, "Still there is not accommodation for more than half the Irish Catholics in New York."[39]

Amidst such odds as he was fighting, Dubois almost lost his Cathedral in March, 1834. A great fire raged throughout the neighborhood destroying the homes of a hundred families and the school belonging to the orphanage. Sparks landed and caught fire on St. Patrick's roof. An immigrant lad, William O'Brien took off his coat and tied it around a leaking water hose. He then climbed to the roof. Barefoot, he stamped on flames and tore out burning shingles until the building was saved.

Dubois moved toward the realization of his prime goal—a seminary and college for his diocese. In 1832 he found an ideal spot; a one hundred and sixty acre farm on the Hudson River at Nyack, thirty miles north of the city. It boasted a stone quarry which promised an income of $1,500 a year, an apple orchard, a large pond fed by a mountain spring, and—like Mount St. Mary's—it was nestled into a hill which gave protection from winter winds. Lafayette, along with Washington, had once used the farmhouse as quarters during the Revolutionary War. A daily steamboat made the site easily accessible from the city. Dubois bought the farm and began building a domed, eighty-foot stone building with two wings extending on either side.

The *New York Weekly Register and Catholic Diary* gave him constant support and appreciated the blessings of such an establishment ("... To the Right Rev. John Dubois do we owe all this. A name with which we inseparately [sic] associated some of the most interesting recollections of Catholicism in the United States.")[41] But, the project was, like Dubois' other projects, fought by those directly under his command. In 1834 when building was halted at a second story level for lack of funds and Dubois appealed in a pastoral letter for help, Levins scorned the project to Cullen in Rome:

"Bishop Dubois has no funds. He cannot derive any from the Catholic Community. They will not contribute for he is disliked, unpopular, hated. The fault is his own. His favorite theme is abuse of the Irish people and Irish priests."[42]

Father John McGerry and the newly ordained John McCloskey were placed in charge of the handful of students gathered into the old farmhouse during construction. McGerry who was trusted by Dubois, but whose letters show him to have constantly abetted Power and Levins, wrote to Rome that because the Bishop was "far advanced in years the people have no confidence in him." He insisted on the need of "popular bishops":

"For we have so much intercourse with Protestants of every possible denomination that it is absolutely necessary we have men able to meet them in every possible way either by word or writing. This is not in the power of a French man; for they can never learn to speak or write our language correctly, much less elegant."[43]

Power, concurring with all this, declared that the "aged bishop" had sunk the diocese into debt by buying a useless farm. Contradicting himself in the same letter then, he projected the possibility that if he were given authority—such as Kenrick had been given over Conwell in Philadelphia the farm might turn into a valuable property.

"I will within my own family," he assured Cullen, "find funds to complete the work . . ."[44]

If his own priests proclaimed his college site a folly the Nativists saw more clearly the future effects of Dubois' work. The *New York Christian Intelligencer,* under a heading: 'Monastery and Nunnery at Nyack' proclaimed:

"There is a deep scheme in fixing these 'cage of unclean birds' at that spot. Probably on the whole shores of the Hudson from New York to Albany there is not an accessible district in which it would be practicable for the Jesuit seducers more easily to effect their proselytizing schemes or more extensively and permanently to distil their fatal poison."[45]

The New York *Observer* reported that a "Rev. Mr. Dewing who is located as he himself put it under the frowning battlements of the Jesuit college at Nyack" tried to put a warning about the institution in an Albany paper and was refused by the editor who feared such a volatile contribution.

"And let it be remembered," said the *Observer,* overlooking the Nativists' consistent record of inflamatory prose, "the articles alluded to were calm, discreet, judicious statements, free from personalities of any kind."[46]

Levins blamed Dubois for poor relationships both within and without the Church.

"The law of Charity is unceasingly outraged by Bishop Dubois," wrote Levins to Cullen, "He acts like a crazed man."

Levins made the serious charge that Dubois had set out on his routine diocesan visit in the summer of 1834 forbidding his city priests to go on sick calls. They could accept baptisms and marriages for that meant money, but priests were forced to tell parishioners "The Bishop forbade them to attend the sick." As a result Levins said:

"The Catholics curse him, execrate him, and say he is a French infidel in disguise. The Protestants laugh at us, mock us and call our religion venal."

John Power cosigned these charges, adding "not a tittle set forth is not true to the letter."[47]

In the lack of any evidence other than their words, the allegations of these witnesses who lived sedentary city lives must be weighed against the life of a man who once fainted at morning prayers after having travelled all night to and from a sick call, was revived and conducted the service, a man now in his seventies who set out on his routine summer journey over hundreds of backwoods miles to act as a missionary priest as well as bishop.

The Catholics were indeed being mocked. Brownlee called upon Protestants to raise a Crusade against them:

"It involves not only the deepest interests of our holy religion," he declared, "but the very existence of our liberties and the perpetuity of our Republic."[48]

Brownlee fought against Levins and Power—face to face in debates and in print. John Hughes was gaining nationwide fame jousting with Princeton's Rev. John Breckinridge. *The Churchman*, organ of the Episcopalians, greeted an encyclical of Gregory XVI by calling the papacy the "scourge of Rome"—"a power which has once subjugated the civilized world." Yet in the midst of this, in June 1834, while conducting a war of words with the *New York Weekly Register and Catholic Diary, The Churchman* gave proof that Dubois evoked not laughter, but respect from some Protestants. Reporting that Dr. Whittingham of St. Luke's Church in the city was embarking for Europe to recover his shattered health the paper noted:

"One circumstance particularly gratifying to himself may be mentioned as evidence that the greatest kindness of personal intercourse may subsist among Christians who differ most widely in religious opinions. The Right Rev. Bishop Dubois of the Roman Catholic Church gave him a general letter addressed to all archbishops, bishops, clergy and laity of the Roman Catholic Church, commending him and the brother who accompanied him to their good will and kind offices."[49]

At Cold Spring Dubois dedicated a Church which had been built with donations from a Protestant, Gouverneur Kemble. The *Protestant Vindicator* declared Kemble a 'nothingarian' and spat "he would just as willingly have aided a Mohammedan Mosque or a Chinese Pogoda."[50] Giving evidence that many Protestants were above Nativists' sentiment, many of them joined in the ceremony. One observer described Dubois as "the amiable and venerable bishop whose grey hair added dignity to his devotion."[51] The band from the nearby U.S. Military Academy provided music. This was all too much for the Scottish born Brownlee. His *Protestant Vindicator* screamed:

"We demand to know by what authority the musicians of West Point were ordered to play "Yankee Doodle," "Hail Columbia," and other tunes on the Lord's day, in a temple of Idolatry."[52]

In mid-October, back in the city, Dubois clashed with Levins in an incident which erupted their smoldering feud into public view once and for all. Considering Levins' earlier charge about sick calls, it is important for

the record that the texts of the notes passed back and forth between the
bishop and his subordinates are preserved in the records of the Propaganda
Fide:

> Dubois to Levins: Oct. 14, 1834
>   The bearer says that you refuse to attend the sick call on
> the ground that it is not your duty. I command you to attend
> under pain of suspension, ipso fact. You must learn your
> duty. I attended one call this morning. You shall attend
> yours or go somewhere else.
>   +John, Bishop of New York

> Levins to Dubois: Oct. 14, 1834
>   I have received your imperious note. Should I receive
> another couched in such terms I tell you I will not attend
> what belongs to your house. If you wish for war, at once
> declare it. I am ready. I exceedingly regret I cannot comply
> with your kind, courteous and charitable request "to go
> some where else." I know it would afflict you. I could
> retort if I pleased. Last night near 12 o'clock I had to attend
> a cholera* call which was at your door before 10 o'clock. I
> refer you to Doctor McCaffrey.
>   I am yr obedient servant,
>   Thomas C. Levins

Dubois had suspended Levins briefly once before in 1832 and had
quickly accepted his apology. Now, with Levins blunt denial of Dubois'
ecclesiastical authority, the bishop had no other choice before him if he
was to have any authority at all in the future:

> Dubois to Levins: Oct. 15, 1834
>   When a priest has the presumption (to use no harsher name)
> to threaten his bishop with war because this superior
> commanded him under pain of suspension to attend a sick call
> which he could, but would not attend, without assigning
> any reasonable excuse for doing so, it is high time to break up
> all connection between such a man and his Superior.
> Accordingly Reverend Sir, I withdraw your faculties and
> consequently I interdict you from all pastoral functions in
> this diocese.
>   +John, Bishop of New York

------

*The cholera had broken out again that year but in no where near the force it had in 1832.

The ministers sponsoring *The Protestant Vindicator* gloated over the suspension from spiritual matters of the man who had so often lampooned them through his Sheet Anchor Brotherhood.

"Is Berkeley McAlpin the Jesuit whom the Romish prelate of this city, Mr. Dubois, has lately stopped from singing Mass and making Holy Water?"[54] they asked.

Still, if Dubois ruled in spiritual concerns, he had no sway otherwise. Levins was popular with Catholics of means in the city, Dubois was not. 'War' it became indeed. The trustees of St. Patrick's humiliated the bishop by immediately appointing the suspended Levins as head of their school. Public emotions in support of the colorful Levins created an atmosphere of danger around the cathedral. One of the Sisters at the orphanage remembered:

"Affairs grew so bad that Bishop Dubois was advised not to stay in his house at night for fear of mob violence and for some nights he went and stayed at Doctor Bedford."

The sisters, she added, began to call the Bishop "the man of the iron will."[55]

Saint Patrick's trustees then called upon Dubois and threatened him with suspension of his own salary. They knew the man very little. Simon Bruté, who had just been made Bishop of Vincennes, had commented that Protestants provided well for their clergymen "while literally our Catholics do nothing."

"Since twenty-three years I have been teaching," he wrote, "I have never received a dollar salary and I sacrificed like Mr. Dubois all I had."[56]

All that he had . . . . After a life of constant travelling and privation Dubois was threatened with the loss of a handful of coins. This material nadir point of his life offered him his greatest moment for the sake of history. Standing up to these little men he calmly brushed aside their threats.

"Gentlemen," he said, "I have seen the horrors of the French Revolution and could meet them again. I am an old man. I can live in a cellar or a garret. But gentlemen, whether I come up from my cellar or down from my garret, you must remember, I am still your bishop."[57]

In the Spring of 1835 Bishop Simon Bruté passed through New York on his way to beg funds in Europe and was frustrated to learn that Dubois was somewhere in the midst of his vast diocese. He visited with the Sisters of Charity and told them to express to his "brother of the Mountain"— "how severe the trial was for me not to see him and have the moment of the heart in heart before crossing the high seas."[58]

At least Bruté got to share such a moment with the sisters, all of whom had been trained under his spiritual care at Emmitsburg. So too, even in the worst of times, these sisters were the greatest source of Dubois' pride. He had been the spiritual and physical architect of the order since he had moved out of his cabin to make room for Mother Seton and her first sisters.

He still watched over the community's growth, advised them, even scolded them when he felt it was necessary. They were his children.

"My heart is at St. Joseph's as long as I live," he wrote, in the mid eighteen thirties, "and I would be happy its material substance would lie there after my death. It would secure me the prayers of the angels who surround the place."[59]

The sisters had balked at the idea of taking care of male orphans. Dubois' handling of this is of special interest because the issue would come up again during the administration of his successor. Then, John Hughes would push the sisters so roughly into following his will that he would end up splitting the one community into two separate religious orders. Dubois, in his day, put the matter to rest by chiding the sisters as a father.

"I am truly sorry to see that so important and so interesting an undertaking as the one I proposed to our good sisters should fall through for want of their own sisters' cooperation," he wrote, "for fail it must if they don't take charge of those poor orphans who will be scattered, lose their religion and morals, and stand in judgement against us for having forsaken them."

To these pleadings he added one crystal clear point of common sense.

"Our sisters attend the infirmary," he reminded them, "where *men* are and these are small innocent children."[60]

The sisters, at length, agreed.

Again, Dubois pushed when the sisters held back from assigning their best teachers to the free school at the Cathedral.

"In a city like this the eyes of the public are fixed upon our schools," he told them, ". . . sectarian malignity would delight in publishing an individual comparison between their [Protestant free school's] very able teachers and our ignorant sisters . . ."

They could never turn him down.

Always, even when he was scolding he would worry about them individually.

"Sister Margaret," he would advise ". . . must be allowed some rest."

"What is the matter with my dear Sister Stanislaus? She looked formerly so hearty . . . I see a whole generation of my dear daughters disappearing gradually and I am afraid I will soon be a stranger to all."[61]

Because he was the father of women's religious orders in the United States, Dubois must have been appalled by one direction Nativism took in the mid-thirties—the attack upon sisterhoods. A tame exposé called *Six Months in a Convent* inspired Brownlee and Company to adopt a wandering young Canadian streetwalker with her infant child, and spin a wild sexual fantasy about her imprisonment in a Montreal convent. They released what became a runaway best seller, *The Awful Disclosures of Maria Monk.* Almost immediately proven a hoax by a fairminded Protestant editor in New York, the book, along with Maria on the lecture circuit, became gospel for Nativists.

The Journal of Commerce assured its readers that "inmates of convents are completely at the mercy of the priests." Maria was just one more girl who had been "compelled to minister to their priestly lusts."[62]

The Protestant Vindicator matched the story to the ravages of the inquisition and opined:

"Is there a genuine Romish prelate or Jesuit priest, or sincere Papist in America who would not consider it the greatest privilege and noblest act of his life if it was in his power to torture every Christian female in the United States exactly in the same way."[63]

The Scottish immigrant James Gordon Bennett, whose *New York Herald* would revolutionize the newspaper industry and set trends for the popular press for a century, was a Catholic and had once been a seminarian. The death of his brother in the seminary made him bitterly anti-clerical and though he remained in the Church he spent a lifetime roasting the clergy to keep them in line.

"The atrocities of the nunneries in Canada spring from the system of government which the Vatican has endeavored to establish in this free land," he told the public, "It is entirely of French and Italian origin. In this city, Bishop Dubois, a mere creature in the hands of the Roman Pontiffs, has been doing and is doing all he can to keep the Catholic Church in the United States under the iron tyranny of Rome and all her worst systems and dogmas. On the contrary, the Irish clergy here and several of the Irish boards of trustees to the Catholic Churches have been aiming for years to establish the independence of their Church against the power of Rome."[64]

If Nativists quickly applauded this Catholic who attacked his priests, they just as quickly learned to hold their applause. Bennett soon enough showed that he was not so much pro-Nativist as pro-selling papers. People loved scandal, and they loved to hear scandal about Protestant ministers as much as they did about Catholic priests. While Maria was still under the guardianship of her clerical sponsors, she got pregnant again. With a Yo-ho-ho, Bennett happily set the blessed event before the public:

"This lively black-eyed virgin is again in that condition in which, as the heathen poets say, 'ladies are who love their lords.' In plain parlance, the sweet, the amiable, the pious, the religious, the enchanting Miss Maria Monk is again enciente . . . She intends to give birth—not as formerly to a young Catholic priest, but to a lovely, interesting and never yielding Presbyterian Parson . . . Since she has been in this city she has been in company with the Rev. William K. Hoyt, the Rev. Mr. Bourne, the Rev. J.J. Slocum, the Rev. Mr. Theodore Dwight, and we don't know how many other reverends besides."

"Lay it on thick, sweet Saint," he urged Maria.[65]

Another American saint, the Reverend Lyman Beecher, whose moralizing kin were famously antislavery, anti-alcohol, anti-immigrant and anti-

Catholic, played W.C. Brownlee's part in Boston. In the same month, August 1834, that Dubois' completed chapel at Nyack was consecrated, Beecher preached a series of Anti-Romish harangues in Boston. In this atmosphere a mob marched to nearby Charlestown and burned an Ursuline Convent school to the ground.

The Nativist press quickly took the offensive.

"The whining cry of persecution has been uttered in long and doleful strains," said *The Christian Intelligencer,* "for the purpose of enlisting the sympathies of the people."[66]

The *Protestant Vindicator* claimed that the "well timed blaze" was "a ruse de guerre, the work of Papists," so that "a greater sum than is lost may be obtained for an enlarged and more costly nunnery as an associate for the Jesuit monastery at Nyack."[67]

Fire was in the air. Not long after the Charlestown conflagration a boy in Auburn, N.Y. was caught igniting a blaze under a Catholic church during Mass.[68]

Watching Dubois' college become a reality, the New York *Christian Intelligencer* issued a warning to "our Reformed Dutch Brethren who dwell on the west side of the Tappan Sea."

"Can a man take fire in his bosom and his clothes not be burned?" asked the paper, ". . . We desire our Protestant brethren to rest assured that it is just as impossible to carry fire, or to walk upon burning brands without being burned as to have any sort of connection with Jesuit priests and immoral nuns without contamination."[69]

In late summer of 1835 a great fire in New York City levelled some $750,000 worth of property. Twenty printing offices were destroyed including *The Herald,* the *Weekly Register and Catholic Diary* and the *Protestant Vindicator.* Every faction was in a position to decide that God's wrath fell on the just and the unjust alike. On a bitter cold night in December an even worse conflagration tore through shipyards, vessels and whole city blocks in the oldest section of the city—a section which had no Catholic churches. If Dubois breathed a sigh of relief after both these blazes, he soon received a shock which must have made him think he was reliving a nightmare. As had happened to his new structure at Mount Saint Mary's, a fire broke out in his almost completed—and uninsured—Nyack college. It burned to its foundations. As with the Mountain fire, it was claimed that the Nyack blaze was the fault of a workman—this time heating glue. The fiery rhetoric, the Nativist calls for the destruction of the building, made the case for arson strong. As with the Mountain fire there was never any conclusive way of finding out what happened.

Histories in which Dubois appears almost always conclude that this fire broke his spirit. He did not rebuild. A wealthy benefactor, Cornelius Heeney, offered lots in Brooklyn for a new college project, but he wanted to keep title to the land during construction. Having suffered enough from trustee problems, Dubois let the project drop. He rocked backward in shock, but then his indomitable spirit reawakened as it always had.

"The conflagration of my college and seminary has by no means discouraged me," he wrote to Purcell, "It seems that I am to be tried in this world—as by fire. May I be less tried so in the next."

Though he insisted that he was "far from viewing this event on this gloomy point of view," he allowed himself, speaking to this younger bishop whom he loved, more bitterness than he had ever expressed in his life.

"I was misinformed," he wrote, "about the population which is composed of stupid, ignorant, black Dutch fanatics under the influence of Brownlee and Company, and who had threatened to burn it as the nunnery was."

He then announced his intention to sell the farm and buy "another place already established, to which I will gradually add other buildings."[70]

While Dubois sought to build, his flock squared off in ever more violent confrontations with the Nativists. In 1835 in Philadelphia John Hughes met John Breckenridge in a second series of debates. In New York W.C. Brownlee set forth a tirade against Catholics before a well-packed house. Halfway into his talk he discovered that the house was packed well with Irishmen. A lusty brawl erupted in which the auditorium was all but destroyed.

John Dubois, who had never in his life entered into the game of polemics, issued a statement in which he said that "inflaming the worst of passions" with such meetings could only lead to the "perpetration of riot and outrage." He cautioned Catholics to ignore provocations "however uncharitable so ever they may be."[71]

Riot and outrage became the order of the day throughout the spring elections. While Whigs packed slates with Nativist candidates, the Democrats with their heavy Irish constituency packed the areas around polling places and intimidated voters. The Democrats won. Angry Nativists talked up an attack on St. Patrick's Church and one June evening some six thousand Catholics gathered to fend off a mob. They dispersed only when Thomas Levins convinced them of the ability of the police to protect the area.

When the *Journal of Commerce* and the *Courier and Enquirer* accused the Irish of controlling elections, Bennett in his *Herald* turned this against Dubois.

"The Irish portion of the clergy has been, during the late riots, the only stay to their madness and ferocity," he declared, "Where was the Bishop and his flatterers on Tuesday evening when the Rev. Mr. Levins (who for his personal independence now lies under an empty interdict) by his patriotic and persuasive efforts stayed the madness of the hour, talked to his countrymen with the tongue of eloquence and kept the city quiet in the neighborhood of Prince Street? Where was the Bishop then? Hanging at some old lady's apronstrings."[72]

An anti-Catholic sheet, *The Downfall of Babylon* went so far as to defend the old bishop.

"Bishop Dubois is a Frenchman and we have ever looked upon him as a pure man and sincere Christian," the paper noted, "He, we are confident, has in no way interfered in our elections though it is within our knowledge that he has reason to lecture the Irish priests under his charge upon the impropriety of their meddling with politics."[73]

Dubois' great problem was with his priests, and not just those who were Irish. The first several decades of the nineteenth century saw a continuing of misfit clergymen leaving the strong structures of the European Church to seek their fortunes in the priest-starved, loosely regulated Church in the United States. Almost every diocese had its share of wandering friars who fed the fuels of scandal.

While in Europe Dubois had accepted the application of a seminarian named Tervouren, hoping that he would serve the large German population in New York. When he arrived as a deacon, Dubois ordained him and sent him to Albany where Tervouren bought, but did not pay for, expensive clothes. He complained he was sick, and as Dubois recorded, "that discharge proved to be Venereal disease." He then printed "an infamous piece about Rev. Mr. Power," which, significantly, Dubois would not quietly condone. He slapped Tervouren into his seminary at Nyack "to repent." There he stole several hundred dollars and booked passage for Europe under the name Fernando.[74]

If Dubois was bent upon defending Power's reputation, Power was infinitely more bent on doing so. He wrote to Anthony Kohlmann saying that John England has informed him "of the many objections of the Holy See against my administration," especially because of his acceptance, during Dubois absence, of unworthy priests.

"I should be more than human," he protested, "if I could escape being imposed upon, exposed as I have been in this city to the applications of all the imposters who arrive in this country."

Ironically, the complaints about Power had come not from Dubois, but from Power's co-administrator Felix Varela. Apparently Power was aware of Dubois' non-complicity for he would have been quick to complain of it. Still, he attempted to exonerate his own misjudgements by amplifying upon the Bishop's record. His litany gives a sad picture of what one had to deal with in acquiring clergymen.

—"Let Doctor Dubois be asked how he came to receive without a single line of recommendation the Rev. P. O'Riley, a Dominican, who shares more of his confidence than I do ... I am well aware of his efforts to blacken me.

—Let Doctor Dubois be asked in like manner how he could have ordained Tervouren whom he brought from Rome, notwithstanding the scandal he gave before his ordination by staying in bed every morning during his retreat and never appearing at Mass though in perfect health. This same Tervouren broke open the bishop's money chest on the night of Good Friday last and eloped to Europe with nearly $400—of the money of the propaganda!!!

—Let him be asked why he kept in his own house for the space of two years and more the old priest Duffy, a vile drunkard who to our shame and disgust had often to lie like a pig in the entry not being able to go upstairs to his bed.

—Let him be asked why he employed Rafferty, a Franciscan who lately arrived here from Lisbon and who ran mad through the country ...

—Let him be asked why he employed Paul McQuade whose departure from Newark, New Jersey was for a crime which I would blush to mention."[75]

Power's unblushing tirade against Dubois' ability to judge others was not written in love. Writing, in love, Dubois expressed much the same opinion of another bishop.

"Our good friend Dr. Bruté is not expert in judging men and his extreme charity blinds him," he told Purcell, "He is the last man upon whose recommendation I would receive any clergyman. The only case when I would listen to him is when he would turn me against anyone. When he condemns you may be sure that he is right for he leans always towards blind indulgence."[76]

Bruté in Europe had, however, failed to accept a Bohemian seminarian who had applied and then awaited his response in Paris.* The young man's home diocese was overstaffed preventing his ordination. Inspired by the missionary appeals made by his seminary rector, Rev. Andreas Reiss, he had impetuously started out for America without proper dimissorials from his bishop. On the surface of the case he might have been no different than any of the adventurers who had already caused so much trouble. Dubois, however, was desperate for German-speaking priests. Unbeknownst to the seminarian who had set sail from Le Havre with no place to go, the Bishop of New York had answered a letter from Father Reiss, saying he would accept this ill-organized and adventurous youth.

In the spring of 1836 he arrived in the city and wandered about in a driving rain with one dollar in his pocket. He spent the night at an inn, and the next morning found the house of Bishop Dubois. Explaining his case, the short, fresh faced, twenty-five-year-old asked to borrow money that he might travel westward to be a missionary for Indians.

*Bruté was in Rome.

To his surprise the bishop smiled and told him that he would give him money to go westward, but to Buffalo where he wanted him to serve as a priest to the German immigrants. In the meantime he boarded him in his own home and, as a test before ordination, assigned him to Father John Raffeiner at the German parish of St. Nicholas in the city. There, reflecting the priority Dubois placed upon the education of children, he was told to prepare a class to receive first Holy Communion.

He worked well. On June 25th, less than a month after his arrival Dubois ordained him a priest. His first Mass was a festival for children; at it his students received the Eucharist for the first time. The case gave evidence that a bishop sometimes has to take a gamble with candidates. This priest worked out well. His name was John Nepomucene Neumann. He eventually became Bishop of Philadelphia. Like Elizabeth Seton whom Dubois established in her apostolate, Neumann lived a life of such heroic sanctity that in the century after his death he was canonized a saint by the Catholic Church.

"Our good and esteemed brother in New York is also in trouble," Bruté wrote his friend Bishop Rosati, "It's with his own clergy. I have counselled him early to have a coadjutor under him, but whom would be agreeable to him, to strengthen him. But his demand must come from himself although it appears that his enemies flatter themselves that they are doing the counselling . . ."[77]

Bruté worried more about Dubois' enemies than Dubois did, and told his brother that he was sure someone was breaking into his room to examine his correspondence. Dubois brushed this off ("It has been the case once but I prevented it"). The leak in information was evident to him. John England, he explained, "is devoted to Rev. Mr. Power." The Bishop of Charleston made a habit of passing along to his friend information which bishops shared confidentially with one another as peers.[78] That was all.

Power still saw himself as material for a bishopric, and his constant popularity with the public encouraged him. He was an excellent preacher. On one occasion after he gave a charity sermon a fashionable lady took off a diamond ring and threw it into the collection. When Georgetown gave him a doctor of divinity degree, John England's *U.S. Catholic Miscellany* said that "disrespect to others" was not meant as it modestly weighed Power's contribution to Catholicism in New York.

"He is its life and soul,"[79] declared England's paper.

Power was beside himself when yet another Frenchman, Bruté, was made bishop. He complained to Father Cullen that given the "eccentric" conduct of Bruté, "his learning appears to be like a lamp in a sepulchre."[80]

For a decade's time he had fought against Dubois. Now that Dubois was convinced that "near the grave as I am"[81] a coadjutor bishop was needed, Power might well have regretted that he had not ingratiated himself to the old man. There was no way that Dubois was going to be convinced that Power should be his auxiliary. He tried once again—this time with something of a last chance desperation—to stack opinion against Dubois' wishes, writing to Rome himself and employing his allies to do the same. John McGerry admitted, at least, that the great problem lay in Dubois not being helped "by those who should be his advisors." His remedy, however, would have been no remedy.

"Could it be the very Rev. Dr. Power were appointed his coadjutor and all would then go well."

"Unfortunately," he added, "there are those who endeavor to persuade the good bishop to the contrary."[82]

By this time the good bishop did not need to be persuaded. He opened his mind to John Purcell. Dubois would generally address a mountaineer as 'My dear child.' Now that Purcell had grown into a peer as a bishop the affectionate Frenchman began his letter to him, "My dear little brother":

"I was going to write a formal Latin letter to you respecting the application which I had made to the Congregation de Propaganda Fide for a co-adjutor when my good angel checked me saying, is it so that you must do for a bosom friend?"

Dubois then described his "very delicate situation."

"An immense population, chiefly Irish, headed by an ambitious, crafty, unhappily unprincipled though very talented and on this account very popular clergyman who has used every means to lower in public estimation every clergyman who he thought might be in his way to the episcopal throne . . ."

Without hesitating he told the County Cork-born Purcell: "I wish to gratify the Irish as much as possible," but added:

"You know the clannish disposition of the Irish for their countrymen how worthless so ever they may be. I pointed the necessity of sparing that propensity by the appointment of an *Irish name* and at the same time the importance of having that *name* corrected by American habits and education."

Even then he was bypassing his own wants. Had he wished a "friendly companion, I would have preferred Mr. [Charles Constantine] Pise, the child of my early affection." He could see however that Pise was "giddy, light, too fond of company" and lacking "that vigor of mind to ride the storm."*

---

*That Pise was a light weight and would have been prey to ridicule is evidenced by the constant lampooning opportunities he afforded James Gordon Bennett. Observing that this clergyman's "sonnetts, madrigals and poetic effusions" had "bewitched half the maiden ladies about town" Bennett decided: "The celibacy which the Church of Rome inflicts upon her ministers has a favorable effect in preserving their amorous feelings always fresh, delicate and blooming. Their whole life is a honeymoon. Look at the Protestant clergy. They marry as the heathen does and hence they become commonplace and dull as plodding husbands generally are."[84]

Instead he opted for a Pennsylvania-born member of St. Vincent de Paul's Vincentian fathers, John Timon "Whom I never saw and know only by reputation."

"By presenting Mr. Timon of an Irish family and born in this country," he decided, "we reconcile both parties."[83]

Not if Power could help it. When John McCloskey left to study in Italy, he carried with him letters from his bishop. Unbeknownst to Dubois he also carried letters from Power ("What my convictions are, you already sufficiently know,"[85] the young priest assured the Vicar General.) McCloskey's duplicity won him some frosty advice from a cardinal when he arrived in Rome.

"I am credibly informed," McCloskey wrote Power, "that owing to particular circumstances with which I am not acquainted, the Cardinals in general have become more cautious in conversing with private clergymen on ecclesiastical matters of any importance."[86]

Power tried to get Cullen to work against Dubois' petition.

"If his wishes be acceded to by the Holy See," he wrote, "time will show the result . . . the utter destruction of Catholicity and good will towards the Holy See here."[87]

Timon was kept for a position of authority within the Vincentian order. Thus, in another petition Dubois asked for the gentlemanly Francis Kenrick of Philadelphia. As an alternative he mentioned the possibility of the now famous, two-fisted John Hughes.

England was off to rescue his friend. In New York, writing ahead that he was on his way to Rome, and adding the "hope for his own sake that Doctor Dubois is only deranged," he predicted the complete ruin of the diocese "under its present (shall I call it?) system."

"The great object of the bishop," he said "is to shut out the only man who, in my opinion, ought to be at the head of the Church here—of course you know I mean Power."[88]

Bennett, aware of the ongoing Power struggle, added public fuel to the fire after England spoke at St. Patrick's. Hailing him as "the greatest Catholic orator perhaps of this or any other country," the *Herald* editorialized:

"We wish Bishop England were the metropolitan of this diocese and Bishop Dubois were at his former occupation, embroidering petticoats for the Blessed Virgin."[89]

Bruté, as Bishop of Vincennes, sent his opinion of the matter. In his usual rambling, self-contradictory style he both endorsed Power and yet stipulated: "There should be no nomination of a coadjutor against his [Dubois'] will." However muddled his prose, Bruté left no doubt as to whose corner he was in.

One ought not to forget," he admonished, "that already since 1791, for forty-five years, Monseigneur Dubois has

been a special benefactor and the chief of our founders of
Churches in America—known to all for his Faith, discipline,
doctrine, piety, zeal, poverty, complete self abnegation,
the indefatigable father and teacher of young clergy for
twenty-five years—likewise the real founder of the Sisters of
Charity although the first plans were initiated through
Monseigneurs Dubourg and Carroll with the celebrated
convert to the Faith the widow Seton.[90]

In April, 1837, the bishops met for another provincial Council at Baltimore, and a foremost piece of business was the nomination of Dubois'
coadjutor. He remained in New York, sending as his procurator Felix
Varela. At the council, Varela wrote bitterly to Dubois that John England
barred his acting as a true representative and had him "reduced to the
status of a non-entity."[91]

Still, the victory was not to be England's. The constant machinations of
his candidate had not helped his reputation. John Hughes, present at the
council as a theologian, had observed earlier to one of the bishops that
Power was "guilty of transactions which would go to show a want of in-
tegrity in matters even of the spiritual order which would destroy all confidence."[92]

The observation was significant because Power would soon become
Hughes' subordinate. Philadelphia's fighting pastor was riding a crest of
popularity owing to the Breckinridge debates and, when the decision was
made, he was the man nominated for New York. John England balked.

"I have on that account not signed the recommendation," he wrote, "—
as the object is to shut Power out and I fear the discontent of the people."[93]

Contentment was not what New York was made of at the moment. As
the Council convened the nation was sliding a total financial crash, result-
ing in no small amount from Jackson's war with the Bank of the United
States. Hard times exacerbated feelings which were already hard. Nativism
had not softened. The *Protestant Vindicator* declared that evidence given
by a janitor proved that there were "dungeons under the Prince Street
Masshouse."

"What means these walls thirty-five feet below the surface of the
ground," the paper reasoned, ". . . and what means the vaults if they are
dungeons."[94]

Not long afterwards the cathedral was broken into, the tabernacle torn
open and a ciborium stolen. The enclosed hosts were strewn about the
building.

Trustees continued to flaunt their financial power. When he sent a newly
ordained priest as an assistant to Utica in December 1836, the trustees
refused to allot the young man a salary and Dubois had to reassign him.
After two years of fighting with the trustees at St. Joseph's in Manhattan,
the pastor, James Cummiskey resigned. They sued him for eighteen hundred

dollars in back rent. His annual salary was eight hundred dollars. Dubois assigned Pise in his place and when they hassled the new pastor, Dubois suspended all sacred functions. The trustees set up a committee to guard against Pise leaving with the furniture. The *Protestant Vindicator* hailed this as "A little revolution in New York Popery."

"The very bishop, the vicar of the pope—yes—even him have the trustees set at defiance," the paper declared, "The brave Irish laymen sustained their claims as trustees and gained a victory."[95]

Levins remained a thorn in Dubois' side. During the several years of his suspension he tried at first to placate the bishop. Forgetting that they had been his exact words, he apologized in 1835 to Dubois for "expressing in a moment of great irritation words which were interpreted by you into a 'declaration of war'."[96]

He asked to say Mass again. Dubois insisted upon one very proper condition: that he quit the cathedral for any other church in the city. He also insisted upon a condition reflective of the pennypinching bent which had always grated upon his subordinates—that Levins return a cassock that belonged to St. Patrick's.[97]

Levins hedged at leaving the cathedral. It was his turf. To move would have been a public admission that he was at fault. The feud continued with Levins still under suspension. In the interim he was employed as an engineer during construction of the Croton aqueduct. He also continued as head of the parish school, and published a surprisingly docile newspaper *The Green Banner* which even printed Dubois' pastoral letters. Levins pleaded to Rome that Dubois had readily forgiven other priests "notoriously guilty of the most gross offenses against morality" while insisting "that he would lay my non restoration as an injunction on his successor in the diocese."[98]

There was no doubt that the confrontation between Levins and Dubois had become a problem of personalities. Unfortunately for Dubois, Rome saw this but failed to see that Levins' refusal to leave the cathedral was a public issue directly involving Dubois' spiritual authority. In December of 1836 Dubois received word from Rome that he was to reinstate Levins. It was an utter defeat of a leader before his subordinates.

In frustration, he balked, and sent off a letter in the slow moving mails asking that his own reasons be reconsidered.

In that same month Dubois issued a statement forbidding the formation of a group organized for the purpose of debates: "The New York Catholic society for the promotion of religious knowledge."

"How can it be supposed," he asked "that young men whose education is chiefly mercantile or mechanical can come with sufficient preparation to the discussion of a question that requires vast erudition with a degree of research which they cannot possess?"

Labelling this a "bona fide interdict" of "a foreigner by birth," the *Journal of Commerce* asked in turn:

"Now when these laymen, the servants, the slaves (Do I slander them?) of a foreign master boast to you of religious liberty, what kind of definition do you think they can give of it."[100]

The *Protestant Vindicator* urged rebellion: "Come forward and boldly tell the tyrant, your soi-disant bishop, that you will read and discuss . . . or come forward and tell the public that you have surrendered your liberties into the tyrant's hands."*[101]

Combining both the Levins and debating society issues the *Herald* admitted that "Mr. Levins might have erred, perhaps injured his religious superior," but found it unjust "that a man of erudition should be controlled by one so inferior to him."

The bishop, Bennett decided "has done more in one month to injure the Catholic cause in this city than Brownlee, Hoyt, Slocum and Co could effect in a year with all the prostitutes in the Five Points at their heels."

"You have occupied the stage long enough," the *Herald* ordered Dubois, "and tired your audience though you could never either delight or instruct them. Now, make your exit."[102]

His college burned to the ground, trustees and priests arranged against him, his authority in shambles, Dubois left the city on his routine diocesan visitation. It was more than just duty which impelled him to go; in the outer regions of his diocese, where priestly visitations were infrequent and where he was more of a missionary than an administrator he had always been a welcome sight to his people.

During his visitation of 1837, a young priest, probably William Quarter, accompanied him and sent home regular reports of the Bishop's progress.

At Rome, N.Y., Dubois visited the church, "a small wooden building situated between the canal and the village" and gave the large assembled crowd his advice on how to answer the current rage of Nativist calumnies.

"Do well," he told them, "and thereby silence the ignorance of foolish men."

The community provided the bishop with a carriage to his next stop. At Turin, thirty miles further north in Oneida County, he preached on the feast of his lifelong spiritual guide St. Vincent de Paul.

"It would seem," understates his chronicler, "as if the festival brought

---

*Ironically, not long after this Brownlee's *Vindicator* betrayed a clericalism at least as strong as that of which it accused the Catholic bishop. Noting that "a few years ago [Dr. Brownlee] caused a challenge to be entered before the public, against Bishop Dubois and his priests," the paper explained: "This was done to bring out a responsible name, as Dr. Brownlee would not enter the lists with a Roman Catholic layman."

back to the bishop's recollection some pleasing reminiscences of bye gone days."

The young priest marveled at the growth of religion around Rochester, Buffalo, and the western districts of the state. Lancaster was blocked to the bishop by rains which made the roads impassable. With the difficulties of bad weather and the worse roads, Dubois' assistant expected his superior to be exhausted "at his advanced age. But so far from being the case, the flush of rude health is still on his cheek, his voice bespeaks a vigorous constitution."

Whenever he administered the Sacrament of Confirmation he exhorted, in "moving language the children that were assembled around him, on the importance of careful preparation. He addressed the adults on the duties of their respective stations in life."[103]

Back in the city in September Dubois rejoiced to Rose White that a school had been completed at the orphanage to replace one lost in fire. It was ready to receive "my innumerable poor little children who . . . have been wandering around like so many birds out of the nest."

"Next Sunday a week," he reminded her, "will be the fiftieth anniversary of my ordination to the priesthood. What an account I will have to render."

For once, New York rose to an occasion on his behalf. He hoped that some of the priests whom he had trained at the Mountain might come but doubted that they could, "scattered as they are throughout the various parts of the states."[104]

Nonetheless thirty-four priests were on hand, a considerable number given the inconveniences of travel. Five thousand people came to celebrate at St. Patrick's, and as many as could fit inside listened to John Hughes preach.

The *U.S. Catholic Miscellany,* understating the event noted:

"To be engaged for fifty years in discharging the functions of the Holy ministry in a country like this is certainly no ordinary occurrence."[105] Which was to say nothing of the French Revolution and his ministry to an insane asylum previous to that, in Paris.

67

New York City (Broadway) in 1834, as it looked in Bishop Dubois' final years. (Drawing by T. Horner)

68

When John Dubois was Bishop of New York, anti-Catholic agitation occasioned fierce debates in the press and on stage. After his death, as these 1844 woodcuts indicate, mob violence increased and more Catholic property was attacked and destroyed.

69

TRUTH IS POWERFUL,

AND WILL PREVAIL.

VOL. V. NEW-YORK, SATURDAY, SEPTEMBER 5, 1829. NO. 36.

IRELAND.

POOR LAWS—MEETING AT CLARA.

[FROM THE DUBLIN REGISTER]

The general feeling of the Irish peasantry for that all-important measure, a modified system of poor laws, was very fully developed in the neighbourhood of Clara on Thursday last.

Samuel Robinson, Esq., one of the Society of Friends, having by a life of philanthropy endeared himself to the sharp-sighted and intelligent peasantry for miles around his residence, at Clara, had

greater rent for their lands, and still, strange to say, they are reluctant to promote employment or alleviate the distress of the Irish poor, although by absence from this soil they are free both here and elsewhere from all manner of taxation. Let us, therefore, my beloved countrymen, inform the people of England, our best friends, that our landed proprietors are like the dog in the manger—they will neither improve their own estates nor allow their poor countrymen to do it for them; but light will, it must, break forth.

Look my countrymen, to the reported proceedings of the Imperial Parliament, and there view with delight the positions taken in your respect by H. V. Stuart, Charles Brownlow, James Grattan, the

There are many more adducible arguments, the recital of which would still further prove the great necessity of a modified system of poor laws; but, suffice it to draw your attention before I conclude, to the United States of America, which, I hope will arouse the apathy of those in influence here—where 30 years since stood an immense forest, is now the great town of Utica, having two daily posts, with nineteen public coaches, running in and out of it every day, whose poorest inhabitants can purchase in quantities, beef, butter, flour, sugar, coffee and tea—whilst the most of you, my struggling and beloved countrymen, are confined to a *lumper potatoe*; therefore, throw yourselves on the mercy of the British nation, let

70

The Truth Teller, *an Irish-Catholic newspaper published in his own diocese, did little to support Bishop Dubois, and was often hostile to him. James Gordon Bennett (1795–1872)* below *was a Catholic who founded the New York* Herald. *His paper consistently lampooned the Catholic clergy.*

71

72

73

Bishop Dubois made several missionary journeys throughout his vast diocese. Above left, he was in Rochester, N.Y. at least four times and would have known St. Patrick's (second church, 1832); above right, St. John's Church, Newark, New Jersey (1828) helped with funds intended for building a seminary; below, St. Vincent de Paul Church in Rosiere, N.Y. (Ogdensburg Diocese) where Bishop Dubois laid the cornerstone for the Church in 1832.

74

NEW-YORK WEEKLY REGISTER

AND

CATHOLIC DIARY.

" ALL THINGS WHATSOEVER YOU WOULD THAT MEN SHOULD DO UNTO YOU, DO YOU ALSO TO THEM."

VOLUME III.]	SATURDAY, NOVEMBER 15, 1834.	[NUMBER 7.

CHURCH OF OUR LADY OF COLD SPRING.

(Drawn by Weir—engraved by Adams.)

We herewith present our readers with a sketch by our friend Weir, of the Catholic chapel of " Our Lady of Cold Spring," one of the most classical and beautiful little churches we have ever seen. The building is of brick, coloured with a composition which gives it the character and appearance of a light, yellowish-brown stone; and the portico, which is of the Tuscan order, of the most correct proportions. Its situation, opposite West Point, on a high rock overhanging the Hudson, and surrounded by majestic mountains, is extremely well chosen; and the traveller, sailing up and down the river, cannot but be struck with its romantic beauty.

It was our fortune to be present at the consecration of this little temple, a few weeks since,* by the Right. Rev. Bishop Dubois, assisted by the Rev. Messrs. Power, Varela, and O'Reilly. The scene was most impressive. It was a calm sabbath morning, full of quiet and repose, accompanied by a slight haziness of the atmosphere, that communicated a soft and gentle hue to the surrounding hills, and disposed the mind to corresponding impressions. It was in the midst of the most majestic of His works, that a temple was to be consecrated to the God of nature and of nations. The area within being insufficient to contain the visitors and congregation, many of the latter might be seen kneeling without on the hard rock, and offering up their silent devotions. Religion never looked more solemn or more divine, than when its rites were thus administered on the rock of ages. Choristers responded to the strains of the amiable and venerable bishop, whose gray hairs added dignity to his devotion, and a fine band of music attended, whose notes might be heard in the recesses of the mountains. It was a scene we shall not soon and wish never to forget, for it was full of lofty inspiration, accompanied by associations of religion, of charity, and of philanthropy.

We could not help cherishing the hope, that the erection of this chaste and elegant little building, might form the commencement of an era of good-will amongst all religious denominations. It seemed to us like the temple of peace; as the shrine where all who worship the same God, and depend for salvation on the same Saviour, might come and lay down that load of unchristian antipathies which has separated mankind into inveterate factions, and deluged the earth with blood. Its history should be told, that the example may be followed.

The village of Cold Spring and its neighbourhood, from various causes, had become the

* Sunday the twenty-first of September.

residence of a large number of poor Irish Catholics, and though there are churches of various denominations at that place, there was not one to which they could resort without hearing their faith questioned, and the objects of their veneration called by the most approbrious names, agreeably to the orthodox practice of too many of the preachers of that religion which is all charity, all philanthropy, all love to our fellow-creatures.

These people were too poor to provide themselves with a place of worship, and to none are the rights of their religion more important to their social habits and morals, than the labouring classes of the Catholic church. In this state of things, a gentleman, having large interests in the neighbourhood, Mr. Gouverneur Kemble, (we hope he will pardon us for mentioning his name,) came forward to their assistance. He gave them the ground on which the church stands, and a considerable portion of the means for its erection, besides furnishing the plan, and giving a paternal superintendence to its progress and completion. The indefatigable exertions of the Rev. Mr. O'Reilly, pastor of the congregation, supplied the remaining funds. Mr. Kemble is a Protestant, and so are we; but this shall not prevent our bearing testimony to the liberal and philanthropic spirit, which, overlooking the metaphysical refinements of religion, resorts to its spirit and essence, and recognizes all the worshippers of one Creator, and one Saviour of the world, as fellow-creatures and fellow-christians, who, however they may differ in modes and forms, look up to the same eternal source in this life, and the life everlasting.

Convenience and necessity are often found in conflict with the natural taste of mankind for the picturesque and beautiful; and in nothing

more remarkably so, than in the location of religious edifices. If it were possible, we would always have our houses of worship isolated from the busy haunts of traffic and of pleasure. In cities this can never be effected; but in the country we delight to see the sanctuaries of religion standing apart from amid the common scenes and objects of worldly care and interest and occupation. They should be held sacred from all sights and sounds of earthly import; the solemn stillness of their presence can only harmonize with the murmur of the breezes, the mysterious rustling of the foliage, and the thousand soothing tones of nature's music. The walk to the house of God should be through smiling fields, shaded by the verdant luxuriance of forest trees—the atmosphere that floats around should be the pure, fresh air of heaven, breathing serenity and peace; the objects that it offers to the eye should be only such as invite to serious meditation, with no intruding incident or object of the world's contaminating impress, to break the chain of humble aspiration, that would lead to heavenly things. The throne of religion is man's heart; but nature, in her calm, untrammelled beauty, is religion's meetest empire.

From Andrews' Orthodox Journal.

CATHOLIC INSTITUTIONS AT MANCHESTER.

The disappointment and mortification we experienced at sending before the public an engraving of St. Patrick's Catholic Church at Manchester, without an accompanying description of the noble edifice, have been in some measure alleviated by the receipt of some information of the progress which Catholic education is making in that town. Such information must afford unspeakable delight and gratification to the sincere friend of useful instruction and unerring truth; and it is therefore with great pleasure we communicate the same to our readers. The enemies of our unspotted and invulnerable Church are reluctantly compelled to acknowledge, and they do so with bitter and sorrowful lamentations, that she is making the most marvellous progress throughout this island. To Catholics it is not so much a matter of wonderment, since infinite wisdom has declared that her sound shall be heard to the utmost corners of the earth, and that the powers of hell shall not prevail against her. In the primitive ages, she spread herself to every quarter of the globe, notwithstanding the sword of the heathen powers was let loose upon her children, and the earth was deluged with their blood. In these our own days we behold her triumphant not only over penal laws and sanguinary persecutions, but over the basest calumnies and falsehoods, for-

75

The New York Weekly Register and Catholic Diary *was a Catholic weekly which supported Bishop Dubois. The issue* above *describes his appearance at Cold Spring, New York to dedicate the new church in 1834.*

Mother Mary Rose (Landry) White (1784–1841) a Sister of Charity, directed the Orphan Asylum in New York.

76

Below, *Rev. John McCloskey (1810–1885), an alumnus of the "Mountain" as he appeared in 1835. He became Archbishop of New York and the first American cardinal.*

77

78

A French cartoon (above) depicted the dreaded Asiatic Cholera in the form of the devil. It spread throughout New York in 1832 causing the death of thousands. Below, fire was an ever-present danger in New York. In the famous fire of 1835, in which much property was destroyed, Catholic institutional property was spared.

79

DIOCESS OF NEW YORK.

In 1810, his holiness Pope pious the seventh created the See of New York, and appointed for the first Bishop thereof Right Rev. Luke Concanon, who was succeeded by the Right Rev. John Connolly, upon whose demise the present Prelate, the Right Rev. John Dubois was promoted to the Episcopal chair, and consecrated in Baltimore, by the Most Rev. Ambrose Marechal, in 1826. This Diocess comprises the State of New York, and the Eastern part of New Jersey.

CHURCHES IN THE STATE OF NEW YORK.

The Cathedral, is a magnificent edifice, one hundred and twenty feet long by eighty feet wide, and capable of containing six thousand persons. It is served by the Right Rev. Bishop, Rev. C. Levins, &c. Mass daily.

Saint Peters is served by the very Rev. John Power, N. G. &c. Mass daily.

Saint Mary's is served by Rev. W. Quarter, &c. Mass daily.

Christ Church is served by Rev. F. Varella, &c. Mass daily.

St. John's Church, Greenwhich Vlliage, James Cummiskey.

St. James', Brooklyn, Long Island, is served by Rev. John Walsh.

The Congregation at Poughkeepsee, is served by the Rev. J. Reilly.

The Congregation at Albany, is served by the Rev. C. Smith.

At Troy, by the Rev. J. Shanahan.

At Lansingburg. by the Rev. John Shanahan.

At Buffaloe, by the Rev. N. Mertz.

At Carthage, by the Rev. James Cahill.

At Ogdensburg, St. Laurencer Co. by the Rev. J, Salmon.

At Rochester, by the Rev. J. F. McGerry.

At Salina, by the Rev. F. Danshue.

At Shenectady by the Rev. Charles Smith, once a month.

At Utica, by the Rev. John Reilly.

NEW JERSEY.

The Congregation at Newark, is served by the Rev. G. Pardow.

Trenton, by the Rev. P. Rafferty.

Above, *the entire listing for the Diocese of New York in 1834, taken from the* Catholic Directory *of that year. It consisted of merely one page, although its territory included all of New York State and part of New Jersey.*

CHAPTER 15

The Spotless Life and Apostolic Labors of My Old Father

It was not displeasing to Dubois when John Hughes was appointed as his coadjutor, for as Bruté noted, "he is fond of Mr. Hughes."[1] Yet, Hughes, who instinctively knew the workings of power, was wary of what his position might be in New York. For years in Philadelphia he had watched Kenrick as coadjutor, embarrassed and put at a public disadvantage by crazy old Conwell. The octogenarian bishop repeatedly announced to the public that full authority had been returned to him. He aligned himself with the trustees who had been his previous enemies, and once even had Bishop Kenrick's furniture moved out of the episcopal house while he was on a diocesan visitation.

Hughes, in his usual blunt manner wrote to Dubois and questioned him about their working relationship. Surprised—a little hurt—Dubois answered that he would never encroach upon Hughes' rights and privileges:

> That scandals should have arisen between Bishop Conwell
> and his coadjutor, who is ex-officio sole administrator of
> the diocese, is no small wonder, with a man of the bishop's
> disposition; but I am neither reduced to the nullity of Bishop
> Conwell—a circumstance rather painful to human
> pride—nor would I be disposed to struggle for the mastery
> if I had been placed in his situation. I would have considered

this nullity as a warning from the divine goodness that
henceforth all my time must be exclusively devoted
to my preparation for death . . .[2]

Whatever drama might have been enacted with the genteel Dubois and
the roughened street fighter Hughes together as a team, it was never played
out. In the first week of 1838, in St. Patrick's Church Dubois consecrated
as bishop the Irish youth whom twenty years earlier he had hired as an
overseer. In the last week of January Dubois and his coadjutor consecrated
St. Paul's Church in Brooklyn. Together then, they visited Philadelphia.
While there Dubois suffered a minor stroke. Though told by those around
him that he was seriously ill, the old man refused to hear of it. He had
never in his life given into illness, and he would not let it slow him down
now. Marshalling his energies, he returned to New York and tried to
resume work. Within two weeks of his return he was felled by another, far
more serious stroke. This time his body and even the energies of his mind
would not respond to the demands of his spirit. For weeks he lay in bed,
bewildered, his memory failing to serve him yet his perception of the present
remaining clear. His right side was partially paralyzed.

So, too, was the business of the episcopacy. John Hughes pressed him
to delegate his responsibilities. Stubborn as always, Dubois refused. He
would exercise his authority as he always had, as soon as his energies returned. In May he suffered yet another stroke. The limits to which he could
carry on a visitation of his diocese now consisted in being helped across
the street to the orphanage. There, seated outside in the sunlight, he played a
grandfather's role with the children. Beginning with the summer of 1838,
John Hughes was the missionary bishop whom Catholics might expect to
see travelling the backwoods of the large diocese.

As winter returned Dubois felt that he had the strength and was determined to preside at episcopal functions. As remembered by a Sister of
Charity:

"For the priests to get the bishop and crozier up to the platform from
his throne, took full five minutes, to pronounce the words five more, to
guide the tottering steps back to the seat five more, while we spectators
had a quiver in our hearts all through, dreading what might happen."[3]

Yet, on another occasion, *The Truth Teller* though it found the bishop to
be "very feeble" reported:

"His voice is not strong but yet effective, his singing is very correct and
his piety calculated to impress those present with a reverence for his
person."[4]

To a report from Hughes of his brother's condition Bruté answered,
"what you say of Bishop Dubois affected me to tears."

The painful picture of such sufferings brought a sharp contrast to his
mind:

"... the painful task of three or four lines for him who made, you know, so readily and properly the immense correspondences of the Mountain, ... so remarkable for his letters to parents, his views, his manner of treating their sons with their very affection. Ah Bishop Dubois, Mr. Dubois! What a life! Now I have to wipe my eyes, else I can't write."[5]

John Hughes may have been carefully solicitious when writing to Bruté, but this man of natural leadership abilities wanted to exercise needed authority. He was frustrated. The diocese cried out for strong discipline.

The long running rebellion of the Irish clergy was exacerbated by the easy going manner in which Dubois had accepted wandering clergymen.

"The good bishop, though possessing discrimination enough," wrote Hughes to Purcell, "too often allowed the heart rather than the judgement to decide on such applications."[6] Hughes would never rule by the heart.

To Samuel Eccleston the new Archbishop of Baltimore, Hughes wrote: "I am bound to unburden my mind . . .[Bishop Dubois'] impressions on all subjects are feeble and brief. In a word his mind is so relaxed that, whatever he was heretofore, he is that no longer. As to myself, I have not been and am not now of any more use in the matter of assisting him than when I was in Philadelphia. He never asks my opinion but on the contrary seems glad of every opportunity to prove to himself and others that he does not stand in any need of it."[7]

At the beginning of 1839, after Dubois had another, near fatal attack, Hughes wrote to the Propaganda Fide. He was no John Power, malicious and willing to carve away Dubois' reputation with lies. Hughes was in pursuit of an object: control of authority in New York. Dubois simply stood in the way. Coldly, Hughes laid out facts about the old man's "practical determination to leave undone what he cannot do himself." He wanted, almost demanded, that authority be given to himself for the good of the Church.

"Of course all the honors should remain with the Bishop. I speak only of the powers for the active government of the diocese. I have no hesitation in saying that Bishop Dubois has been incompetent to discharge them, at least since this time twelve months. And if he were conscious of his true state I do not see how in conscience he could continue to attempt or pretend to do it."[8]

At this precise moment a situation arose which demanded a strong hand. The war of several years duration waged between Levins along with the cathedral trustees against the bishop, once again erupted in active battle. The still suspended Levins, as head of the parish religious school, not only fired a teacher hired by Dubois, but employed a constable to enter and evict him from his classroom. When Hughes from the pulpit the next Sunday demanded an apology from the trustees, Levins tested the strength of this newcomer by brazenly passing out, between Masses, leaflets explaining his position.

Within days New York resounded with the mortar blast of a pastoral letter, signed by John Dubois but written in a blistering style which was the very antithesis of what the diocese was accustomed to hearing from their bishop.

"A civil officer . . . ," the letter charged, "entering the sanctuary of religious instruction and seizing or ready to seize one of the teachers with the same hands which perhaps had been last employed in grasping the night vagabond or the public thief! What an example for these children. What a humiliation to our religion in the midst of a community prejudiced against it."[9]

Hughes called for a meeting of parishioners, and before an assemblage of some seven hundred people he excoriated the trustees. This Irishman, who was a master at demagoguery, spoke to his own and likened the trustees to the British parliament using the civil law to destroy the Catholic religion. Under such a system, he warned, "there is no security. They may send their constable when and where they will to remove Catechist, priest, or bishop . . ."[10]

No one dared to oppose this strong charismatic leader. He threw out a series of counter-resolutions to be endorsed by those faithful to proper authority. A frightened John Power scurried to be the first to sign. The trustees gave in to Hughes' will: Levins was finished. Placing the man squarely under his thumb, Hughes reinstated him and then—no ifs, ands or buts,—shipped him up the river—and out the way—to a Church in Albany. In one night's work John Hughes had reached out and grasped absolute authority. He would maintain that grasp without once relaxing it among the Catholics of New York for a quarter of a century.

All of this was accomplished under the name of John Dubois. To Mark Frenaye, the adventurer who had been returned to his faith by the gentle Dubois, the flushed warrior Hughes exulted: "The poor old bishop is revenged for their treatment of him. He can hardly believe it."[11]

In spring Dubois was taken on a visit to Emmitsburg. When his carriage arrived from Gettysburg, several of the sisters ran halfway down to the gate to greet him. He remained for a week. One of the sisters noted that he was "very feeble." He had to rest frequently. On Sunday he wanted to say Mass at the Mountain chapel which he had built in the full vigor of manhood. Now he was unable to climb the path, and had to be persuaded to say Mass at the bottom of the hill.[12]

In Vincennes, Bruté himself seriously ill, wrote to one of the Sisters of Charity:

"Oh the situation of our common friend and father; the father, indeed who gave to our Church of America such a family as yours, and that numerous clergy, the hundred almost wanting, his children priests . . . The last faint effort, however, of his humbled state; all rejoicing to perceive and improve the moments left to perfect his sacrifice . . . Bishop Dubois—such a model of duty, best duty, and all duty to the last."[13]

"... all duty to the last." Just as the brothers Dubois and Bruté had mutually complained about their shared stubborn streaks and foibles of every order, so too Bruté's praise was easily turned back upon himself. He died on June 26, 1838, actively serving his people at Vincennes even in his final illness.

In August, Archbishop Eccleston received an order from Rome removing Dubois from the jurisdiction of his diocese. Because this order followed near enough in memory to the removal of Conwell, a careful distinction was made. It was to be given out that the faithful Dubois had asked for retirement. The archbishop decided not to forward the letter but to personally carry it to New York. Providentially, Hughes was away and even more providentially Dubois' "little brother" John Purcell was in the city. Nonetheless, there was no way to prepare the old man for the news. He was stunned.

"What wrong have I done?" he pleaded, "They cannot take away my authority unless I am guilty of a crime. I will never give it up, never."[14]

They reasoned with him. Purcell finally got down on his knees and begged his old teacher to see what had to be done. What was at stake was not an individual good but the good of the Church. Dubois could not turn away from this. As he used the third person so often in his pastoral letters, so he afterwards described his own submission.

"He obeyed the bit," he wrote, "but not till he had covered it with foam."[15]

He could not conceal his resentment about Hughes, who had fought so eagerly to grasp power. Untypically, after a lifetime of effusively making peace after differences with others, he could not warm up to the cold "Mr. Hughes,"—the title which he thereafter used in referring to him. Immediately after this the new bishop took up the project of a college and bought, in place of the Nyack farm, an estate at Rose Hill at Fordham. When the announcement was made to the public and Hughes given total credit for the plan, someone mentioned to Dubois that the public did not yet really know who Hughes was; Dubois responded drily:

"Ah, but they soon will know him."[16]

His life's work was finished. He had once told Hughes that if he ever became a "nullity" such as Conwell he would take it "as a warning from the divine goodness that henceforth all my time must be exclusively devoted to my preparation for death ..."

This was the only work to be left to him.

In May of 1838 Talleyrand died. The wily old chameleon had beaten the hand of every regime in France since he had scandalized the Paris of Dubois' youth. As he was dying he was reconciled to the Church, but as the Abbé who annointed him reached for the palms of his hands, the rite for a layman, Talleyrand stopped him, turned to him the back of the hands and said:

"You forget, I am a bishop."[17]

If Dubois heard this story he might have wondered that the mercy of God so easily let a man have his cake and eat it too.

Dubois had poured himself out for the Church and had been cast aside in his old age. Talleyrand, whose exile to American had coincided with Dubois; had used the Church—as he had all society—to foster his own advantage. After decades of living without the Church he had died grabbing on to the prerogatives of a bishop. Nonetheless, if he wondered at this at all, the seventy-five-year-old Dubois had seen far too many ironies in life to care.

Purcell was haunted by the emotional scene of which he had been part. He unburdened himself to another bishop:

". . . The spotless life and apostolic labors of my old father deserved that his grey hairs should be brought down with more honor to the grave. I had lamented Bishop Bruté's death almost inconsolably. But compared to such a fate it is rather to be envied."[18]

Almost immediately after gaining full authority, Hughes left on a begging tour of Europe. In Rome the brash young bishop had an audience with Gregory XVI. Before Hughes could set forth himself and what he planned to do in New York, the Pope stopped him and asked about Bishop Dubois. This was the man who as head of the Propaganda Fide had made himself Dubois' "special friend" during his Rome visit. He had signed the order for the old man's forced retirement. Now he quickly reminded Hughes that he was still Dubois' "special friend" and charged him to bring Dubois his blessings and affection.

Hughes' absence for the better part of a year gave Dubois a reprieve before total retirement. Small notices dotted throughout the newspapers gave evidences that he was still capable of the sacramental work of a bishop. In May of 1840 the *U.S. Catholic Miscellany* reported that he confirmed two hundred people at St. James Church in the City: "He presided at High Mass, visited the Sunday schools in the evening, sang vespers and gave benediction of the Blessed Sacrament."[19] In July the *Catholic Register* noted that he consecrated a church in Williamsburg, New York, and administered Confirmation.

He was not the only who was busy. John Power had found an issue with which to exercise leadership. During that spring he began to rally support against the anti-Catholic policies of the public school system. John Hughes arrived back home two days before a public meeting called by Power. He liked the issue and decided that if anyone was going to voice leadership in such a campaign it would be himself—and only himself. John Power was finished as a public figure.

This issue—with its resultant banning of religious instruction from state

funded schools—brought about public clashes and full scale riots throughout the 1840s. It heightened John Hughes' popularity with Catholic immigrants ("New York has long had need of such a man . . ."[20] declared the
callous *U.S. Catholic Miscellany* while Dubois was still up and about)
and won him the full hatred of Nativists. James Gordon Bennett who hated
him simply for his clerical exercise of power, discovered an interesting
point in Hughes' history and began to declare to the world that the Irish
bishop was nothing more than "the gardener of Bishop Dubois."[21] The
New York Common Council tried to use Dubois to insult Hughes when
the Prince de Joinville arrived from France. Ignoring Hughes, who had
called upon the royal family while in Paris, the Council invited Dubois to
a public banquet. Dubois ignored the invitation.

Hughes steadily ignored Dubois. He never accorded him any emeritus
status in the diocese. Like John Power who also had gotten in his way,
Dubois was simply shunted aside. Once Hughes was in office, Dubois might
as well have been dead for all he was referred to by the acting bishop. In
the last year of Dubois' life, Hughes consecrated the city's first French
national parish, calling the Church of St. Vincent de Paul "a center around
which the scattered children of France would hasten to congregate."
Hughes told the long story of what the United States, north of the Potomac,
owed to French missionaries, beginning with the early Jesuits and bringing
his audience up through such great men as Bishop Cheverus. He never
mentioned Dubois.[22]

Dubois remained aloof from "Mr. Hughes." He would admit of his in-
firmities to visiting friends, but if, as did happen, the young bishop entered,
the old man would abruptly insist that he was "quite well."[23]

It was in April 1842, the month in which Bishops Henry Conwell and
John England both died, that Dubois had his own life threatened in an
attack upon the bishop's residence by a Nativist mob, angry at John
Hughes' tampering with civil politics. Thoroughly frightened by this incident, Dubois was again encouraged to go on a visit to the one place where
he had lived in a truly happy atmosphere—his Mountain.

He arrived in late springtime and remained for over a month. He was
extremely feeble and stayed at St. Joseph's convent where a bed was placed
for him in Mother Seton's old room. To get about he had to lean on the
arm of one of the sisters. He insisted on getting up with the community at
the first bell, but when he said Mass the sisters scheduled a second liturgy
to save him the labor of giving out Communion. Dubois quickly caught on
to the trick and asked Mother Xavier if it was a new custom that the sisters
attend two daily Masses. After that a compromise was reached. An assistant came to the Bishop's Mass and gave out Communion.

As idyllic as his situation once again was, he reacted quickly when it
was suggested that he remain permanently. No. He had to return to his
diocese. As if afraid they might forcibly detain him, he made immediate

arrangements to leave for New York. Once there he wrote, in a clear hand, one last 'thanks' to the Sisters of Charity. The letter showed that his illness never impaired his courtly manners.

"Although I have no news to communicate or to receive I cannot let this opportunity pass without expressing my gratitude for the many favors I received at your house during my stay there . . . Be also the interpreter of my gratitude to all my Sisters and particularly to the one who was so troubled by me. I hope to trouble her again next year. You and they will always be present in my mind, in all my prayers, and I will always pray for you."[24]

He would trouble no one the next year. His strength ebbed away. Yet even within a week of his death he pushed his meager energies to get out of his house in order to visit friends. More and more, prayer became his refuge and only apostolate. In December the Sisters from the orphanage took turns caring for him in his room, for he was as weak as an infant.

Catherine Seton, who claimed him as father far more intimately than many of these whom he lavishly called his "Children" took her turn with the sisters. She was there five days before Christmas when it became obvious that he was going to die. At times in his final hours he was delirious. He kept thinking that he was at his Mountain and that he had to get up and go out to the Valley to say Mass for the sisters. At the very last, as John Hughes recorded, "his mind was perfectly clear and tranquil . . . He knew everyone though he could not speak much." What speaking he did was to God. He prayed in a whisper. Someone held a crucifix to his lips. He kissed it. Then he was gone.[25]

New York was not overly interested in the funeral of John Dubois. In the space of the five years since his stroke he had easily been forgotten as the public focused its eyes on the great career of John Hughes. Dubois, even while he lived, belonged to a chapter of history already closed. The notice of his passing in the New York papers was buried under the ongoing polemics between Protestants and Catholics, Nativists and immigrants. The Catholic Bennett did, however, catch one odd omission on the part of "the gardener of Bishop Dubois." Reporting the Funeral Mass the *Herald* noted:

"Of the deceased, Bishop Hughes spoke little."

Hughes coldly told those present that Bishop Fenwick of Boston, who was to have preached, had not arrived and that he "would not, owing to the length of time the service already had occupied, and other causes, undertake himself the melancholy task. The Eulogy of the departed, he said, would be pronounced at some future day in that church by one who could do full justice to the theme."[26] Instead, he used his oratorical genius to defend the right of Catholics to pray for the dead.

Hughes had never forgotten or forgiven the humiliating fact that Dubois had made him, as an uneducated and unproven youth, work his way into Mount St. Mary's as a gardener. Once, when someone pointed out that Dubois had, at that time, done him a great kindness Hughes snapped:

"It was a regular contract between us, in which neither was required to acknowledge any obligation to the other."[27]

Hughes in 1842 made it obvious to the world that he felt none.

Dubois had once given directions that after death his body be placed not in one of the vaults directly under the Cathedral, but under a place prepared beneath the sidewalk in front.

"Bury me," he said "where the peole will walk over me in death as they wished to do in life."[28]

One of the Sisters of Charity described the scene which followed the funeral:

"I had never seen the entrance, a stone trap door that we walked on every day, opened before. Down I followed the bearers with many other fearless ones, forty or more stone steps and stood watching by torch light while they placed the venerated remains in the tomb directly under the middle entrance of the church."[29]

The remains were not long venerated. Just as in old age Dubois had been quickly forgotten, his burial place was forgotten by New Yorkers. Not until one hundred and thirty-four years later would diocesan historians become curious about the whereabouts of his remains and instigate a search for them.

Nonetheless if New York erected no memorial to John Dubois, it was obvious at the time of his death to those who cared, that he left the same kind of living memorial that is bequeathed by a good parent unknown to the public but loved by his children. William Quarter, who hero worshipped his old father, gave the eulogy refused by Bishop Hughes. At a Memorial Mass for Dubois he pointed out that as an emigré of the French Revolution the dead prelate was mourned by no blood relatives "in this land of exile."

"But," he said, "would you know the family of the Right Reverend John Dubois? Look at the crowd of priests and levites filling that sanctuary . . . Look at those Sisters of Charity . . . Look at the orphan boys and girls . . . The tears of this immense gathering for whom our faithful shepherd toiled as long as toiling was possible to exhausted mortality, attest that he whom we love leaves a very large family."[30]

81

Above, *John Hughes (1797–1864), another alumnus of Dubois'*
"Mountain" became the administrator of the Diocese of New York
when the old Bishop was too ill to run affairs properly. This
picture is from an early painting by the noted artist G.P.A. Healy.

Archbishop Samuel Eccleston
(1801–1851) personally travelled
from Baltimore to inform Bishop
Dubois that he had been "retired"
from New York in 1839.

82

Above, *Mount Saint Mary's College, as drawn by its president, Thomas R. Butler (1834–1838). At* top left *is the old Church on the Hill;* below *that is the original cabin. The large building in the* center *is known as Dubois Hall (1826); the low building to its right was not actually built when this picture was drawn. When it was erected some years later it included another story in height to match Dubois Hall. Projecting into the foreground is the "White House" (1809) where Dubois lived after moving out of his primitive cabin.* Below, *an engraving of Mount Saint Mary's College, Emmitsburg, drawn by James Hickey about 1842. He was an art instructor there for 45 years.*

And I will give to thee the keys of the kingdom of heaven: And whatsoever thou shalt bind upon earth, it shall be bound also in heaven; and whatsoever thou shalt loose on earth, it shall be loosed also in heaven. Ch.XVI.V.19.

85

THE
KEY OF HEAVEN;
OR,
A MANUAL OF PRAYER,

Corrected, Improved, and Enlarged.

CONTAINING MANY
PRAYERS AND DEVOTIONS NOT IN FORMER EDITIONS.
ALSO,
AN EXPLANATION OF THE PRINCIPAL FESTIVALS
OF THE MASS, SIGN OF THE CROSS,
HOLY WATER, INDULGENCES,
&c. &c.

RECOMMENDED BY THE
Right Rev. JOHN DUBOIS, *Bishop of New York;*
AND REVISED BY THE
Very Rev. JOHN POWER, *Vicar-General.*

FIRST AMERICAN (STEREOTYPED) EDITION.

PRINTED FOR, AND PUBLISHED BY JOHN McSWEENY,
30 *Madison street*, *N. York.*

MDCCCXXXIX.

Above, *the title page of a devotional prayer book compiled by Father Power, and approved by Bishop Dubois;* below *Bishop Dubois' official seal, and his signature as Bishop of New York.*

86

87

88

Above, *Old St. Patrick's, N.Y.C. Convent and Girl's School, completed in 1826, the year Bishop Dubois came to New York;* at right, *the Cathedral rectory on Mulberry Street where Dubois lived after 1836. The entire Old Cathedral complex is now on the National Register of Historic Places.*

89

90

Above, *a portion of the death notice of Bishop Dubois (1842), and* at left, *Sister Catherine Seton (1800–1891), a Sister of Mercy, who attended Bishop Dubois in his final hours.*

91

Right, *Old St. Patrick's Cathedral, NYC (rebuilt in 1868), shown from the Mulberry Street entrance.*

92

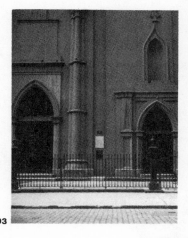

93

At left, *portion of the opposite entrance on Mott Street;* below, *the "lost" gravesite of Bishop Dubois is now marked by the white plaque on wall. Actual grave is under the white marble slab on step.*

94

95

To honor its founder on the occasion of the 175th anniversary of the college, a new statue of John Dubois was dedicated on October 23, 1983 at Mount Saint Mary's, Emmitsburg. The bronzed-aluminum figure was cast in Italy, and is of heroic stature—seven feet tall. It stands at the main entrance to the campus, and was donated by Dr. Francis Bonner, Jr. (MSM '64), in memory of his father Dr. Francis Bonner (MSM '36).

Notes

PREFACE

[1]Interview with Sister Martha Daddisman, recorded July 1, 1877, St. Joseph's, Emmitsburg.

[2]*The Catholic Expositor and Literary Magazine,* Jan. 1843, vol. 3, p. 243.

[3]John Gilmary Shea to James F. Edwards, Aug. 16, 1890, Notre Dame.

CHAPTER 1
The Child of the Ancien Régime

[1]Robert R. Palmer, *The School of the French Revolution,* Princeton, 1975, p. 77–78.

[2]*Ibid.,* p. 54–66.

[3]*Ibid.,* p. 79–80.

CHAPTER 2
The Deluge

[1]Gouverneur Morris, *A Diary of the French Revolution,* Boston, 1939, vol. II, p. 255.

[2]Louis Gottschalk (Ed.), *The Letters of Lafayette to Washington,* N.Y., 1944, p. 297.

[3]Howard C. Rice, Jr., *Thomas Jefferson's Paris,* Princeton, 1976, p. 117.

[4]Jean Matrat, *Robespierre, or the Tyranny of the Majority,* New York, 1971, p. 56.

[5]W.E. Woodward, *Lafayette,* New York, 1938, p. 154.

[6]J.F. Bernard, *Talleyrand,* New York, 1973, p. 88.

[7]M. Ch. Hamel, *Histoire de L'Eglise de Saint Sulpice,* Paris, 1901, p. 239–240.

[8]P. Pisani, *L'Eglise de Paris et La Revolution,* Paris, 1908, vol. II, p. 198.

[9]_____, *Histoire des Evenements Arrives sur La Paroisse S. Sulpice Pendant La Revolution,* Paris, 1792, p. 51.

[10]Hamel, p. 246–247.

[11]Gottschalk, p. 355–356.

[12]James R. Bayley, *A Brief Sketch of the Early History of the Catholic Church on the Island of Manhattan,* New York, 1870, p. 104. Bishop Bayley wrote: "Bishop Bruté mentions in one of his notes that during the height of the reign of terror, Robespierre, meeting Mr. Dubois, invited him to breakfast with him, and that it was by his connivance that he was able to escape from France."

CHAPTER 3
Politics and Politicians of This World

[1]Madame La Tour du Pin, *The Memoirs of Madame La Tour du Pin,* Edited and Translated by Felice Harcourt, New York, 1969, p. 227.

[2]The Duc de Broglie, *Memoirs of the Prince de Talleyrand,* London, (no date), p. 176.

[3]Mme. La Tour du Pin, p. 273.

[4]*The Virginia Gazette and General Advertiser,* Richmond, August 3, 1791.

[5]Henry Ammon, *James Monroe; The Quest for National Identity,* New York, 1971, p. 87.

[6]W.P. Cresson, *James Monroe,* Chapel Hill, 1946, p. 115.

[7]Samuel Mordecai, *Richmond in Bygone Days,* Richmond, 1860, p. 162.

[8]*The Virginia Gazette . . .* May 30, 1793.

[9]*The Virginia Gazette . . .* July 13, 1791.

[10]*Journal of the House of Delegates,* 1791, Microfilm, Virginia State Library. No pagination. *The Virginia Gazette . . .* December 6, 1791.

[11]*Ibid.,* September 28, 1791.

[12]*Ibid.,* September 28, 1791.

[13]*Ibid.,* August 24, 1791; August 3, 1791.

[14]*Ibid.,* October 12, 1791.

[15]*Ibid.,* September 28, 1791.

[16]Mary M. Meline and Edward F.X. Sweeney, *The Story of the Mountain,* Emmitsburg, 1911, vol. I, p. 6.

[17]*Ibid.*

[18]John McCaffrey, *The Jubilee at Mount St. Mary's,* New York, 1859, p. 245.

[19]Thomas O'Brien Hanley, SJ (editor), *The John Carroll Papers,* Notre Dame, 1976, Vol. III, p. 515–516, John Carroll to Charles Plowden, September, 1791.

[20]Mme. La Tour du Pin, p. 246.

[21]*Ibid.,* p. 239. Talleyrand, *Memoirs,* vol. I, p. 176.

[22]*The Virginia Gazette . . .* October 20, 1791.

[23]*Ibid.,* December 28, 1791.

[24]*Ibid.,* January 23, 1793.

[25]Mme. La Tour du Pin, p. 244.

[26]*The Virginia Gazette . . .* February 13, 1793.

[27]Ammon, p. 104; Stanilaus M. Hamilton, *The Writings of James Monroe,* New York, 1898, vol. I, p. 251.

[28]John Dubois, Retreat to Sisters; handwritten note, St. Joseph's, Emmitsburg, 1823.

[29]*The Virginia Gazette . . .* May 30, 1793.

[30]Peter Guilday, *The Life and Times of John Carroll,* New York, 1922, vol. II, p 405.

[31]Mme. La Tour du Pin, p. 271.

CHAPTER 4
We Poor Backwoods Clowns

[1]Guilday, vol. II, p. 167.
[2]Annabelle Melville, *John Carroll,* New York, 1957, p. 87.
[3]*Ibid.,* p. 95.
[4]*Ibid.,* p. 208.
[5]Guilday, p. 322; Melville, p. 97.
[6]T.J. Williams, *History of Frederick County, Maryland,* Hagerstown, 1910, vol. I, p. 135.
[7]Memoirs of Mary Brawner, written August 23, 1853, Mount St. Mary's, Emmitsburg.
[8]John Dubois to Anthony Garnier, April 18, 1816, Sulpician Archives, Paris.
[9]*Frederick Town Herald,* May 6, 1809.
[10]*Ibid.,* June 26, 1802; April 22, 1809.
[11]John Gilmary Shea, *The Life and Times of the Most Rev. John Carroll,* New York, 1898, vol. II, p. 311.
[12]John Dubois to James Monroe, March 12, 1802, Virginia State Archives.
[13]John Dubois, Retreat notes for sisters, June 9, 1822, St. Joseph's, Emmitsburg.
[14]Melville, p. 131.
[15]John Dubois to John Carroll, July 10, 1804, Archdiocese of Baltimore Archives.
[16]John Dubois to John Carroll, January 4, 1808, Baltimore.
[17]"Biographical Sketch of the Right Rev. John Dubois," U.S. Catholic Directory, 1845, p. 43–57.
[18]John Dubois to John Carroll, July 10, 1804, Baltimore.
[19]John Dubois to John Carroll, March 14, 1807, Baltimore.
[20]*Ibid.*
[21]John Dubois to John Carroll, November 11, 1805, Baltimore.
[22]*Ibid.*
[23]Memoirs of Mary Brawner, 1853, Mt. St. Mary's, Emmitsburg.
[24]Meline & Sweeney, vol. I, p. 11.
[25]John Dubois to John Carroll, Mary 14, 1807, Baltimore.
[26]John Dubois to John Carroll, January 14, 1808, Baltimore.
[27]John Dubois to John Carroll, November 11, 1805, Baltimore.

CHAPTER 5
On Condition That I Would Not Have to Conduct It

[1]John Carroll to Charles Plowden, September 24, 1796, quoted in Joseph Ruane, *The Beginnings of St. Sulpice in the United States,* Washington, 1935, p. 99; John Carroll to Charles Grassi, September 24, 1813, Melville, p. 155.
[2]Resolutions of the faculty of Georgetown College, December 3, 1798, Ruane, p. 86.
[3]James Emery to William DuBourg, April 1, 1800. Ruane, p. 101.
[4]James Emery to William DuBourg, October, 1800. Ruane, p. 111.
[5]James Emery to William DuBourg, January 28, 1802. Ruane, p. 114.
[6]James Emery to William DuBourg, February 26, 1804, (Sulpicians, Baltimore).
[7]John Dubois to Ambrose Maréchal, November 23, 1812, (Sulp. Balt.).
[8]James Emery to John Carroll, April 14, 1801, (Sulp. Balt.).
[9]John Dubois to Ambrose Maréchal, November 23, 1812, (Sulp. Balt.).
[10]*Ibid.*
[11]Meline & Sweeney, vol. I, p. 15.
[12]John Dubois to Ambrose Maréchal, November 23, 1812, (Sulp. Balt.).
[13]*Ibid.*

[14]*Ibid.*
[15]*Ibid.*
[16]*Ibid.*
[17]*Historical Statistics of the United States,* U.S. Dept. of Commerce, Bureau of the Census, Washington, 1976, p. 147.

CHAPTER 6
Mother is a Saint

[1]*The Frederick Herald,* August 20, 1808.
[2]John Carroll to Anthony Garnier, February 14, 1809, *Carroll Papers,* vol. III, p. 80.
[3]John Dubois to John Carroll, March 21, 1809, Baltimore.
[4]John Carroll to Leonard Neale, August 24, 1809, *Carroll Papers,* vol. III, p. 94.
[5]Annabelle M. Melville, *Elizabeth Bayley Seton,* New York, 1951, p. 135.
[6]Joseph I. Dirvin, C.M., *Mrs. Seton,* New York, 1962, p. 171.
[7]John Carroll to William Strickland, December 8, 1808, *Carroll Papers,* vol. III, p. 75.
[8]John Carroll to Patrick Kelly, January 15, 1808, *Carroll Papers,* vol. III, p. 37–38.
[9]Simon Bruté, *Mother Seton,* Published privately, 1884, p. 277.
[10]John Carroll to Robert Molyneux, June 19, 1808, *Carroll Papers,* vol. III, p. 63–65.
[11]Melville, *Elizabeth Bayley Seton,* p. 132.
[12]*Ibid.,* p. 133.
[13]Sarah Trainer Smith, "Philadelphia's First Nun," p. 417–522, *Records of the American Catholic Historical Society of Philadelphia,* 1894, vol. V, p. 417.
[14]Dirvin, p. 225.
[15]*Ibid.,* p. 228.
[16]*Ibid.*
[17]*Ibid.*
[18]Elizabeth Seton to Julia Scott, May 9, 1809, Joseph B. Code, *Letters of Mother Seton to Mrs. Julianna Scott,* New York, 1960, p. 180. Sarah T. Smith, p. 428.
[19]Meline & Sweeney, vol. I, p. 43–44.
[20]Elizabeth Seton to John Carroll, August 6, 1809, Baltimore.
[21]Melville, *Seton,* p. 154.
[22]Elizabeth Seton to Julianna Scott, September 20, 1809, Code, p. 189.
[23]Meline, vol. I, p. 43–44.
[24]Melville, *Seton,* p. 167.
[25]Elizabeth Seton to John Carroll, August 6, 1808, Baltimore.
[26]Elizabeth Seton to John Carroll, September 8, 1809, Baltimore.
[27]John Dubois to Elizabeth Seton, October 8, 1809, St. Joseph's.
[28]Elizabeth Seton to John Carroll, September 8, 1809, Baltimore.
[29]Melville, *Seton,* p. 171.
[30]D. Doran, *Annals of the English Stage,* London, 1871, vol. VI, p. 434.
[31]*New York Diary* (1791) clipping in Melmouth folder in New York Public Library, undated.
[32]George C. Odell, *Annals of the New York Stage,* New York, 1927, vol. I, p. 332.
[33]*Ibid.,* vol. II, p. 180.
[34]*Ibid.,* vol. II, p. 54.
[35]*Ibid.,* vol. I, p. 332.
[36]*Ibid.,* vol. II, p. 213.
[37]John Dubois to Charlotte Melmouth, November 28, 1809, St. Joseph's.
[38]Melville, *Seton,* p. 363.
[39]Odell, vol. II, p. 392.
[40]John Dubois to Charlotte Melmouth, November 28, 1809, St. Joseph's.
[41]Rose White's Journal, unpaged, St. Joseph's.

42John Cheverus to Elizabeth Seton, January 24, 1810, St. Joseph's.
43Elizabeth Seton to John Carroll, June 15, 1810, Baltimore.
44Dirvin, p. 285.
45Elizabeth Seton to John Carroll, May 13, 1811, Baltimore.
46Melville, *Seton,* p. 178.
47*Ibid.*
48*Ibid.,* p. 163.
49*Ibid.,* p. 180.
50Elizabeth Seton to John Carroll, May 13, 1811, Baltimore.
51Elizabeth Seton to John Carroll, September 5, 1811, Baltimore.
52John Carroll to Elizabeth Seton, September 11, 1811, Baltimore.
53Sister Mary Agnes McCann, *The History of Mother Seton's Daughters,* New York, 1917, vol. I, p. 23.
54*Ibid.*

CHAPTER 7
You Remind Me of Nothing Else But God

1Simon Bruté, *Memoirs of the Rt. Revd. Simon William Gabriel Bruté*, Edited by James R. Bayley, New York, 1876, p. 41.
2Meline and Sweeney, vol. I, p. 42.
3*Ibid.,* vol. I, p. 43.
4*Ibid.,* p. 48.
5Elizabeth Seton to John Carroll, August 9, 1811, Baltimore.
6Elizabeth Seton to John Carroll, August 9, 1811, Baltimore.
7Bruté, *Memoirs,* p. 111.
8*Ibid.,* p. 151.
9*Ibid.,* p. 111.
10*Ibid.,* p. 122.
11*Ibid.,* p. 214.
12*Ibid.,* p. 154.
13*Ibid.,* p. 145–147.
14*Ibid.,* p. 109.
15*Ibid.,* p. 151.
16*Ibid.,* p. 152.
17*Ibid.,* p. 139–140.
18*Ibid.,* p. 118–123.
19*Ibid.,* p. 158.
20*Ibid.,* p. 163.
21*Ibid.,* p. 164.
22*Ibid.,* p. 212.
23*Ibid.,* p. 25.
24*Ibid.,* p. 36.
25Sr. Mary Salesia Godecker, *Simon Bruté de Remur,* St. Meinrad, 1931, p. 54.
26Ruane, p. 241.
27*Ibid.,* p. 242.
28*Ibid.,* p. 238.
29John Carroll to John Dubois, December 22, 1811, Sulpicians, Baltimore.
30Dirvin, p. 316.
31Melville, p. 189.
32John Dubois to Simon Bruté, May 7, 1812, Elizabeth Seton Guild, Emmitsburg.
33Godecker, p. 61.
34John Carroll to John Tessier, September 13, 1812, Sulpicians, Baltimore.

CHAPTER 8
The Little Bonaparte

[1]Meline & Sweeney, vol. I, p. 56.
[2]Ruane, p. 245.
[3]John Dubois to Gen. Robert Harper, May 7, 1817, Mount St. Mary's.
[4]Ruane, p. 175.
[5]Meline & Sweeney, vol. I, p. 57.
[6]Simon Bruté's written account of the state of religion in Emmitsburg, September 17, 1813, Mount St. Mary's.
[7]John Carroll to Raphael Brooke, August 4, 1815, Baltimore.
[8]Ruane, p. 175.
[9]Meline & Sweeney, vol. I, p. 57.
[10]Dirvin, p. 425.
[11]Meline & Sweeney, vol. I, p. 99.
[12]*Ibid.,* vol. I, p. 51.
[13]Melville, *Seton,* p. 235.
[14]Dirvin, p. 343.
[15]*Ibid.,* p. 342.
[16]Melville, *Seton,* p. 235.
[17]*Ibid.,* p. 236.
[18]_____, Rose White, Typed account, p. 25 (St. Joseph's).
[19]Melville, p. 231.
[20]John Hickey to William Hurley, November 25, 1814, Sulpicians, Baltimore.
[21]*Frederick Town Herald,* September 24, 1814.
[22]Rose White, p. 36.
[23]Elizabeth Seton to William Seton, (1815) St. Joseph's.
[24]William Seton to Elizabeth Seton, June 14, 1815, St. Joseph's.
[25]Bruté, *Mother Seton,* p. 297.
[26]*Ibid.,* p. 288–289.
[27]*Ibid.,* p. 305–306.
[28]*Ibid.,* p. 287.
[29]*Ibid.,* p. 288.
[30]*Ibid.,* p. 283–284.
[31]*Ibid.,* p. 281.
[32]Bruté, *Mother Seton,* p. 305.
[33]John Tessier to John Hickey, September, 1815, Mount St. Mary's.
[34]Bruté, *Mother Seton,* p. 282, p. 291–306.
[35]Melville, *Seton,* p. 274.
[36]Richard Seton to Elizabeth Seton, September 3, 1816, Mount St. Mary's.
[37]John Dubois to William Seton, (1816) Mount St. Vincent's College Archives.
[38]Melville, *Seton,* p. 246.
[39]John Dubois to William Seton, (1816) Mount St. Vincent's.
[40]William Seton to John Dubois, January 26, 1817, Mount St. Mary's.
[41]Richard Seton to John Dubois, June 20, 1817, Mount St. Mary's.
[42]Richard Seton to Elizabeth Seton, July 24, 1817, Melville, *Seton,* p. 376.
[43]Melville, *Seton,* p. 272.
[44]John Dubois to Catherine Seton, December 22, 1818, Mount St. Mary's.
[45]John Dubois to Catherine Seton, September 26, 1819, Mount St. Mary's.
[46]Reminiscences of Sister Martha Daddisman, recorded, July 1, 1877, St. Joseph's.
[47]John Dubois to Simon Bruté, January 10, 1816, Meline & Sweeney, vol. I, p. 68–69.
[48]Simon Bruté to Monsieur Ducleux, July 17, 1815, Sulpician Archives, Paris.
[49]Theodore Maynard, *The Reed and the Rock,* New York, 1942, p. 123.

[50]Ruane, p. 250.

[51]*Ibid.*, p. 271.

[52]John Tessier to John Hickey, April 1, 1818, Sulpicians, Baltimore.

[53]John Dubois to John Hickey, May 5, 1818, Sulpicians, Baltimore.

[54]John Hickey to John Tessier, May 20, 1818, Sulpicians, Baltimore.

[55]Ruane, p. 248.

[56]John Tessier to John Hickey, May 25, 1818, Sulpicians, Baltimore.

[57]Ruane, p. 247–251.

[58]Elizabeth Seton to William Seton, July 1, 1818, Mount St. Mary's.

[59]John Dubois to Ambrose Maréchal, May 29, 1818; June 21, 1818, Baltimore.

[60]Reminiscences of Sr. Helena Elder; recorded in 1883, St. Joseph's.

[61]John Dubois to Ambrose Maréchal, February 10, 1823; February 12, 1819; September 18, 1821, January 25, 1823. Simon Bruté to Ambrose Maréchal, September 17, 1826, Baltimore.

[62]Elizabeth Seton to Ambrose Maréchal, November 6, 1817, Baltimore.

CHAPTER 9
She Did But Follow My Express Prescriptions

[1]Melville, *Seton,* p. 268.

[2]*Ibid.,* p. 289.

[3]*Ibid.,* p. 286.

[4]*Ibid.,* p. 259.

[5]Elizabeth Seton to Anthony Filicchi, June 1, 1818, Copy, St. Joseph's.

[6]Reminiscences of Sister Martha Daddisman.

[7]Note accompanying a petition of Samuel Cooper that he be granted a dispensation from saying the breviary. Propaganda Fide Files, Notre Dame.

[8]Samuel Cooper to Ambrose Maréchal, March 15, 1819, Baltimore.

[9]John Hughes to John Purcell, February 14, 1831, New York Archdiocesan Archives.

[10]Dirvin, p. 365.

[11]Elizabeth Seton to Anthony Filicchi, November 1818, St. Joseph's.

[12]Elizabeth Seton to Simon Bruté, Bruté, *Mother Seton,* p. 243.

[13]Maynard, p. 105.

[14]Elizabeth Seton to Elizabeth Boyle, October 20, 1820, Mount St. Vincent.

[15]Dirvin, p. 445.

[16]*Ibid.*

[17]Meline and Sweeney, vol. I, p. 69.

[18]Melville, *Seton,* p. 298.

CHAPTER 10
The Lord Gave and the Lord Hath Taken Away

[1]John Dubois to Robert Harper, January 7, 1821, Baltimore.

[2]John Dubois to Catherine Seton, (1821) St. Joseph's.

[3]John Dubois to Mrs. Tiernan, February 14, 1821, Mount St. Mary's. _____, *Rose White,* p. 61.

[4]John Dubois to Rose White, undated, St. Joseph's.

[5]John Dubois to Mrs. Tiernan, February 14, 1821, Mount St. Mary's.

[6]_____, *Rose White,* p. 114.

[7]John Dubois to Rose White, undated, St. Joseph's.

[8]Ruane, p. 202.

[9]George Elder to John Dubois, December 27, 1818, Mount St. Mary's.

[10]Meline and Sweeney, vol. I, p. 146.
[11]John Carroll to John Dubois, January 25, 1823, Mount St. Mary's.
[12]Meline and Sweeney, vol. I, p. 140.
[13]Michael Egan to Catherine Seton, June 3, 1824, Mount St. Mary's.
[14]John Purcell to Joseph Wiseman, March 31, 1824, Mount St. Mary's.
[15]Reminiscences of Sr. Helena Elder, (1883) St. Joseph's.
[16]Meline and Sweeney, vol. I, p. 117.

CHAPTER 11
Should You Send Old M. Dubois to New York

[1]Charles C. Pise to Michael Egan, Meline and Sweeney, vol. I, p. 123.
[2]Meline and Sweeney, vol. I, p. 126.
[3]John Dubois to Rose White, September 1824, St. Joseph's.
[4]John Dubois to Ambrose Maréchal, March, 1826. Meline & Sweeney, vol. I, p. 147.
[5]Simon Bruté to Ambrose Maréchal, December 16, 1825, Baltimore.
[6]John Connolly to Propaganda Fide, February 25, 1818, New York.
[7]Ronen John Murtha, OSB *The Life of the Most Reverend Ambrose Maréchal,* Ann Arbor, 1975, p. 221.
[8]*Ibid.,* p. 216.
[9]*Ibid.*
[10]E.M. Harland to John Dubois, March 13, 1824, Mount St. Mary's.
[11]Rev. William Taylor, *An Address to the Roman Catholics of New York,* New York, 1821, p. 3.
[12]John Dubois to John McGerry, September 7, 1820, Mount St. Mary's.
[13]*New York Gazette and General Advertiser,* February 10, 1825.
[14]P. Laurenson to John Dubois, February 16, 1825, Sulpicians, Baltimore.
[15]William DuBourg to U.S. Bishops, October 4, 1825, Sulpicians, Baltimore.
[16]Anthony Kohlmann to Propaganda Fide (1815), New York Archdiocesan Archives.
[17]*National Advocate,* February 1826, clipping in Propaganda Fide files, cut out without date.
[18]John Savage to John Leahy, December 13, 1826, New York Archdiocesan Archives.
[19]William Burke to John McGerry, August 29, 1826, Mount St. Mary's.
[20]Joseph Snyder to John Dubois, August 25, 1826, Mount St. Mary's.
[21]Elizabeth Boyle to John Dubois, September 24, 1826, Mount St. Mary's.
[22]John Dubois to William Grason, August 25, 1826, Mount St. Mary's.
[23]Richard Fresley to John Dubois, September 12, 1826, Mount St. Mary's.
[24]William Burke to John McGerry, August 29, 1826, Mount St. Mary's.
[25]John Hughes to John Dubois, January, 1825, Mount St. Mary's.
[26]John Hughes to Michael Egan, October, 1825, Mount St. Mary's.
[27]John Dubois to John Hughes, October 24, 1826, Mount St. Mary's.
[28]*U.S. Catholic Miscellany,* September 16, 1826.
[29]*Ibid.,* November 18, 1826.
[30]John Dubois to Michael Egan, October 18, 1826, Mount St. Mary's.
[31]*The Truth Teller,* November 4, 1826.

CHAPTER 12
If I Had Help . . .

[1]Albert Ullman, *A Landmark History of New York,* New York, 1939, p. 199.
[2]Martha J. Lamb, *History of the City of New York,* New York, 1877, vol. II, p. 692.
[3]*The Truth Teller,* June 10, 1829.

[4]*Ibid.,* February 14, 1829.

[5]*Ibid.,* September 25, 1825.

[6]*U.S. Catholic Miscellany,* December 2, 1826.

[7]*The National Observer,* quoted in *The Truth Teller,* August 19, 1826.

[8]*The Truth Teller,* August 19, 1826.

[9]John Gilmary Shea, *A History of the Catholic Church Within the Limits of the United States,* New York, 1890, vol. III, p. 196.

[10]*The Truth Teller,* November 11, 1826.

[11]John Dubois to Michael Egan, November 18, 1826, Mount St. Mary's.

[12]*The Truth Teller,* November 18, 1826.

[13]*U.S. Catholic Miscellany,* July 28, 1827.

[14]*The New York Observer,* April 28, 1827.

[15]*The Truth Teller,* August 4, 1827; *The New York Advertiser,* May 4, 1827.

[16]*U.S. Catholic Miscellany,* December 1, 1827.

[17]James Rooney to Michael Egan, June 7, 1825, Mount St. Mary's.

[18]"What the Duke of Saxe Weimar Eisenach saw and said of the Catholics of the United States in 1825–1826." *Historical Records and Studies,* New York, 1911, vol. VII, p. 10.

[19]*U.S. Catholic Miscellany,* July 21, 1827.

[20]*The Truth Teller,* March 3, 1827.

[21]*Ibid.,* March 24, 1827.

[22]John Dubois to Michael Egan, May 31, 1827, Mount St. Mary's.

[23]Michael Egan to John McGerry, July 8, 1827, Mount St. Mary's.

[24]John Dubois to Michael Egan, April 13, 1827, Mount St. Mary's.

[25]John Dubois to John McGerry, June 26, 1827, Mount St. Mary's.

[26]James Rooney to Michael Egan, June 7, 1827, Mount St. Mary's.

[27]*Ibid.*

[28]John Dubois to Michael Egan, June 26, 1827, Mount St. Mary's.

[29]James Rooney to Michael Egan, June 7, 1827, Mount St. Mary's.

[30]John Dubois to Michael Egan, June 26, 1827, Mount St. Mary's.

[31]John Dubois to the Association for the Propagation of the Faith, Lyons, 1830, *Historical Records and Studies,* New York, vol. V, 1909, p. 220.

[32]*Ibid.*

[33]*New York Observer,* February 17, 1827.

[34]1 Nephi 14:11, 1 Nephi 13:8. *The Book of Mormon.* An account written by the hand of Mormon upon plates taken from the plates of Nephi, translated by Joseph Smith, Jr., Salt Lake City, 1920.

[35]John Dubois to the Association for the Propagation of the Faith, Lyons, 1830, *Historical Records and Studies,* vol. V, p. 225.

[36]*Ibid.,* p. 225.

[37]*Ibid.,* p. 227.

[38]Sarah Turner Smith, p. 463.

[39]*U.S. Catholic Miscellany,* July 28, 1827.

[40]*The Truth Teller,* January 12, 1828.

[41]Michael Egan to John McGerry, July 11, 1828.

[42]John Dubois to the Association for the Propagation of the Faith, Lyons, 1830, *Historical Records and Studies,* vol. V, p. 223.

[43]Martin Griffin, "History of the Church of St. John the Evangelist," *Records of the American Catholic Historical Society of Philadelphia,* vol. 20, p. 352.

[44]John Dubois to the Association for the Propagation of the Faith, Lyons, 1830, *Historical Records and Studies,* vol. V, p. 229.

[45]*Ibid.*

[46]*Ibid.*

[47]*Ibid.,* p. 221.

[48]John Power to Henry Conwell, January 31, 1829, New York.
[49]*U.S. Catholic Miscellany,* December 27, 1828.
[50]Simon Bruté to John Dubois, November 15, 1828, New York.
[51]John Power to John McGerry, January 15, 1829, Mount St. Mary's.
[52]John Power to Henry Conwell, January 14, 1829, Propaganda Fide, Notre Dame.
[53]John Dubois to the Propaganda Fide, May 1829, duplicated copy, Mount St. Mary's.
[54]*U.S. Catholic Miscellany,* October 4, 1828.
[55]John Power to Henry Conwell, August 14, 1828, Propaganda Fide, Notre Dame.
[56]John Power to Henry Conwell, September 20, 1828, Propaganda Fide, Notre Dame.
[57]Thomas Levins to Henry Conwell, January 31, 1829, Propaganda Fide, Notre Dame.
[58]John Power to Henry Conwell, January 30, 1829, Propaganda Fide, Notre Dame.
[59]Euphemie Toussaint to Pierre Toussaint, October 19, 1827, New York Public Library.
[60]*The Truth Teller,* June 10, 1826; August 11, 1827.
[61]Unsigned letter to Pierre Toussaint, Undated, (1820s), New York Public Library.
[62]Thomas Levins to Henry Conwell, January 31, 1829, Propaganda Fide, Notre Dame.
[63]John Dubois to John Tessier, February 15, 1829, Sulpicians, Baltimore.
[64]William Quarter to Michael Egan, September 20, 1829, Mount St. Mary's.
[65]*New York Observer,* December 19, 1829.

CHAPTER 13
Home for Another Revolution

[1]John Dubois to Rose White, December 9, 1831, St. Joseph's.
[2]William DuBourg to Simon Bruté, May 5, 1830, Notre Dame.
[3]John Dubois, *Pastoral Letter,* New York, 1834, p. 4.
[4]Vincent Harold to Thomas Levins, September 3, 1830, New York.
[5]John Dubois to Rose White, December 9, 1831, St. Joseph's.
[6]*Ibid.*

CHAPTER 14
Tried in This World As by Fire

[1]John McElroy to John Dubois, June 24, 1825, Mount St. Mary's.
[2]*The New York Observer,* June 29, 1833, December 27, 1834.
[3]*The Sun,* December 13, 1833.
[4]*The Sun,* March 11, 1834.
[5]*Dictionary of American Biography,* "William Craig Brownlee," vol. II, p. 176–177.
[6]Memorial, *W.C. Brownlee—Fourth Son of the Laird of Torfoot,* New York, 1860, p. 78.
[7]*Ibid.,* p. 84.
[8]*The Protestant,* January 3, 1830.
[9]Quoted in *U.S. Catholic Miscellany,* April 3, 1830.
[10]*U.S. Catholic Miscellany,* January 30, 1830.
[11]*The Truth Teller,* July 3, 1830.
[12]Quoted in *U.S. Catholic Miscellany,* September 3, 1831.
[13]*Ibid.,* January 26, 1832.
[14]*The New York Observer,* January 1, 1831.
[15]*The Protestant,* April 16, 1831.
[16]*Ibid.,* May 12, 1832.
[17]*Courier and Enquirer,* November 9, 1831; Andrew Byrne to Francis Jamison, November 16, 1831.
[18]*The New York Observer,* March 16, 1832; *U.S. Catholic Miscellany,* February 16, 1832.
[19]John Dubois to Rose White, December 9, 1831, St. Joseph's.

[20]*U.S. Catholic Miscellany,* January 21, 1832.

[21]*The Truth Teller,* August 18, 1832.

[22]Simon Bruté to Joseph Rosati, September 2, 1832, St. Louis Diocesan Archives.

[23]John Power to the Propaganda Fide, August 16, 1832, Notre Dame.

[24]*The Truth Teller,* February 9, 1833.

[25]Quoted in *The Truth Teller,* February 7, 1827.

[26]*The Sun,* March 19, 1834.

[27]*The Herald,* September 7, 1835.

[28]Philip Hone, *The Diary of Philip Hone, New York [1927], p. 97.*

[29]"Notes from conversations with Mr. Hart," James R. Bayley, *A Brief Sketch of the Early History of the Catholic Church* . . . New York, 1870, p. 108.

[30]John Dubois to Cardinal Weld, September 13, 1836, New York Historical Society.

[31]"Travelers accounts of Catholics in the United States," *Historical Records and Studies,* vol. VII, 1907, p. 9.

[32]Simon Bruté to John Purcell (1833), Cincinnati Diocesan Archives.

[33]John England to Paul Cullen, September 26, 1833, Irish College, Notre Dame.

[34]Francis P. Kenrick to Paul Cullen, March 20, 1834, Irish College, Notre Dame.

[35]John England to Joseph Rosati, March 3, 1835, New York (copy).

[36]John Power to Paul Cullen, September 15, 1833, Irish College, Notre Dame.

[37]*New York Weekly Register and Catholic Diary,* December 14, 1833; handwritten, unsigned account at St. Joseph's.

[38]*The Truth Teller,* November 2, 1833.

[39]*New York Weekly Register and Catholic Diary,* February 1, 1834.

[40]John Dubois to Rose White, February 1835, St. Joseph's.

[41]*New York Weekly Register and Catholic Diary,* May 31, 1834.

[42]Thomas Levins to Paul Cullen, July 18, 1834, Irish College, Notre Dame; John Dubois, Pastoral Letter, 1834.

[43]John McGerry to Paul Cullen, September 15, 1834, Irish College, Notre Dame.

[44]John Power to Paul Cullen, September 15, 1834, Irish College, Notre Dame.

[45]Quoted in *U.S. Catholic Miscellany,* July 2, 1833.

[46]*The New York Observer,* December 20, 1834.

[47]Thomas Levins (and John Power) to Paul Cullen, July 18, 1834, Irish College, Notre Dame.

[48]*The New York Observer,* January 3, 1834.

[49]*New York Weekly Register and Catholic Diary,* June 14, 1834.

[50]*The Protestant,* September 27, 1834.

[51]*U.S. Catholic Miscellany,* October 4, 1834.

[52]*The Protestant,* October 1, 1834.

[53]John Dubois to Thomas Levins, October 14, 1834; Thomas Levins to John Dubois, October 14, 1834; John Dubois to Thomas Levins, October 15, 1834, Propaganda Fide, Notre Dame.

[54]*The Protestant,* November 5, 1834.

[55]Sr. Helena Elder, St. Joseph's.

[56]Simon Bruté to Joseph Rosati, May 2, 1833, St. Louis.

[57]John Gilmary Shea, *History of the Catholic Church* . . . , vol. III, p. 506.

[58]Simon Bruté to Elizabeth Boyle, May 7, 1835, St. Joseph's.

[59]John Dubois to Sr. Josephine, October 1, 1834, St. Joseph's.

[60]John Dubois to "Sr. Superior," October 21, 1832, St. Joseph's.

[61]John Dubois to Rose White, December 18, 1837, St. Joseph's.

[62]*Journal of Commerce,* July 11, 1836.

[63]*The Protestant,* March 23, 1836.

[64]*The Herald,* January 20, 1836.

[65]*Ibid.,* January 23, 1837; September 1, 1837.

[66]*The Christian Intelligencer,* May 2, 1835.
[67]*The Protestant,* September 3, 1834.
[68]*U.S. Catholic Miscellany,* May 29, 1835.
[69]Quoted in *U.S. Catholic Miscellany,* July 2, 1833.
[70]John Dubois to John Purcell, May 20, 1837, Notre Dame.
[71]*The Protestant,* April 1, 1835.
[72]*The Herald,* June 7, 1835.
[73]*The Downfall of Babylon,* July 4, 1835.
[74]John Dubois to John Purcell, December 15, 1834, Notre Dame.
[75]John Power to Anthony Kohlmann, August 16, 1833, Propaganda Fide, Notre Dame.
[76]John Dubois to John Purcell, December 15, 1834, Notre Dame.
[77]Simon Bruté to Joseph Rosati, March 30, 1835, St. Louis.
[78]John Dubois to John Purcell, September 29, 1835, Notre Dame.
[79]*U.S. Catholic Miscellany,* May 39, 1834.
[80]John Power to Paul Cullen, July 25, 1834, Notre Dame.
[81]John Dubois to John Purcell, September 29, 1835, Notre Dame.
[82]John McGerry to Paul Cullen, March 10, 1835, Irish College, Notre Dame.
[83]John Dubois to John Purcell, July 27, 1835; September 29, 1835, Notre Dame.
[84]*The Herald,* March 3, 1836.
[85]John Cardinal Farley, *The Life of John Cardinal McCloskey,* London, 1918, p. 43–44.
[86]*Ibid.*
[87]John Power to Paul Cullen, August 12, 1835, Irish College, Notre Dame.
[88]John England to Paul Cullen, June 23, 1836, Irish College, Notre Dame.
[89]*The Herald,* January 10, 1837.
[90]Simon Bruté to the Propaganda Fide, March 7, 1836, Notre Dame.
[91]Felix Varela to John Dubois, May 18, 1837, Propaganda Fide, Notre Dame.
[92]John Hughes to Anthony Blanc, August 6, 1836, Notre Dame.
[93]John England to Paul Cullen, August 6, 1836, Notre Dame.
[94]*The Protestant,* June 20, 1836.
[95]*Ibid.,* November 8, 1837.
[96]Thomas Levins to John Dubois, January 16, 1835; January 17, 1835, Propaganda Fide, Notre Dame.
[97]John Dubois to Thomas Levins, January 16, 1835, Propaganda Fide, Notre Dame.
[98]Thomas Levins to the Propaganda Fide, June 29, 1836, Notre Dame.
[99]*Journal of Commerce,* December 22, 1836.
[100]*Ibid.*
[101]*The Protestant,* December 14, 1836; November 1, 1837.
[102]*The Herald,* January 11, 1837.
[103]*U.S. Catholic Miscellany,* September 9, 1837; September 23, 1837; August 19, 1837.
[104]John Dubois to Rose White, September 1837, St. Joseph's.
[105]*U.S. Catholic Miscellany,* October 14, 1837.

CHAPTER 15
The Spotless Life and Apostolic Labors of My Old Father

[1]Simon Bruté to the Propaganda Fide, March 7, 1836.
[2]John Dubois to John Hughes, November 6, 1837, New York.
[3]Unnamed sister, notes, St. Joseph's, 1838.
[4]*The Truth Teller,* March 9, 1839.
[5]Simon Bruté to John Hughes, April 19, 1834, New York.
[6]John Hughes to John Purcell, February 24, 1838, New York.
[7]John Hughes to Samuel Eccleston, October 29, 1838, New York.

[8]John Hughes to the Propaganda Fide, January 18, 1839, Notre Dame.

[9]John Hughes, Pastoral (in John Dubois' name), *The Truth Teller,* February 20, 1839.

[10]*U.S. Catholic Miscellany,* March 31, 1839.

[11]John Hughes to Mark Frenaye, March 20, 1838, New York.

[12]_____, *Rose White,* p. 102.

[13]Simon Bruté to Sr. William Anna, January 10, 1834, Elizabeth Seton Guild, Emmitsburg.

[14]Richard Shaw, *Dagger John,* New York, 1977, p. 133.

[15]*Ibid.*

[16]John Hassard, *Life of John Hughes,* New York, 1969, p. 204.

[17]J.F. Bernard, p. 619.

[18]John Purcell to Anthony Blanc, September 3, 1839, Notre Dame.

[18]*U.S. Catholic Miscellany,* May 21, 1840.

[20]*Ibid.,* September 5, 1840.

[21]*The Herald,* November 1, 1841.

[22]*U.S. Catholic Miscellany,* September 3, 1842.

[23]C.G. Herbermann, "Life of Rt. Rev. John Dubois," *Historical Records and Studies,* vol. II, 1905, p. 342.

[24]John Dubois to Sr. Xavier Clarke, July 29, 1842, St. Joseph's.

[25]Unnamed sister, St. Joseph's; John Hughes to Sr. Xavier Clarke, December 21, 1842, St. Joseph's.

[26]*The Herald,* December 24, 1842.

[27]John Hassard, p. 23.

[28]Unnamed sister, St. Joseph's.

[29]*Ibid.*

[30]*Ibid.*

Index